Towards a Realist Conception of Theology

Classic Theology and Contemporary Challenges
Series editor:
Gijsbert van den Brink (VU Amsterdam)
Volume IV

I. Cornelis van der Knijff, *Between Providence and Choice Biography*
II Martijn S. Pouw, *Greatness & Limits of Common Priesthood*
III. Adriaan C. Neele, *That Which We Have Seen*

BERTRAND RICKENBACHER

Towards a Realist Conception of Theology

An Account Based on the Works of Bavinck and Plantinga

Summum

© 2024 Summum Academic Publications – Kampen
www.summumacademic.com

Omslagontwerp: Brainstorm
Opmaak binnenwerk: Gewoon Geertje

ISBN 9789492701596 (hardcover)
ISBN 9789492701602 (paperback)
ISSN 2666-1373
NUR 704

All rights reserved. No part of this publication may be reproduced, translated, stored in a retrieval system, or transmitted in any form by any means, electronic, mechanical, photocopying, recording or otherwise, without prior written permission from the publisher.

Table of contents

Acknowledgements   9

Chapter 1: Realism and Theology:
Background, Scope and Relevance   11
1. Introduction   11
2. Realism in Philosophy and Christian Theology: A Brief Overview   13
    2.1 Sectional Realisms and Their Counterparts   14
    2.2 General Philosophical Realism and Its Alternatives   17
    2.3 Theological Realism and Its Issues   22
3. Anti-Realist and Realist Trends in Contemporary
Theological Studies   28
    3.1 A Definition of Realism and Anti-Realism in Theology   28
    3.2 Questions of Method   31
    3.3 Anti-Realist Trends   32
        3.3.1 *Experiential-Expressive* Anti-Realist Trends   33
        3.3.2 *Cultural-Linguistic* Anti-Realist Trends   37
    3.4 Realist Trends   43
        3.4.1 *Critical Realist* Trends   44
        3.4.2 *Classical* and *Radical* Theological Realist Trends   48
4. *The Bavinck/Plantinga Model for a Realist*
Conception of Theology   51
    4.1 The Research Question   52
    4.2 Methodological Clarifications   55
    4.3 Structure and Content   60

Chapter 2: Herman Bavinck's Defense of a Realist
Conception of Theology   61
1. Introduction   61
2. Dogmatic Theology as a Science   64
    2.1 The *Object* of Theological Science   67
    2.2 The *Method* of Theological Science   68
    2.3 Dogmatic Theology and the Other Sciences   72
3. Realism and the Principles of Theology   76
    3.1 The *Principles* of Theological Science   77
    3.2 Against Rationalism and Empiricism: Realism   80
    3.3 A Form of Realism Sustained by a Classical Logos Theology   86

4. Realism in *Reformed Dogmatics 2: God and Creation*	93
4.1 Realism and the Transcendence of God	94
4.2 Semantic Realism	96
5. Bavinck's Realism Synthesized and Interpreted	98
5.1 Synthetic Remarks on Bavinck's Realism	98
5.2 Is Bavinck a *Critical Realist*?	101
5.3 Is Bavinck a *Theological Realist*?	108

Chapter 3: Alvin Plantinga's Theory of Warrant and Realist Theology — 117

1. Introduction	117
2. Plantinga's Theory of Warrant	119
2.1 Warrant, Proper Function, and Design Plan	121
2.2 From Naturalistic Epistemology to Supernatural Metaphysics	125
2.3 *Where the Conflict Really Lies*	131
3. Human Knowledge of God	137
3.1 The *A/C Model* as an Extension of the Theory of Warrant	140
3.2 The *Extended A/C Model*	144
4. Critical Issues Related to Plantinga's *Extended A/C Model*	150
4.1 Plantinga's "Unresolved Conditional" Method	150
4.2 A Barthian Reading of Plantinga?	156

Chapter 4: A Realist Conception of Theology for the Contemporary Western Context — 163

1. Introduction	163
2. The *Bavinck/Plantinga Model for a Realist Conception of Theology*	164
2.1 Points of Convergence	164
2.2 The Benefit of the *Bavinck/Plantinga Model*	168
2.2.1 How Plantinga Improves Bavinck's General Theory of Knowledge	169
2.2.2 How Bavinck Improves Plantinga's Theological Thought	171
3. The *Bavinck/Plantinga Model* in the Contemporary Realism Debate	176
3.1 The *Bavinck/Plantinga Model* and *Critical Realism*	176
3.2 The *Bavinck/Plantinga Model* and *Theological Realism*	181
3.3 Concluding Observations	184
4. The Wider Scope of the *Bavinck/Plantinga Model*	186
4.1 The *Bavinck/Plantinga Model* as a Work of Retrieval	187

4.2 Retrieval versus "Working under the Conditions of (Post-) Modernity"	194
4.3 Theology as a Meaningful Truth-Seeking Discipline	196
5. Conclusion: Avenues for Further Research	203
Bibliography	207
Index of Names	229
Index of Subjects	231

Acknowledgements

This book, based on my PhD dissertation, represents the culmination of a very long intellectual and personal journey. I am fully aware that this journey would have been impossible without the support of divine providence and the help of many people. My parents Alain (†2015) and Anne (†2022), my wider family and my wife's family, the brothers and sisters of my congregation, as well as many friends and colleagues, have accompanied me through good and bad days.

I am pleased to express my special gratitude to the following individuals who each played a specific role in the achievement of my research:

- Gijsbert van den Brink, my supervisor, for his academic and pedagogical excellence, as well as his human qualities,
- Roger Pouivet, my co-supervisor, for the interest he immediately took in this project and the great accuracy of his comments,
- Michael Rea, the Director of the *Center for Philosophy of Religion* of the University of Notre Dame (USA), for inviting me as a research visitor from August 2013 to January 2014 (which gave me the opportunity to meet several times with Alvin Plantinga), and Joyce Zurawski, the secretary of the Center, who helped us in so many ways as we, a foreign family, settled in South Bend IN,
- Marie-Eve, Gabrielle, Jean-David and Christophe, my four adult and teen children, for their lively and joyful presence, which encouraged me day after day,
- and last but not least, Natacha, my wife. Without her love, her unshakable support and the acceptance of the sacrifices which flow from PhD research (proofreading of the dissertation included), this project would simply never have been brought to an end. This book is dedicated to her.

Chapter 1

Realism and Theology: Background, Scope and Relevance

1. Introduction

The question of the nature and the scope of theology is a broad yet crucial question for theologians. What are we doing when we study theology? Are we talking about *God* and the ways he interacts with the world, or are we dealing with *human beliefs* about God? Is theology a science? If so, what are the criteria which define its scientific character? What are the roles of faith and reason in the practice of this discipline? Might the theologian employ philosophical tools? Do these questions above belong to the field of theology, or are they a preamble to theology? Such interrogations are almost as old as theology itself, and since the seventeenth century and the emergence of modernity in Western countries, they have been increasingly debated. Nowadays they are inescapable for any theologian who wants to practice his or her discipline in a reflexive way.

Issues related to *realism in theology* belong to these types of questions and underlie the work of many contemporary theologians.[1] A shortlist of such important issues includes the following: If God exists, is it possible for human beings to *really* know something about him, and to formulate *true* theological affirmations? Or do human beings only know what they believe or think about God, but not God himself? Are theological statements only ways of describing a conceptual fiction or an inaccessible reality, i.e., God, or is theology a truth-seeking discipline? Answering these questions related to *realism in theology* is difficult for at least two reasons. First, it implies working on numerous complex and interconnected theological fields, such as the doctrine of God (the being and the attributes of God), the doctrine of revelation (in a wide sense that includes notably Christology, the theology of creation and Scripture), and theological anthropology. Secondly, over recent centuries intense

---

1 In this book, I will here and there use the formula *realism in theology* in italics. This formula needs to be understood as a short form of "the realist conception of theology and the issues that result."

discussions over the above-mentioned questions have considerably increased the complexity of the debates, to the point where it is now difficult to master their multiform character.

I nevertheless think that these questions still have to be studied with care, since modern and postmodern thought continues to pose an important challenge to classical Christian faith in relation to such issues.² Going against important cultural trends in Western societies, I do not consider that the *realism in theology* file is closed, or that it is more reasonable to admit the impossibility of knowing anything real and speaking the truth about God. Nor do I agree that the empirical and comparative approach of religious studies is more cogent and responsible than the uncertain practice of theology. I believe instead that realism is an important component of Christian theology that should not be buried too hastily, and that Christian theologians should not be too impressed by modern and postmodern anti-realist conceptions of theology. On the contrary, I assume that it is still an important task for Christian thinkers to develop arguments that promote realism in theology as a viable and cogent intellectual option. In short, I consider that it is possible and desirable to work on answering John Milbank's provocative question: "How should one respond to the death of realism, the death of the idea that thoughts in our minds can represent the way things actually are in the world?"³

The aim of this book is thus to apply an answer to Milbank's question to the field of theological studies by showing how the work of two important thinkers, the early twentieth century Dutch Reformed

---

2 In this book, I regularly use the adjective "classical" with expressions such as "Christian faith" or "Christian theology." Even if this concept is not very precise, it helpfully characterizes forms of Christianity that adhere in a rather straightforward way to the dogmatic content of the Nicene Creed (325). Colin Gunton, in his introduction to the Christian faith, also works with this concept and gives an interesting definition that is directly related to the scope of this research: "The reason for the approach taken in this book is that Christianity is a faith which—among other things—claims certain things to be true: about God, the world and our human species. In recent times a number of strategies have been devised which attempt to bypass or evade Christianity's claim to be true, but they will not finally work [...]. This claim for truth is made first of all by a community of belief known as the church, and takes the form of articulation in creeds and confessions. Over the course of history, there has been—at least until the era we call "modern"—a general and remarkable unanimity about the content and centrality of those creeds." Colin Gunton, *The Christian Faith. An Introduction to Christian Doctrine* (Oxford: Blackwell, 2002), viii-xi.
3 John Milbank and Catherine Pickstock, *Truth in Aquinas* (London and New York: Routledge, 2001), 1.

theologian Herman Bavinck (1854-1921) and the contemporary American analytic philosopher of religion Alvin Plantinga (born in 1932), can mutually strengthen each other. My goal in this matter is to propose a realist conception of theology that is well-informed, coherent and cogent in the contemporary context.

In this first chapter, I present the elements that will allow the reader to seize the background, the relevance and the scope of this research: I begin by drawing a broad sketch of philosophical and theological key issues related to the question of realism (2). This section will outline the general background against which I develop the research. I then narrow the focus onto contemporary theological anti-realist and realist trends (3). The aim of these pages is to put forward the relevance of the research by showing that the topic of *realism in theology* is still debated among theologians and philosophers of religion. After these two contextual sections, I finally present the research question, the method employed, and the structure of this book (4).

2. Realism in Philosophy and Christian Theology: A Brief Overview

The topic of realism has elicited crucial philosophical and theological debates for many centuries and continues to receive much scholarly attention in both fields. As Eberhard Herrmann, speaking of the tradition of analytical philosophy, states:

> One of the most exciting philosophical discussions in the analytic tradition is about the relationship between human consciousness and human language on the one hand and the world on the other. It is a subject that never loses its philosophical actuality. The complexity of the question increases considerably if, moreover, it is assumed that we are not merely part of the world, but are also required consciously to relate to it, and interact with it. More exactly, the discussion focuses on the question whether we can talk unambiguously about objectivity and truth, or alternatively, whether relativism is unavoidable due to the fact that the human perspective is always tied to a certain context.[4]

These very condensed lines make clear the importance, as well as the complexity and interwovenness of the questions related to realism. In fact, the term "realism" does not refer to one particular stance (like "theism" or "rationalism") but covers a whole range of positions, depending

---

4 Eberhard Herrmann, *Religion, Reality and a Good Life* (Tübingen: Mohr Siebeck, 2004), 1.

on the particular domain or debate in which it is used.⁵ Presumably, these positions are mutually related (that is why it makes sense to refer to them using the same concept), but they are by no means identical, nor do they necessarily imply each other.

In what follows, the goal is not and cannot possibly be to provide a detailed historical or systematic account of all theological and philosophical debates in which the term "realism" has played or is playing a role. Rather, I will keep in mind the specific topic of this inquiry, which can be named a "realist conception of theology." I will define this concept more precisely in the course of this chapter, but for now it may suffice to roughly describe it as the view that God is a living being who exists independently of the human mind, who can be known by humans, and about whom true statements can be made. The modest goal in this section is to situate this notion of theological realism within the context of realism-related debates as these take place across the philosophical landscape. In particular, I will mention some of the key issues that play a role in these debates. The account in this section provides samples what can be found in more elaborate ways in many general surveys and handbooks of (the history of) philosophy. Thus, it will hopefully enable the reader to perceive the bigger picture that composes the background of this research.

2.1 Sectional Realisms and Their Counterparts
To start with, the label "realism" has played an important role in some wide-ranging debates that are relatively independent from the theological issues that are of concern in this book, because these debates focus on specific segments or sections of reality. Without trying to sketch these debates even cursorily, I will mention the key issues that are at stake in some of them (and these examples may serve as *partes pro toto*).

First, "realism" became a technical term in the well-known medieval debates on the question of whether the so-called *universals*—properties that can be instantiated by more than one individual entity—exist independently of these entities. The affirmation of this view was called realism.⁶ Today, it is also often referred to as Platonism—Plato being one

---
5 Cf. Christopher J. Insole, "Realism and Anti-Realism," in *The Oxford Handbook of the Epistemology of Theology*, ed. William J. Abraham and Frederick D. Aquino (Oxford: Oxford University Press, 2017), 274.
6 Cf. e.g. Panavot Butchvarov, "Conceptualism," in *The Cambridge Dictionary of Philosophy*, ed. Robert Audi (Cambridge: Cambridge University Press, 1995), 148, and for a more detailed account Gyula Klima, "The Medieval Problem of Universals," *Stanford Encyclopedia of Philosophy* (Winter 2017 edition), Edward N. Zalta (ed.), URL

of its most influential proponents. Its denial used to be called nominalism, i.e. the view that rather than being entities in and of themselves, universals are just names (*nomina*) given by humans. However, such denial could also take the more sophisticated form of conceptualism: universals (like "rectangularity") are mental ideas that enable us to subsume various objects in particular classes according to their similarities and differences. The debate on the nature of universals is still ongoing,[7] but since God is not a universal but a particular—in its capitalized form, the term typically refers to one and only one being—it does not have a clear theological counterpart, and what we call theological realism does not seem to correspond to a particular stance in this debate.

Second, the term realism often serves as the counterpart of traditional *idealism*, i.e. the view that real objects are dependent on, or (in a more moderate version) correlated with perception.[8] The paradigmatic example of this type of idealism is George Berkeley, who famously claimed that *esse est percipi*: to be real is to be perceived. Realists, in this sense, typically *deny* that material objects are dependent for their existence on being perceived (or even perceivable). Again, there do not seem to be relevant theological issues at stake in this debate. As is clear from the case of Berkeley himself, idealism does not exclude (and in his case even requires) theological realism: in terms of which all things exist because they are perceived by God. God, not being a material entity, exists in and of itself. Also, Berkeley believed that God can be known, and that therefore true statements could be formulated about God, and that neither view was inconsistent with his idealism. As we will soon find out, in the course of time traditional idealism developed into a more sophisticated variety that *did* affect the issue of realism in theology. Before examining this version, however, it may be useful to point to some other realisms that do not seem to have any great effect on the prospects of theological realism.

Third, I must mention the notion of *moral realism* in this connection. While, like the other versions of realism discussed here, moral realism comes in different forms, the underlying idea is fairly easy to convey: morality is not just a matter of people's preferences, emotions or social

---

= <https://plato.stanford.edu/archives/win2017/entries/universals-medieval/>.

7 Cf. e.g. Nicholas P. Wolterstorff, *On Universals. An Essay in Ontology* (Chicago: University of Chicago Press, 1970).

8 For example, Paul Guyer and Rolf-Peter Horstmann, "Idealism," *The Stanford Encyclopedia of Philosophy* (Fall 2020 edition), ed. Edward N. Zalta, URL = https://plato.stanford.edu/archives/fall2020/entries/idealism/. Here idealism is chiefly considered a philosophical movement gaining traction in the eighteenth century, though its roots can of course be traced all the way back to antiquity.

constructions, but corresponds to moral facts that exist independently of people's beliefs and attitudes. Most moral realists will add that moral judgments are propositions that have truth value and that it is possible to know at least some moral facts. Moral anti-realists, by contrast, will deny that moral propositions refer to objective facts ("moral subjectivism"), that moral propositions are true ("error theory"), or that moral utterances are propositions with any truth value ("non-cognitivism").[9] Although there are clear parallels between moral and theological realism and anti-realism, as shall be seen in the next section, there does not seem to be an implicative relationship between the two. That is, it is possible to be a moral realist and a theological anti-realist (Iris Murdoch being a case in point). Conversely, it also seems possible to combine theological realism and moral anti-realism (although, admittedly, this is a less likely combination, since those who believe in God usually relate God and the moral good).

Fourth, realism and anti-realism also play a role in reflection on the nature of *science*. Traditionally, the debate here focuses on the status of so-called "unobservables": entities (like electrons, quarks, magnetic fields etc.) that are invoked in scientific theories because of their explanatory and predictive value. Do such concepts correspond to realities outside the mind of the scientists, or are they just tools or instruments that help with understanding and predicting certain phenomena? Scientific realists affirm the former, whereas scientific anti-realists adopt the latter, "instrumentalist" view. One of the best-known instrumentalists is Bas van Fraassen, according to whom science aims at "empirical adequacy," i.e., a theory is empirically adequate "if what it says about the observable things and events in the world, is true."[10] Note that Van Fraassen is agnostic about the truth-value of non-observable entities (such that he might be considered a non-realist rather than an anti-realist), whereas so-called "fictionalists" are more outspoken in denying that unobservables exist or that propositions positing them have truth value.[11] Again, it seems

---

9 Cf. Geoff Sayre-McCord, "Moral Realism," *The Stanford Encyclopedia of Philosophy* (Winter 2020 edition), ed. Edward N. Zalta, URL = <https://plato.stanford.edu/archives/win2020/entries/moral-realism/>. According to a 2009 survey held among 3226 philosophers, some 56 percent of them support or lean towards moral realism, whereas some 28 percent are friends of anti-realism (the others indicating "other"); see https://philpapers.org/surveys/results.pl?affil=Target+faculty&areas0=0&areas_max=1&grain=coarse

10 Bas C. van Fraassen, *The Scientific Image* (Oxford: Oxford University Press, 1980), 12.

11 Arthur Fine, "Fictionalism," *Midwest Studies in Philosophy* 18 (1993), 1–18. See also the overview of the issues in Anjan Chakravartty, "Scientific Realism," *The Stanford*

that this debate does not have a direct bearing on the issue of theological realism. Indirectly, instrumentalism implies a form of skepticism towards unobservables that may easily be seen as also affecting the great unobservable entity of theology, viz. God. Yet there is no implicative relation here, since God is not, to most religious believers, a theoretical concept. Non- or anti-realism with regard to scientific concepts cannot without further argument be extended to God.

This summary of varieties of realism that are relatively independent of the *realism in theology* debate is by no means exhaustive. More instantiations could be mentioned (e.g. mathematical realism, or realism about numbers), but it can be assumed that the conclusions with regard to their relation to theological realism will not be different. Arguably, the reason for this is that these are all sectional forms of realism, i.e. forms limited to a particular section of reality, be it universals, material objects, moral values, scientific theories (or, rather, specific entities posited in such theories) or mathematical concepts. What is true for one section does not necessarily apply to others. That is why no direct implications follow for theology and its subject matter from these sectional realism-debates. Yet, there are also more generic realism issues, which pertain to all of reality, all human knowledge, and/or all our propositions. It seems natural to assume that these issues *do* have a bearing on *realism in theology* debates. Let us therefore now turn to a brief discussion of these more general issues.

2.2 General Philosophical Realism and Its Alternatives
In the previous section I suggested that traditional idealism (as I called it) received an offshoot that would exert a tremendous influence on the realism in theology debates. It is now time to introduce this variety of anti-realism and see what realism means when construed as its opposite. The version I have in mind comes with different names, such as transcendental idealism, critical idealism, constructivism and "creative anti-realism."[12] In its most straightforward form, this position holds that everything that exists depends for its very existence on the workings of our mind. Using specific concepts, or, rather, a complex conceptual framework, we "make" things into what they are—we construe or construct them by means of mental tools that we use to structure and

Encyclopedia of Philosophy (Summer 2017 edition), ed. Edward N. Zalta, URL = <https://plato.stanford.edu/archives/sum2017/entries/scientific-realism/>.

12 "Creative anti-realism" is the term used by Alvin Plantinga. See for example his *Twin Pillars of Christian Scholarship* (Grand Rapids: Calvin College and Seminary, 1990), 14-17.

interpret the raw materials of our experience. Given the fact that we cannot bypass these conceptual tools, we have no direct access to reality as it is in itself and therefore, we cannot make true statements about it.

This view, of course, can be traced back to Immanuel Kant. Yet whereas Kant held that the conceptual tools we use in ordering our experience are universally the same, later constructivists started to differentiate between various conceptual frameworks, even allowing for a myriad of different ways in which people structure their experience, depending on their cultural and social conditions. Both in this "social constructivism" and in its Kantian predecessor we can distinguish at least three dimensions: a metaphysical, an epistemological and a semantic one.[13] Critical idealism and social constructivism have a bearing on how we construe all of reality, on the conditions of possibility for all human knowledge, and on the meaning and truth-value of all our propositional assertions. These same three dimensions can also be detected in their counterpart: general philosophical realism—that is, that form of realism that is not limited to a specific section of reality but extends to all of it. Although these dimensions are often interlocked in intricate ways, this common taxonomy seems still useful for teasing out the various conceptual options on offer. After presenting the main philosophical issues along each of these three lines, in the next section I will start to explore the topic that is at the center of this study: theological realism and its issues.[14]

The first and most fundamental dimension of the question of realism is ontological or *metaphysical*.[15] One can define metaphysical realism as

---

13 Here I follow a common pattern of analyzing general (as well as sectional) realisms and their counterparts. See for instance Insole, "Realism and Anti-Realism," 274-289; Edward Craig, "Realism and Antirealism," in *Routledge Encyclopedia of Philosophy Online* (2020), doi 10.4324/9780415249126-N049-1; Chakravartty, "Scientific Realism," §1.2; David O. Brink, "Moral Realism," in *Cambridge Dictionary of Philosophy*, 511-512.

14 In this book, I follow John Webster's definition of theology proposed in "On the Theology of the Intellectual Life," in *God Without Measure: Working Papers in Christian Theology. Vol. II: Virtue and Intellect* (London and New York: T&T Clark, 2016), 141: "The object of Christian theological inquiry is God and all things in relation to God. This integral object can for purposes of analysis be broken down into two topics. First, theology is inquiry into God in himself, into the eternal, perfect and eternally blessed life of God in the Holy Trinity in his inner works. Second, and derivatively, theology is inquiry into the economy, that is, into the outer works of God as creator, reconciler and perfecter of creatures, and so into the unfolding of created realities as they come from and return to God."

15 In this book, I will follow the article devoted to metaphysics in the *Cambridge Dictionary of Philosophy* and consider the adjectives "metaphysical" and "ontological" as quasi-synonyms, even if one may observe that metaphysics deals with a wider scope

the affirmation that there is an external reality, in the form of a spatiotemporal world, independent of the human mind and its conceptual or social constructions. It is interesting to note that Kant, although he denied the possibility of acquiring knowledge about such an external world, did not deny its existence. In that sense, he was an epistemological non-realist but a metaphysical realist. After Kant, the epistemological dimension of the realism debate took center stage, since few anti-realists (apart from some "solipsists") went so far as to actually deny the existence of a spatiotemporal world. In this context, it is not surprising to notice that twentieth century philosophers and theologians have been deeply preoccupied with epistemological issues. A consequence of this modern heritage on the realism debates is that they are often perceived as mainly epistemological discussions.[16]

Moving on to *epistemological* realism, we may define this provisionally as the view that external reality can (at least approximately) be known as it is. In its most straightforward (classical or "naïve") form, epistemological realism affirms that external reality is intelligible, and that human beings have direct (even if not exhaustive) access to it. Most Greek and medieval thinkers took this position. In spite of some divergences, there is a vast consensus around the idea that the union of the knowing subject and the known object in the act of knowledge produces a quite unmediated knowledge of external reality. From this perspective, the concepts shaped by the human mind have a purely transitive function.[17] In modern times, the Scottish Common Sense philosopher, Thomas Reid (1710-1796), elaborated this view into a full-blown philosophical position.[18] A modern

---

of questions than ontology (which concentrates on the study of being *qua* being). For more details, see Peter van Inwagen, *Metaphysics* (Boulder: Westview Press, 2009).

16 This affirmation is true at least in the Anglo-Saxon philosophical world. In the Continental context, the important influence of post-modernity tends also to put forward semantic issues, as will be shown in the next subsection.

17 As Thomas F. Torrance sums up: "In all our basic acts of perception and knowledge, meaning [...] is displaced away from ourselves, so that when we adopt something, sensible or intelligible, as a sign for something else our attention does not rest upon the sign but on what it indicates or points to: it is, so to speak, a transparent medium through which we operate." See his "Theological Realism," in *The Philosophical Frontiers of Christian Theology*, ed. Brian Hebblethwaite and Stewart Sutherland (Cambridge: Cambridge University Press, 1982), 169.

18 This observation is important in the context of this present research, since Alvin Plantinga, whose work will be studied in this book, perceives himself as an intellectual heir of Thomas Reid. My model for a realist conception of theology can thus be indirectly related to this intellectual tradition. See Terence Cuneo and René van Woudenberg (eds.), *The Cambridge Companion to Thomas Reid* (Cambridge: Cambridge University Press, 2004).

variation on this realist theme can be found in early twentieth century logical positivism (see for instance the theses of the Vienna Circle). A major difference between classical and positivist realism is that the latter, contrary to the former, evacuates the possibility of knowing anything that is not observable (and thus rejects metaphysics, not to mention theology).[19]

The second important stance admits the intelligibility of the world, but affirms that it can be grasped only in an indirect way by human beings. This trend acknowledges that we know the external world only through the screen of concepts and intellectual schemes produced by our mind, but denies that this blocks our access to the spatiotemporal world as it is. The origins of this philosophical position may probably be found in the work of Duns Scotus (c. 1266-1308). Contrary to classical realism, which assumes the unity of the knowing subject and the known object in the act of knowledge, Duns Scotus affirmed that when confronted with external reality, the knowing subject produces a mental image (the *esse repraesentatum*), which becomes the effective object of knowledge (instead of reality itself).[20] It is possible to interpret Kantian idealism as a radicalized modern version of this stance which contributed to widely extending its audience. From a contemporary point of view, this view—often called "critical realism"—can be understood as an attempt to propose a *via media* between classical realism and anti-realism.

The third position to be mentioned here is epistemological anti-realism, which is based on a rejection of the notion of the intelligibility of the world. If external reality is not intelligible, human knowledge is a mere construction of the human mind or human culture (*constructivism*) or an instrument for producing practical results (*pragmatism*). The road towards knowledge of the spatiotemporal world as it is in itself is blocked by the conceptual categories we use to interpret our experiences of it. Yet, as noted, often the basic existence of an external spatiotemporal world is presupposed by epistemological anti-realists. The close relation between ontology and epistemology is obvious here, since it is impossible to know (or to discover) an intelligibility that does not exist in the world. This

---

19 Positivist realism became strongly criticized by philosophers of science in the second part of the twentieth century. The contemporary renewal of the epistemology of theology that is part of the background of my research is to be understood in this wider perspective, and not necessarily as a critique of classical epistemological realism.
20 See André de Muralt, "La doctrine médiévale de l'*esse objectivum*," in *L'Enjeu de la Philosophie Médiévale* (Leiden: Brill, 1993), 90-167.

short description provides the matrix of all forms of epistemological anti-realism that will be described below, both in their idealist and pragmatist versions.[21]

On the *semantic* level, finally, a realist position is one in which the meaning of a statement is determined by what would make that statement true. For example, we know what "the cat is on the mat" means if and only if we know what it is for the cat to be on the mat—that is, only if we know what would make "the cat is on the mat" true. The question of semantic realism seems intimately related to that of epistemological realism, since as human beings we use propositions that express what we know in order to share this knowledge with others. Our knowledge (epistemology) and the expression of this knowledge (semantics) can thus be considered as two sides of a coin. Yet, there is a special twist here in the focus on the concept of truth, which is why semantic realism is also sometimes called "truth-realism" or "alethic realism."[22] Semantic realism, or truth-realism, is the thesis that an assertion is true if and only if what the assertion claims is actually the case. Semantic anti-realism, on the other hand, holds that the truth of a statement depends on whether or not we are justified in uttering it, or have warrant, or enough evidence, to do so. Semantic anti-realists consider that we do not have simple unmediated access to the external world to find out whether or not something "is the case." Thus, as with epistemological anti-realism, there is a subjective element in semantic anti-realism, in that the truth of a statement is dependent on whether one is able to prove or verify that statement or otherwise secure its truth-making conditions.[23]

Obviously, semantic realism issues are connected with the way in which one navigates the classical debate on the three main theories of truth. Semantic realists will usually favor a correspondence theory of

---

21 It is possible to connect the question of epistemological realism to the contemporary analytical debates on the structure (or construction) of human knowledge that oppose *foundationalists* with *coherentists*. As these concepts do not play an important role in this work, they are not included in this synthesis. As an introduction to these debates, one may read the famous article of Ernest Sosa, "The Raft and The Pyramid," *Midwest Studies in Philosophy, Vol. 5: Studies in Epistemology* (Minneapolis: University of Minnesota, 1980), 3-25.

22 "Broadly speaking, the essential thesis of AR [alethic realism] is that whether a statement is true or not is independent of our epistemic means such as justification, warrant, or evidence." Murat Baç and Renée Elio, "Scheme-Based Alethic Realism: Agency, the Environment, and Truthmaking," *Minds and Machines* 14 (2004), 175.

23 Semantic anti-realists such as Michael Dummet, Hilary Putnam and others have different views about what exactly is required here. See Insole, "Realism and Anti-Realism," 287.

truth, whereas semantic anti-realists usually advocate a coherentist or a pragmatist theory, according to which, roughly speaking, a statement is true when it "works." Also, semantic realism issues have a link with discussions on the type of language that is most appropriate to refer to reality—either formal/mathematical language, as the logical positivists argued, poetic language, as the Romantics and Heidegger suggested, or ordinary language, as the later Wittgenstein and his followers proposed. Rather than exploring these debates further, however, I instead examine how the various dimensions of general realism and anti-realism have shaped (or, perhaps, interacted with) the discussion about *theological* realism.

2.3 Theological Realism and Its Issues

Starting with the theological counterpart of *metaphysical* realism, the most obvious question is whether there is a being named *God* whose reality is independent of the human mind and social constructions. Almost all theologians in history have answered this question positively and consider this positive answer a presupposition of their theological work.[24] Of course, atheists disagree. Yet, the discussion about metaphysical theological realism is not identical to the theism-atheism debate. It is important to see that a more subtle question is lurking in the background here, namely: if God exists, could it be the case that the mode of God's existence is external to the human mind? Note that this question may also be answered affirmatively by atheists. Thus, it is possible for an atheist to be a metaphysical theological realist.

Theologians have usually discussed questions related to metaphysical realism in the "Doctrine of God" sections of their systematic theologies, and in separate treatises on what is sometimes called "theology proper." The basic question here is: what can be said about God's *being*? This question has generated varied and vast discussions that can be divided into three categories. First, there have been debates on the cogency of applying the metaphysical concept of *being* to God, from the first centuries' Christianized Neo-Platonist speculations to the twentieth century post-Heideggerian critiques of "onto-theology." Second, there have been vast discussions on the attributes of God and on their relation to God's being, with often fine-grained distinctions being made between,

---

24 An exception can be found in the 1960s post-Nietzschean "Death of God" theology that militated for a Christian atheism. For a more recent illustration, in 2011 the French translation was published of a book by Klaas Hendrikse, a Dutch "atheist pastor": *Croire en un Dieu qui n'existe pas: Manifeste d'un Pasteur athée* (Genève: Labor et Fides, 2011).

for example, God's communicable and incommunicable attributes. Finally, moving from generic to specifically Christian theism, the theological tradition added to these considerations reflections on the Trinitarian nature of God.[25]

Other metaphysical realism questions emerge when one considers theology not only as the *science of God* but also as the discipline that studies God's relation with the world and human beings, or the world and human beings in light of their relation with God. On these questions, classical Christian theologians generally made two important ontological assertions. First, they believed that the world, understood as God's creation, bears an imprint of its creator; and this imprint is the origin of the intelligibility of the world. In the Augustinian tradition, this intelligibility was understood in Platonist terms (the intelligibility of the creation lies in participation with the supreme intelligibility of God). In the Thomistic tradition, and in Aristotelian terms, the intelligibility of the creation is to be found in concrete beings and can be related to God by the study of causality. These classical affirmations of the intelligibility of the world are generally presented in the sections on *general revelation* or the *doctrine of creation* in systematic theologies.

Second, while thinking about the Incarnation, the providential actions of God, and Jesus' miracles as narrated in the gospels, theologians usually regarded these notions as extra-mental ontological realities also. That means that they considered the external world ontologically open to God's direct action. This ontological stance led them to develop an utterly realistic understanding of God's relation to the created world. After the seventeenth century scientific revolution, however, this assumed openness of the world to God's direct action became very much subject to debate. The modern naturalistic ontology conceived the natural world as a closed and deterministic system governed by inviolable scientific laws. This ontology became more and more influential, and the scope of its determinism more greatly extended.[26] Several theologians who were impressed by this naturalistic (or "scientistic") worldview developed an anti-realist understanding of world's openness to God's action. The work of Rudolf Bultmann (1884-1976) is a seminal illustration of this approach.

---

25 For a contemporary introduction to these three categories of questions, see chapters 2 and 3 of Cornelis van der Kooi and Gijsbert van den Brink, *Christian Dogmatics. An Introduction* (Grand Rapids: Eerdmans Publishing, 2017).

26 The non-deterministic character of some contemporary scientific theories (such as quantum mechanics, on certain interpretations) does not necessarily modify this statement, since numerous scientists still presuppose a naturalistically closed world that excludes the direct intervention of a supernatural being.

Since the natural world is an ontologically closed reality, the biblical narratives that present direct actions of God have to be understood in an anti-realist symbolic way that allows the seizing of their existential dimension.[27]

Turning now to the theological issues related to *epistemological* realism, we may observe that, due to the unique nature of its primary subject matter (viz. God), theology had started to face the challenges of "naive" epistemological realism long before the Kantian turn in philosophy. All along theologians had to do justice to the biblical (and more broadly monotheistic) affirmation that God is both knowable *and* incomprehensible. In Christian theology, the classical solution to the epistemological tension generated by this dual affirmation was to distinguish between two types of theology that were supposed to exercise a constant regulative function over each other. *Cataphatic* (or affirmative) theology had to make clear what could be known of God as revealed in Jesus Christ, while *apophatic* (or negative) theology had to always recall the fundamental limitations of human knowledge of God.[28] In the Middle Ages, theologians elaborated on this patristic heritage and developed what is called the *triplex via*, composed of the *via affirmationis*, the *via negativa*, and the *via eminentiae*, that is "a process in which affirmative and negative discourse about God taken together signifies the most effective way of approaching God."[29]

During the Reformation, while mainly relying on patristic and medieval developments, Martin Luther and John Calvin developed slightly different concepts to deal with the tension. Luther introduced an explicit dialectic between what he called the *hidden God* and the *revealed*

---

27 See, for example, Rudolf Bultmann, "Neues Testament und Mythologie. Das Problem der Entmythologisierung der neutestamentlichen Verkündigung," in *Kerygma und Mythos. Ein theologisches Gespräch*, ed. Hans Werner Bartsch (Hamburg: Herbert Reich Evangelischer Verlag, 1960), 15-48. Bultmann is characteristic here of the post-Kantian position in theology more generally conceived: the phenomenal world is an ontologically closed reality, and theology, as a discipline that aims at noumenal realities, should abandon claims to ontological realism in order to work on the level of religious experience or ethical involvement.
28 For a specific approach of apophatic theology, read Denys Turner, *The Darkness of God. Negativity in Christian Mysticism* (Cambridge: Cambridge University Press, 1995). For a well-balanced theological synthesis of *cataphatic* and *apophatic* theologies among the church fathers, see Justin Popovitch, *Philosophie Orthodoxe de la Vérité*, tome 1 (Lausanne: L'Age d'Homme, 1992). section I 1.
29 Paul van Geest, *The Incomprehensibility of God. Augustine as a Negative Theologian* (Leuven: Peeters, 2011), 37.

God.[30] God's transcendence is always hidden in his revelation, and God can only be seized by faith through the experience of the cross.[31] Calvin borrowed from his humanist education the classical rhetorical concept of the *accommodation* of the speaker to the listener and applied it to God. The result was an important epistemological (and semantic) doctrine called *accommodatio Dei*: in order to make himself known to human beings, God accommodates himself to our limited faculties.[32] Elaborating on this doctrine, shortly after the Reformation the Reformed scholastic theologians introduced a distinction between what they called *archetypal* theology and *ectypal* theology. By archetypal theology they meant God's perfect self-knowledge, by ectypal theology, the derived and imperfect knowledge of God that is accessible to humans.[33] Thus, from the patristic era to the Reformation and beyond, classical Christianity developed in various ways a moderate realist epistemological understanding of theology that was always accompanied by an anti-realist coloration generated by God's transcendence. This tension has elicited the finest Christian reflections on theological epistemological realism over the centuries, and the aim here is to work from this perspective while developing my own realist conception of theology.

In the context of the modern epistemological philosophical debates mentioned in the previous section, the solutions proposed by classical

---

30 See John Dillenberger's classic: *God Hidden and Revealed. The Interpretation of Luther's Deus Absconditus and its Significance for Religious Thought* (Philadelphia: Muhlenberg Press, 1953) and cf. Alister McGrath, *Luther's Theology of the Cross. Martin Luther's Theological Breakthrough* (Oxford: Blackwell, 1985). McGrath sums up Luther's stance as follows: "In the single event of revelation, the eye of faith discerns the *Deus revelatus*, where sense-perception can only find the *Deus absconditus*" (165).

31 This Lutheran Christological approach exercised a deep influence on Karl Barth's theological epistemology in his *Church Dogmatics* II.1. See John Webster's synthesis in *Barth* (London and New York: Continuum, 2004), 81-82.

32 See Jon Balserak, *Divinity Compromised. A Study of Divine Accommodation in the Thought of John Calvin* (Dordrecht: Springer, 2006) and Paul Helm, *John Calvin's Ideas* (Oxford: Oxford University Press, 2004), 184-208. According to Helm, the central idea of Calvin's religious epistemology is "that much of our knowledge of God is due to God's gracious accommodation of himself to our straitened epistemic condition" (184).

33 See Richard A. Muller, *Dictionary of Latin and Greek Theological Terms Drawn Principally from Protestant Scholastic Theology* (Grand Rapids: Baker Books, 1985): "Theologia archetypa: *archetypal theology*, the infinite knowledge of God known only to God himself, which is the archetype or ultimate pattern for all true theology" (299-300); "Theologia ectypa: *ectypal theology*; i.e., all true finite theology, defined as a reflection of the divine archetype. *Theologia ectypa* is, therefore, a broad category into which all knowledge of God available to finite minds is gathered" (300).

Christian theologians have lost their influence and new tendencies have appeared. The first of these was the emergence of rationalist approaches in theology that tended to underestimate the incomprehensibility of God. The appreciation of reason in science and philosophy impacted theology and contributed to the building of logical systems that were supposed to exactly mirror the divine nature and actions.[34] This tendency can be illustrated by the vast metaphysical and philosophical theology systems of the seventeenth century, and also, in a somewhat paradoxical way, by early twentieth century fundamentalist approaches, which often display a similar overconfidence in human reason. The second tendency, no doubt in part provoked by the first, was precisely the opposite, namely downplaying the possibility of human knowledge of God by one-sidedly emphasizing the apophatic dimension of theology. In many post-Kantian forms of theology, this shift led to the "anthropologizing" of theology, which came to be perceived as the study of the human experience of the divine.[35] In this context, one can observe a remarkable convergence between generic epistemological anti-realism and apophatic theologies, thinly concealed by latter's apparently humble Christian recognition of God's transcendence. In short, since the modern loss of balance, theologians have been under pressure from both trends of underestimating or overestimating God's incomprehensibility.[36]

Just as was the case with epistemological realism, the problems of *semantic* realism had been discovered and addressed by theologians long before Kant. This, again, was due to the peculiar nature of their main object, namely an incomprehensible God. Indeed, theology is probably

---

34 William C. Placher has described this phenomenon in *The Domestication of Transcendence. How Modern Thinking about God Went Wrong* (Louisville: Westminster John Know Press, 1996).

35 Cornelis van der Kooi aptly summarizes the impact of the Kantian epistemological revolution on theology as follows: "In his [Kant's] thinking, and in particular in his epistemology, the turn from a theocentric view of the world to an anthropocentric point of departure comes to be seen. Knowledge is henceforth no longer knowledge of the preternatural, of divine truth. With modern philosophy knowledge comes to be ever more strictly regarded as knowledge that is limited to human, earthly things, and has the status of an object, which does not extend beyond the limited horizon of human faculties." Cornelis van der Kooi, *As in a Mirror. John Calvin and Karl Barth on Knowing God* (Leiden and Boston: Brill, 2005), 225.

36 §27 of Karl Barth's *Church Dogmatics II/1* (179-254) is a significant attempt to maintain the classical balance between the incomprehensibility and the knowability of God in a modern context. Its influence on twentieth century theology can hardly be overestimated.

the only discipline that claims to talk about an incomprehensible object.[37] If the epistemological question that puzzled theologians concerned what it meant to know a God who was both incomprehensible and knowable, the semantic question was "How can one truthfully speak of such a God?" In a sense, both questions were addressed along the same lines. When the church fathers developed their distinction between apophatic and cataphatic theologies, this was also a *semantic* distinction: while speaking about God in order to make true statements about who, what, or how God is, one should always remember that God is *not* captured by such statements, since God is above human predication. The same proviso is expressed in the medieval *triplex via*, the Lutheran dialectic of the revealed and the hidden God, the Calvinist doctrine of divine accommodation, and the post-Reformation distinction between archetypal and ectypal theology.

Yet, the study of the semantic aspect of theological realism also led to a specific contribution that played an important role in Christian theology for centuries. Using the concept of *analogy*, medieval theologians, in particular Thomas Aquinas (1225-1274), developed an authentically theological semantic theory.[38] Without going into details, the aim of this theory was to form a conception of theological discourse that avoided both equivocity and univocity. Aquinas's theory steered a judicious middle course between these two extremes by suggesting that our words and concepts do not retain the same meaning when applied to God. Neither do they become entirely vacuous, since there is an analogy, or partial similarity, between God and the world. In this way, premodern theology avoided the problems raised by both naïve semantic realism and semantic anti-realism. In modernity, however, the epistemological tendency to underestimate God's incomprehensibility was naturally accompanied by a more univocal use of language in theology, whereas the tendency to overestimate God's incomprehensibility came with an equivocal conception of theological discourse. Hence, the classical synthesis broke down.

We have seen that on the epistemological side, modern theologians have been deeply challenged by notions of divine revelation and human knowledge of God. On the semantic side, the debate has focused on the nature of religious truth and religious language. In this debate, semantic

---

37 Eberhard Jüngel develops these questions with care in sections 3 and 4 of *God as the Mystery of the World. On the Foundation of the Theology of the Crucified One in the Dispute Between Theism and Atheism* (London and New York: Bloomsbury T&T Clark, 2014).

38 For a recent presentation of this subject, see Roger M. White, *Talking about God. The Concept of Analogy and the Problem of Religious Language* (Farnham: Ashgate, 2010).

theological realists can definitely acknowledge coherentist and pragmatist dimensions of what it means for a theological statement to be true. At the same time, however, they hold that true theological statements somehow correspond to the reality of God. Like their philosophical counterparts (as discussed in the previous session), they are friends of the correspondence theory of truth. Similarly, they may value highly non-cognitive modes of language such as myths, symbols, poetry, existential concepts etc., but, at the end of the day, they will contend that theological discourse is, or can be, "reality-depicting," in which case it conveys knowledge about God. In such ways, the semantic dimension of theological realism is intimately connected with its metaphysical and epistemological components.

3. Anti-Realist and Realist Trends in Contemporary Theological Studies

Having proposed a synoptic outline of the main key issues of the realism debates in philosophy and theology, in this section I narrow the scope of the presentation and focus on the contemporary theological discussions related to this research. By doing this, I move from the sketch of a general background to more immediate questions that will clarify the relevance of the project. The aim of this section is to show that the *realism in theology* file is open and still generates lively and important academic discussions. I therefore believe that it is useful to work on the elaboration of a cogent model for a realist conception of theology in the Western contemporary theological context. Before entering the core of this section, I start by clarifying more precisely my use of the concepts of "realism" and "anti-realism" (3.1). Secondly, I briefly present some important methodological choices I have made in my presentation of realist and anti-realist trends (3.2). I then describe what I hold to be the main contemporary anti-realist trends (3.3), before finally synthesizing the main realist trends (3.4).

3.1 A Definition of Realism and Anti-Realism in Theology
As shown in the previous section, there are many different forms of realism and anti-realism. One may adopt a general realist approach, or prefer sectional definitions, such as realism in mathematics, the experimental sciences, the human sciences, etc. One can be a realist in one domain and not in another one (for instance, one can be a realist in the experimental sciences and not in theology). And a realist as well as an anti-realist can ultimately adopt (subtly) different attitudes towards the ontological, epistemological and semantic dimensions of the question.

    A difficulty to be stressed before going further relates to questions of labels and which appears when one deals with contemporary works on realism. Numerous thinkers who seem to adhere to significant elements of anti-realist conceptions of theology are reluctant to be called *anti-realists*, and generally want to be designated with "softer" labels (the most striking example being *non-realism*). And conversely, many thinkers who seem to adhere to an apparently thoroughly realist conception of theology tend to integrate some traditionally anti-realist elements in the presentations of their systems. Between radical anti-realism and classical common-sense realism one can thus find a grey-scale image composed of non-realists, critical realists, symbolic realists, pragmatic realists, non-metaphysical realists, narrative realists, postmodern realists, non-foundationalist realists, etc.[39] It is not my purpose to study the intellectual, academic, editorial or psychological motivations that lead to this conceptual maze, but we nevertheless have to be aware of this situation before studying contemporary realist and anti-realist trends in theology.

In order to deal with workable concepts, I adopt Christopher Insole's clear-cut definition of realism and anti-realism in theology:

> I understand any approach to the practice of religion to be anti-realist *if and only if* it denies at least one of the following *four criteria for a realist construal of religious discourse*
> A) there is an indispensable core of religious utterances that are fact-asserting, not merely expressive (from here on I will refer to this core as "statements"),
> B) statements are made true by a non-epistemic state of affairs (the way the world is, rather than by standards of "ideal justification"),
> C) what is the case is independent of human cognition,
> D) we can, in principle, have true beliefs about what is the case independent of human cognition.
>
> Religious anti-realism involves a denial of at least one of these claims for religious statements.[40]

---

39 To take only contemporary examples, see among others, Andrew Moore's defense of *narrative realism* in Chapter 7 of *Realism and Christian Faith. God, Grammar, and Meaning* (Cambridge: Cambridge University Press, 2003), or Eberhard Herrmann, who argues in Part IV (116-181) of *Religion, Reality, and a Good Life* (Tübingen: Mohr Siebeck, 2004) for a "pragmatic realism with respect to religion," or Karin Johannesson who argues for a "non-metaphysical realism" applied to religious belief in chapter 6 of *God Pro Nobis. On Non-Metaphysical Realism and the Philosophy of Religion* (Leuven: Peeters, 2007), see especially pages 237-241.
40 Christopher J. Insole, *The Realist Hope. A Critique of Anti-Realist Approaches in Contemporary Philosophical Theology* (Aldershot and Burlington: Ashgate Publishing, 2006), 2. This definition is inspired by William Alston's important article "Realism and the Christian Faith," *International Journal for the Philosophy of Religion*, 3 (1995), 37-55.

This clear-cut definition of realism and anti-realism in theology has several advantages. First, it fits the content of the previous section, since it includes the three above-discussed dimensions of the realism debates: there is a structured reality which is independent of human cognition (the metaphysical dimension C), which, in principle, can be known (the epistemological dimension D), and described by "objectively" true factual propositions (the semantic dimension of A and B). Second, it is careful enough to allow for the possibility (already encountered in the previous section) that atheists can also adhere to theological realism. Even though they will reject most (if not all) theological statements as false, they may still acknowledge that such statements are "fact-asserting" (criterion A), rather than symbolic or something like that. Third, Insole stipulates a clear guideline for the unambiguous use of the concept of anti-realism in theology: irrespective of how one self-identifies, if one denies at least one of the criteria A-D, one counts as an anti-realist. Fourth, it firmly embeds the realism-in-theology debate in "the practice of religion," thus highlighting that it is not just an academic discussion but has much wider ramifications.

I am also sympathetic to Insole's strategy towards the lexical confusion that reigns in realism discussions:

> None of the theological thinkers I critique in this book as representing "anti-realism" would so style themselves. They prefer in general to be realists, or beyond the terms of the realist/anti-realist debate. I do not in fact much mind what anyone calls themselves. Depending on various self-stylings this book could be read as a "critique of certain sorts of realisms, and third-positions above realism and anti-realism which adopt a denial of one or more of A to D."[41]

Clarifying the concepts of realism and anti-realism in this way is not conducted with the aim of exercising a policing function over the *realism in theology* debates. The purpose is instead to display the wider conceptual frame that underlies this research.

Finally, apart from a very specific philosophical position, realism, in each and any of its forms, can also be seen more loosely as indicating a certain attitude, or stance, or "spirit." In this connection, Crispin Wright's synthetic remark on realism touches the nerve:

---

41 Insole, *The Realist Hope*, 3.

> Realism is a mixture of modesty and presumption. It modestly allows that humankind confronts an objective world, something almost entirely not of our making, possessing a host of occasional features which may pass altogether unnoticed by human consciousness and whose innermost nomological secrets may remain forever hidden from us. However, it presumes that we are, by and large and in favourable circumstances, capable of acquiring knowledge of the world and of understanding it.[42]

Even though I would replace the word "presumption" with "confidence," these lines display the spirit of realism in a way that characterizes my own perspective on the question.

3.2 Questions of Method

In this section, I present the main contemporary anti-realist and realist trends in theology by using an ideal-type (or paradigmatic) method. I describe the main characteristics of the various trends and briefly mention the work of thinkers who are particularly representative of these, without addressing questions that are too specific or formulating value judgments. By "contemporary" I mean the period starting around 1970. From the 1960s onwards, major renewals in the fields of the philosophy of science and the theory of knowledge deeply reshaped the intellectual landscape (the demise of the positivist conception of science; the development of new pragmatic models of science, with, for example, the work of T. S. Kuhn; the renewal of Kantian perspectives on science with the work of Karl Popper, etc.).[43] Theologians rapidly realized that these intense debates in philosophy and science could not be without consequences for their discipline. Thus, they started to rework the main questions related to the epistemology of theology, among which was the crucial question of realism. The various trends that will be described in this section can be understood in the light of this renewal.[44] Since both Bavinck and Plantinga

---

42 Crispin Wright, *Realism, Meaning and Truth* (Oxford and Cambridge: Blackwell, 1993), 1-2.
43 For a clear general introduction to these renewals, see Alan Chalmers, *What is this Thing Called Science?* (Maidenhead: Open University Press, 2013).
44 For a contemporary introduction to these developments in the philosophy of science and their impact on theology, see Gijsbert van den Brink, *Philosophy of Science for Theologians. An Introduction* (Frankfurt am Main: Peter Lang, 2009). For two significant historical sources, see Ian Barbour, *Issues in Science and Religion* (Englewood Cliffs: Prentice Hall, 1966) and Wolfhart Pannenberg, *Theology and the Philosophy of Science* (Philadelphia: Westminster Press, 1976).

are Protestants, and since Roman Catholics and Protestants no longer treat most issues related to realism in theology in significantly different ways, I will mainly concentrate on Protestant theology.[45] Eastern Orthodoxy will not be included, since the main *realism in theology* issues are typically Western concerns.

The chosen ideal-type method presents a limit one should be aware of. Many existing approaches do not necessarily fit perfectly in the described ideal-type, so there is a risk of oversimplification. An author can barely belong to a certain paradigm, or can borrow elements from different ideal-types, or can even move from one type to another. I nevertheless do not consider this limit to be too problematic, since I do not study thinkers for their own sake, but only as types of important anti-realist or realist trends in theology. Thus, the next chapters are further embedded in their proper context. In this way, the *simplifications* generated by working with typologies are not necessarily *oversimplifications*, in the sense that they need not distort the described realities, but may just as well enlighten them by stressing the main contours of a discussion.

3.3 Anti-Realist Trends

Anti-realist conceptions of theology play an important role in the contemporary Western context and thus deserve attention. I will propose two ideal-types (or paradigms, or models) inspired by the famous meta-theological typology contained in George Lindbeck's *The Nature of Doctrine*.[46] Lindbeck calls the first ideal-type the *experiential-expressive* model. He uses this term to describe systems that take their roots in the soil of the post-Kantian philosophy of religion and that have notably flourished in the Continental philosophical tradition. The second ideal-type is the *cultural-linguistic* model. This model originates in the Anglo-

---

45 The following is a list of interesting introductory material to contemporary Roman Catholic theology in relation to the questions that are the concern of this work: Fergus Kerr, *Twentieth-Century Catholic Theologians. From Neoscholasticism to Nuptial Mysticism* (Malden and Oxford: Blackwell Publishing, 2007). David F. Ford and Rachel Muers (eds.), *The Modern Theologians. An Introduction to Christian Theology since 1918* (Malden and Oxford: Blackwell Publishers, 2005, 3rd ed.). In this book, read in particular the articles devoted to Henri de Lubac, Karl Rahner, Hans Urs von Balthasar and on "Roman Catholic Theology after Vatican II." Hans Boersma, *Nouvelle Théologie and Sacramental Ontology. A Return to Mystery* (Oxford: Oxford University Press, 2009). Kevin J. Vanhoozer, *The Cambridge Companion to Postmodern Theology* (Cambridge: Cambridge University Press, 2003), and in particular Stephen Long's article devoted to radical orthodoxy.
46 George A. Lindbeck, *The Nature of Doctrine. Religion and Theology in a Postliberal Age*, 25th Anniversary edition (Louisville: Westminster John Knox Press, 2009), 16ff.

Saxon pragmatic tradition and can be related in different ways to the thought of Wittgenstein. These two models have in common a rejection of classical metaphysics (almost a commonplace in twentieth century philosophy and theology), and an anthropocentric conception of theological work. They nevertheless also present significant differences. In this subsection, I will first deal with the *experiential-expressive* model, and then with the *cultural-linguistic* model.

3.3.1 Experiential-Expressive Anti-Realist Trends
The first contemporary anti-realist trend in theology presented, the *experiential-expressive* trend, has deep roots in Continental modern philosophical and theological traditions, since it has its main origin in Kant's critical philosophy. I will start by clarifying the two title concepts ("experiential" and "expressive") and then briefly mention two important thinkers who represent in a paradigmatic way this first anti-realist trend.

The first concept is "experiential" and is related to epistemology. The core idea is that theology does not produce any knowledge of God, but rather describes the human experience of the divine.[47] Religion may be perceived as existential (a life-changing experience), mystical (a sort of fusion with the absolute), or ethical (social involvement), and theology articulates these extra-cognitive experiences. This leads to the closely-related second concept, "expressive," which is related to semantics. Since human beings have no cognitive access to God, they cannot formulate true propositions about him. The function of religious language (or theology) is then to *express* in a metaphorical, symbolic, or mythical way the human experience of the divine. It has no referential dimension, but is utterly phenomenological: the aim is to describe the various shapes of human religious experience.[48] This trend can thus be considered anti-

---

47 See Kant's famous formula at the end of the "Preface to the Second Edition" of the *Critique of Pure Reason*: "I have therefore found it necessary to deny *knowledge*, in order to make room for *faith*." Immanuel Kant, *Critique of Pure Reason* (London: Macmillan, 1933), 29.

48 For instance, the Swiss theologian Pierre Gisel affirms: "Par-delà tant une *théorie de la religion* qu'une *théorie du christianisme* ou d'autres [...], il y a à profiler et à déployer une *vision de l'humain* comme tel, sachant que ce qui est en cause dans le religieux et ses symbolisations – l'absolu, la limite, l'altérité, l'excès, etc. – est en fait une donnée humaine et que, dans une religion, pour exemple le christianisme, se joue une manière de le traiter ou, plutôt, d'y avoir affaire qui *déborde* tout ce qui s'en dit, s'en vit, s'en normalise ou s'en institutionnalise. [...] Sur cet axe, la réflexion théologique, requise, se fait, formellement, philosophie : réflexion humaine sur l'humain, sur ses conditions et sur ce à quoi il a affaire, ce qui le définit." Pierre Gisel, *La Théologie* (Paris: Presses Universitaires de France, 2007), 32.

realist, not in the sense that it denies any reality to God or to human experience of God (from a metaphysical perspective), but in the sense that it does not consider theology a discipline capable of formulating true propositions about God (in an epistemological and semantic way).

It is useful to distinguish two tendencies within this first contemporary anti-realist trend. The first tendency is clearly post-Kantian and insists in a radical way on the transcendence, the mystery and the unknowability of God. God is the ultimate unspeakable noumenal reality. In order to illustrate this stance, I will paradigmatically refer to the work of the former Harvard Divinity School professor, Gordon Kaufman (1925-2011). This author published several books on this question and his work is generally considered a major contribution to this trend.[49] The second tendency is more post-Hegelian and develops an immanent understanding of God: God is within human beings and has no other external reality. Therefore, theology can only be understood as a form of anthropology. I will illustrate this trend by briefly referring to the emblematic work of the Anglican priest and professor at the University of Cambridge, Don Cupitt (born in 1934). This thinker gained an audience with the *Sea of Faith* movement he founded,[50] and still represents a milestone in contemporary anti-realist studies (even if he calls himself a *non*-realist).

The first experiential-expressive anti-realist tendency can be exemplified by the work of Gordon Kaufman.[51] I have chosen two quotations from the

---

49 I could also have chosen John Hick as a representative thinker of this post-Kantian anti-realist conception of theology. The relevant works of these thinkers can be found in the bibliography. A detailed critical analysis of the works of Kaufman and Hick can be found in Insole's *The Realist Hope*. In relation to the third chapter of this book, it is worth noting that Plantinga criticizes with care Kaufman and Hick's anti-realism in *Warranted Christian Belief* (New York: Oxford University Press, 2000), 31-63.

50 While Don Cupitt is the prominent figure of the Sea of Faith movement, other names can be mentioned in this context: Hugh Dawes, David A. Hart, Anthony Freeman and Graham Shaw. See the bibliography for more details. This movement also has a website: http://www.sofn.org.uk.

51 Because this book is in English, Anglo-Saxon figures are used to illustrate its affirmations. We should nevertheless be aware that the first form of experiential-expressive anti-realism, defended by the entire hermeneutic tradition, played a very important role in Continental theology, both Protestant and Roman Catholic. For instance, it is difficult to overestimate the role played in France, as well as in other countries influenced by the phenomenological turn, by Paul Ricoeur or Jean-Luc Marion, two philosophers very much interested in theological questions such as the transcendence of God, revelation, or the nature of religious language. Their works have contributed greatly to the development of post-Kantian forms of epistemological and semantic theological anti-realism.

important work of this scholar in order to illustrate what I consider to be the paradigmatic traits of this approach. The first quotation presents his insistence on the radical unknowability of God:

> The real referent for "God" is never accessible to us or in any way open to our observation or experience. It must remain always an unknown X, a mere limiting idea with no content. It stands for the fact that God transcends our knowledge in modes and ways of which we can never be aware and of which we have no inkling. [...] Any supposed knowledge of God always remains unverifiable and controversial and may be completely mistaken. It is part of the profound mystery and meaning to which the word "God" points that man can never claim here adequacy of understanding and certainly no mastery or control. "... how unsearchable are his judgments, and his ways past finding out" (Rom. 11:33 KJV). The religious significance of the unspecifiability of the real referent for "God" is precisely this sense of an unfathomable depth of mystery and meaning.[52]

In these lines, the classical balance between the incomprehensibility and knowability of God is broken, as well as the patristic dialectic between apophatic and cataphatic theologies described in the previous section. A pervasive insistence on the impossibility of formulating anything true about God replaces these older theological stances, and the reference to Paul's Epistle to the Romans is not counter-balanced by other biblical passages that deal with God's revelation. Finally, the reference at the end of the quotation to the concept of "meaning" is to be understood in light of the wider discussions on the distinction or opposition between *meaning* (as a coherentist concept) and *truth* (as a concept that refers to an objective reality).

The second quotation puts forward another central trait of this anti-realist trend, that is, an anthropocentric and constructivist understanding of theological work:

> What sort of cosmic vision should we construct in our theological search for orientation in life? [...] (2) Since it is an orientation *for human beings* in the world that we are seeking, we want a picture or a map which takes into account our specifically human needs, capacities, and opportunities. [...] It should be a vision of human life and the world, in short, which can facilitate and promote human existence within the actual ecosystem

---

52 Gordon D. Kaufman, *God the Problem* (Cambridge: Harvard University Press, 1972), 85.

within which we live; in this respect our metaphysical/theological construction will necessarily be anthropocentric in its purpose and in its emphases.[53]

In these lines theology is considered in a constructivist way, as a mere production of the human mind. This is the first side of this anthropocentric conception of theology. The second is that theology is not oriented towards the formulation of true propositions about God and his relation to the world, but is reduced to the expression of a vision of the human being in the world that promotes a good and responsible life.

The second *experiential-expressive* anti-realist tendency can be exemplified by the work of Don Cupitt. Like the former, this approach develops an experiential rather than cognitive understanding of religion and theology, and therefore also considers theological discourse as mainly expressivist. It also adopts a strongly anthropocentric conception of theological work, in the two ways outlined in the previous paragraphs. The main difference between the two tendencies is that the latter does not insist on God's unattainable transcendence in a post-Kantian way, but on God's immanence in a post-Hegelian way. God can be identified with human experience of spiritual freedom. Therefore, theological language that refers to God as an apparently external reality has to be interpreted in a symbolic way in order to express human spiritual liberation.

Three illustrative passages follow. The first quotation shows how Cupitt identifies human spiritual experience with God from an immanent perspective:

> A human being is a self-conscious subject emerging from nature and continually striving to enlarge the scope of his consciousness, and with it his freedom. [...]
> The ultimate goal of this endeavour is the God of religion. In religion we celebrate the triumph of a free, universal, disinterested sovereign consciousness which is spirit because it is wholly autonomous and emancipated from the constraints of natural necessity. It is lord over nature, holy, exalted, lucid, self-possessed, blissful and unlimited in its range.[54]

---

53 Gordon D. Kaufman, *In Face of Mystery. A Constructive Theology* (Cambridge and London: Harvard University Press, 1993), 257.
54 Don Cupitt, *Taking Leave of God* (London: SCM Press Ltd, 1980), 163. This is a recurring idea in Cupitt's books. Here are some other brief quotations: "What then is God? God is a unifying symbol that eloquently personifies and represents to us

In the second quotation, Cupitt presents his expressivist view of Christian theology:

> And what is God? The Christian doctrine of God just is Christian spirituality in coded form, for God is a symbol that represents to us everything that spirituality requires of us and promises us.[55]

Finally, we find in Cupitt's approach the same strong anthropocentric understanding of the theological task found in Kaufman and other post-Kantian anti-realists:

> The first *conscious* believers are appearing, people who know that religion is just human but have come to see that it is no less vital to us for that. Religion has to be human; it could not be otherwise, for it would not work as religion unless it were simply human. Coupled with all this a large-scale philosophical shift, the so-called "end of metaphysics." We have come to see that there can be for us nothing but the worlds that are constituted for us by our own languages and activities. All meaning and truth and value are humanly constructed and could not be otherwise.[56]

3.3.2 Cultural-Linguistic Anti-Realist Trends

Lindbeck calls the second main contemporary anti-realist trend in theology the *cultural-linguistic* model. This second model is not to be opposed to the first, since as Lindbeck himself states, "there is a sense [...] in which experience and expression are no less important in a cultural-linguistic model than in an experiential-expressive one."[57] The *cultural-linguistic* model indeed also valorizes the religious experience

---

everything that spirituality requires of us. The requirement is the will of God, the divine attributes represent to us various aspects of the spiritual life, and God's nature as spirit represents the goal we are to attain. Thus the whole of spiritual life revolves around God and is summed up in God. God is the religious concept, reified." (*Taking Leave of God*, 9); "I continue to speak of God and to pray to God. God is the mythical embodiment of all that one is concerned with in the spiritual life. He is the religious demand and ideal, the pearl of great price and the enshriner of values. He is needed—but as a myth" (*Taking Leave of God*, 166).

55 Cupitt, *Taking Leave of God*, 14.
56 Don Cupitt, *The Sea of Faith* (London: SCM Press Ltd, 1994), 18-19. He affirms at page 239: "Theology must be translated into spirituality. Hence the attack on metaphysics and objectivity, and in the long run the development of a non-realist interpretation of religious belief. If this is so, then Christianity's own inner logic points in the direction of an anthropocentric and voluntarist view of life, a radical Christian humanism."
57 Lindbeck, *The Nature of Doctrine. Religion and Theology in a Postliberal Age*, 22.

against any theological cognitive ambitions and develops an expressivist understanding of religious language. It is also based on the demise of classical metaphysics in theology and on an anthropocentric approach of theology.

The differences, writes Lindbeck, are rather to be found in a "reversal of the relation between the inner and outer."[58] The following lines characterize this reversal:

> A religion can be viewed as a kind of cultural and/or linguistic framework or medium that shapes the entirety of life and thought. [...] It is not primarily an array of beliefs about the true and the good (though it may involve these), or a symbolism expressive of basic attitudes, feelings, or sentiments (though these will be generated). Rather, it is similar to an idiom that makes possible the description of realities, the formulation of beliefs, and the experiencing of inner attitudes, feelings, and sentiments. Like a culture or language, it is a communal phenomenon that shapes the subjectivities of individuals rather than being primarily a manifestation of those subjectivities.[59]

Contrary to the post-Kantian anti-realist trends, which generally hold that religious experience comes first, and is then expressed in symbolic, mythical or metaphorical forms, the *cultural-linguistic* model implies that it is precisely this complex symbolic world formed by a communal theological tradition that shapes the religious experience. In the end, the result is similar since it leads to an anti-realist conception of theology. The reference in these lines to Wittgensteinian concepts such as "language game" or "form of life" is not due to chance, since this second anti-realist trend is as much influenced by the work of this philosopher as the first trend was inspired by the work of Kant. Finally, the pragmatic coloration of this trend has to be stressed: "To become religious [...] is to interiorize a set of skills by practice and training. One learns how to feel, act, and think in conformity with a religious tradition that is, in its inner structure, far richer and more subtle than can be explicitly articulated."[60]

---

58 Lindbeck, *The Nature of Doctrine. Religion and Theology in a Postliberal Age*, 22.
59 Lindbeck, *The Nature of Doctrine. Religion and Theology in a Postliberal Age*, 19.
60 Lindbeck, *The Nature of Doctrine. Religion and Theology in a Postliberal Age*, 21.

This second contemporary trend is nowadays more fashionable than the first among anti-realist scholars. The following presentation of the *cultural-linguistic* model distinguishes three main groups. The first group adopts a neutral descriptive approach of religion and theology, in a genuinely post-Wittgensteinian way. This stance is paradigmatically illustrated by the work of D. Z. Phillips (1934-2006).[61] The second tendency is the appropriation of the model by those commonly known as the post-liberal theologians. To illustrate this stance, I refer to the work of a founder of that movement, Hans Frei (1922-1988). Thirdly, I sketch the *cultural-linguistic* model in its atheist version with the presentation of theological fictionalism. The paradigmatic figure here is Robin Le Poidevin (b. 1962). Taken together, these three groups cover a very broad and important field in anti-realist studies.

The first *cultural-linguistic* anti-realist tendency explicitly follows the tracks of Wittgenstein,[62] and is best represented by the work of D. Z. Phillips. One can indeed find in this philosopher's work numerous important Wittgensteinian themes applied to religious belief and theology. First is an affirmation of the merely descriptive character of philosophical work applied to religion: "Philosophy is neither for nor against religious belief. After it has sought to clarify the grammar of such belief its work is over."[63] Second is pragmatic indifference to the older realism debates (which is one of the main themes of Wittgenstein's *On Certainty*): "Theological non-realism is as empty as theological realism. Both terms are battle-cries in a confused philosophical debate, which is not to deny that these slogans may cause all sort of trouble for believers

---

61 Some post-Wittgensteinian Roman Catholic theologians or philosophers of religion work in a way that differs from that of D. Z. Phillips. See for instance: Elizabeth Anscombe, *Faith in a Hard Ground. Essays on Philosophy and Ethics* (Saint Andrews: Imprint Academic, 2008); Elizabeth Anscombe, *From Plato to Wittgenstein* (Saint Andrews: Imprint Academic, 2011); Herbert McCabe, *Faith within Reason* (London and New York: Continuum, 2007); Herbert McCabe, *On Aquinas* (London and New York: Continuum, 2008).

62 For general introductions, see: Fergus Kerr, *Theology after Wittgenstein* (Oxford and New York: Basil Blackwell Ltd, 1986); D. Z. Phillips, and Mario von der Ruhr (eds.), *Religion and Wittgenstein's Legacy* (Aldershot and Burlington: Ashgate Publishing, 2005); Norman Malcolm, *Wittgenstein. A Religious Point of View? Edited with a Response by Peter Winch* (London and New York: Routledge, 1993). For a detailed critique of D. Z. Phillips' work, see Insole, *The Realist Hope*.

63 D. Z. Phillips, *Faith and Philosophical Enquiry* (London: Routledge and Kegan Paul, 1970), 109.

and unbelievers alike."[64] And third is a clear presentation of what is probably the core of the Wittgensteinian approach:

> The criteria of what can sensibly be said of God are to be found *within* the religious tradition. This conclusion has an important bearing on the question of what account of religion philosophy and theology can give. It follows from my argument that the criteria of meaningfulness cannot be found *outside* religion, since they are given by religious discourse itself. Theology can claim justifiably to show what is meaningful in religion only when it has an internal relation to religious discourse. Philosophy can make the same claim only if it is prepared to examine religious concepts in the contexts from which they derive their meaning.[65]

This stance is not anti-realist in the sense that it necessarily denies God's existence, but in its appropriation of a pragmatic definition of truth and its insistence on the concept of "meaning." Concepts such as "fact," "true," or "real" are defined by the way they are used in different language games ("meaning is use"), and there is no higher external reference point that allows anyone to formulate true propositions about God (or anything else) in a way that transcends communal or cultural particular views.[66]

The second *cultural-linguistic* anti-realist tendency is developed by the post-liberal theologians.[67] It differs from the first tendency since the thinkers who work from this perspective are unambiguously involved in

---

64 D. Z. Phillips, *Wittgenstein and Religion* (London: Macmillan, 1993), 35.
65 Phillips, *Wittgenstein and Religion*, 3.
66 David F. Ford sums up Wittgensteinian anti-realism nicely in his *Theology. A Very Short Introduction* (Oxford: Oxford University Press, 2013), 22: "We are all involved in complex 'languages' through which our understanding, behavior, and imagination are shaped. Christianity is one such language game, it has its own integrity, and you should not judge it by rules of other games any more than you would apply the rules of chess to tennis. Therefore it cannot be adequately explained in terms of other language games such as atheist materialism or Islam or secular feminism. The task of theology is to make clear what sort of 'game' Christianity is and to draw the consequences for living within it. It is pointless to try to justify Christian faith in alien terms—that would be to switch games."
67 These thinkers have sometimes been called *narrative theologians* or *Yale School theologians*. George Lindbeck belongs to this theological family, as do George Hunsinger, William C. Placher and Ronald F. Thiemann. For introductory readings, see: George Hunsinger, "Postliberal Theology," in *The Cambridge Companion to Postmodern Theology*, ed. Kevin J. Vanhoozer (New York: Cambridge University Press, 2003), 42-57; James Fodor, "Postliberal Theology," in *The Modern Theologians. An Introduction to Christian Theology since 1918*, ed. David F. Ford and Rachael Muers (Malden and Oxford: Blackwell Publishing, 2005), 229-248.

the Christian faith.[68] They nevertheless follow the same trend, since most of these thinkers could have written the lines of D. Z. Phillips quoted above. I have chosen to refer briefly to Hans Frei's seminal work, *The Eclipse of Biblical Narrative*, to illustrate this tendency.

The Eclipse of Biblical Narrative is a work in historical theology that investigates how biblical hermeneutics have radically changed in modern times. But in parallel with this historical scope, Frei develops his own theological agenda. He frequently mentions what he calls the "reversal in the direction of interpretation" that occurred in modernity:[69]

> It is no exaggeration to say that all across the theological spectrum the great reversal had taken place; interpretation was a matter of fitting the biblical story into another world with another story rather than incorporating that world into the biblical story.[70]

The main theological preoccupation of post-liberal theologians is to reverse once more the "direction of interpretation" without going back to pre-modern hermeneutics. This program is made possible by an adhesion to a cultural-linguistic understanding of theology. Biblical narratives produce a world that shapes believers' understanding of external reality and life in a fundamental way. Theology is then understood as the discipline that makes clear the grammar and the rules of this biblical world in order that believers might understand more deeply in which reality they live.[71] Yet contrary to pre-modern theologians who spontaneously admitted that biblical narratives refer to external reality in a realist way, the post-liberals constantly avoid dealing directly with the question of the external reference of biblical narratives.[72] It is *in fine* not

---

68 It is noteworthy that the work of post-liberals is probably the only anti-realist trend studied in this section that is not anthropocentric. Without entering into the details, this is probably due to the influence of Karl Barth's theocentric thought on post-liberal theologians such as Hans Frei and George Hunsinger.
69 Hans Frei, *The Eclipse of Biblical Narrative. A Study in Eighteenth and Nineteenth Century Hermeneutics* (New Haven and London: Yale University Press, 1974), 9.
70 Frei, *The Eclipse of Biblical Narrative. A Study in Eighteenth and Nineteenth Century Hermeneutics*, 130.
71 Nicholas Wolterstorff sums up this whole view in one formula: "Living within a Text." See: Nicholas Wolterstorff, "Living within a Text," in *Faith and Narrative*, ed. Keith E. Yandell (Oxford: Oxford University Press, 2001), 202-213.
72 This question of the external reference of the biblical narratives has generated many debates. For contributions of well-known theologians *pro* and *contra* (George Lindbeck, Alister McGrath, George Hunsinger, Miroslav Volf, et al.), see: Timothy R. Phillips and Dennis L. Okholm (eds.), *The Nature of Confession. Evangelicals and*

so difficult to read post-liberal theologians in a postmodern way: the believer experiences and practices faith, and lives in a world shaped by the biblical narratives, and as the world is structured by narratives, storytelling and other worldviews, the question of the external reference of the biblical narratives is to be considered a false problem typical of modern foundationalism—a problem that should be ignored.[73]

The third and last cultural-linguistic anti-realist tendency is commonly known as *theological fictionalism*. Unlike post-liberal theology, this stance is developed by atheists. The purpose is to offer a positive way of understanding religious belief from an atheist point of view, and will be illustrated by the work of Robin Le Poidevin.[74]

Theological fictionalism relies deeply on an instrumentalist conception of knowledge (which means that theories are "fictions adopted because they are useful, not because they are true descriptions of the world").[75] From this perspective, theology has nothing to do with formulating true propositions about God but instead looks like a game of make-believe:

> To engage in religious practice [...] is to engage in a game of make-believe. We make-believe that there is a God, by reciting, in the context of the game, a statement of belief. We listen to what make-believedly are accounts of the activities of God and his people, and we pretend to

---

Postliberals in Conversation (Downers Grove: InterVarsity Press, 1996). One can also notice the similitude of the debates generated by Lindbeck's *The Nature of Doctrine* and T. S. Kuhn's *Structure of Scientific Revolutions*, with Lindbeck and Kuhn's shared uneasy attitude towards the question of external reference, and more generally that of *realism*. In this context, read Lindbeck's "Afterword. Interreligious Relations and Christian Ecumenism: Revisiting Chapter 3 of *The Nature of Doctrine*," in *The Nature of Doctrine*, 25th Anniversary edition, 125-140. Finally, it is interesting to see that the type of theology promoted by Hans Frei in his famous *Types of Christian Theology* (New Haven and London: Yale University Press, 1992) is also not very clear on the question of the external reference of theological discourse.

73 This is the core of the research of Robert Andrew Cathey, *God in Postliberal Perspective. Between Realism and Non-Realism* (Farnham: Ashgate Publishing, 2009). Frei's favorable reference to Auerbach's famous work of literary criticism, *Mimesis*, at the very beginning of *The Eclipse of Biblical Narrative* tends to confirm this interpretation. One may gain the impression that the meaning of biblical narratives is definitively more important than their truth.

74 Two other important proponents of this trend are Peter Lipton and Andrew Eshleman (see the bibliography).

75 Robin Le Poidevin, *Arguing for Atheism. An Introduction to the Philosophy of Religion* (London and New York: Routledge, 1996), 111.

worship and address prayers to that God. In Walton's terms,[76] we locate ourselves in that fictional world, and in doing so we allow ourselves to become emotionally involved, to the extent that a religious service is capable of being an intense experience. [...] What remains, when the game of make-believe is over, is an awareness of our responsibilities for ourselves and others, of the need to pursue spiritual goals, and so on.[77]

Even though in the game of make-believe we find in religion and theology no more truth content than in any other game, it is nevertheless useful since it may generate positive attitudes towards other people and nature. This anti-realist trend is the most radical stance identified in this subsection.

3.4 Realist Trends
Although the anti-realist trends in theology are important nowadays, they are not unopposed. One can indeed observe numerous theologians and philosophers of religion who are not satisfied with anti-realism, since they hold that formulating true propositions about God and his action in the world is an essential dimension of Christian theology. Having presented the main anti-realist trends, this subsection is devoted to outlining the main realist trends in the contemporary Western theological world.

Here I adopt the same method as for the anti-realist trends and work with two main ideal types. The first ideal type presented is *critical realism*. The main characteristic of this approach is its sensitivity to the twentieth century critics of scientific positivism and its project of applying the main lines of this scientific epistemological renewal to theology. I have called the second ideal type *theological realism*.[78] This trend refuses to start with pre-theological philosophical or scientific categories and attempts to develop a realist conception of theology based on thoroughly theological

---

76 See Kendall Walton, "Fearing Fictions," *Journal of Philosophy* 65 (1978), 5-27; Kendall Walton, "How Close are Fictional Worlds to the Real World?" *Journal of Aesthetics and Art Criticism* 37 (1978), 11-23.
77 Robin Le Poidevin, *Arguing for Atheism. An Introduction to the Philosophy of Religion*, 118-119. The pragmatic dimension of the last sentence can be stressed by a quotation from pages 111-112: "By having an image of the goodness of God before us, we will be encouraged to lead a less selfish, and therefore more fulfilling, life. The idea of God, rather than God himself, is thus an instrument through which good can be realized."
78 I use this label here in a slightly more specific sense than in the previous section, where it covered all realism-in-theology positions. I do not know of a better term for the specific nature of classical and post-Barthian takes on realism.

concepts. These two major trends play an important role in the perspective of this research, since they constitute the background against which I develop my own argument.

3.4.1 Critical Realist Trends

The first realist ideal type is *critical realism*. As a philosophical and scientific movement, critical realism has its own history that will not be studied in this section. From the beginning of the twentieth century until today, critical realism has often been intimately related to epistemology debates in the context of the natural sciences and in this context has often been called *scientific realism*.[79] The critical realism presented in the following paragraphs developed mainly from the 1970s to the 1990s in Anglo-Saxon discussions on the philosophy (and more particularly the epistemology) of science in general, and theology in particular. As mentioned above, a radical renewal occurred in these fields during these decades, with the demise of the modern phenomenon of positivism (which came to be assimilated with *naïve realism*) and the strongly postmodern development of instrumentalist theories. Theologians and scientists such as Ian Barbour, Arthur Peacocke, and John Polkinghorne studied with care what was happening on the stage of the epistemology of the sciences and started to work applying these developments to the epistemology of theology.[80] Their works have been a source of intellectual renewal for many theologians.

The distinctive trait of *critical realism* (in general and applied to theology) is the will to find a *via media* between *naïve realism* and *instrumentalism*. Ian Barbour, a founder and leading figure of this movement, defines critical realism as follows:

---

79 For a detailed introduction, read Ilkka Niiniluoto, *Critical Scientific Realism* (Oxford: Oxford University Press, 1999).

80 See Ian G. Barbour, *Issues in Science and Religion* (Englewood Cliffs: Prentice-Hall, 1966); Ian G. Barbour, *Myths, Models, and Paradigms. A Comparative Study in Science and Religion* (New York: Harper and Row, 1976); Arthur Peacocke, *Intimations of Reality. Critical Realism in Science and Religion* (Notre Dame: Notre Dame University Press, 1984); John Polkinghorne, *Scientists as Theologians: A Comparison of the Writings of Ian Barbour, Arthur Peacocke and John Polkinghorne* (London: SPCK, 1996); John Polkinghorne, *Belief in God in an Age of Science* (New Haven: Yale University Press, 1998). For introductions to critical realism that integrate theological perspectives on the question, see Gijsbert van den Brink, *Philosophy of Science for Theologians. An Introduction* (Frankfurt am Main: Peter Lang, 2009), 237ff; Alister E. McGrath, *A Scientific Theology (Volume 2): Reality* (London and New York: T&T Clark, 2006 [2002]), chapter 10; Paul D. La Montagne, *Barth and Rationality. Critical Realism in Theology* (Eugene: Cascade Books, 2012).

Like the naïve realist (and unlike the instrumentalist), the critical realist takes theories to be representations of the world. He holds that valid theories are true as well as useful. To him, science is discovery and exploration as well as construction and invention. The scientist, he insists, seeks to understand and not just to predict or control. Unlike the naïve realist, however, the critical realist (along with the instrumentalist) recognizes the importance of human imagination in the formation of theories. He acknowledges the incomplete and selective character of scientific theories.[81]

Barbour continues, affirming altogether that scientific theories are constructions, "abstract symbol systems" created by the human mind, and that these constructions are nevertheless not merely arbitrary, since they have to be compatible with observations made on an objective external reality.

In a short but enlightening way, Alister McGrath locates theological critical realism as follows:

In recent years, the term "critical realism" has come to be used within theological circles to designate a style of realism which is sensitive to the historically situated and personally involved character of theological knowledge, while resolutely declining to let go of the ideals of truth, objectivity and rationality.[82]

---

81 Ian G. Barbour, *Myths, Models, and Paradigms. A Comparative Study in Science and Religion*, 37. Another facet of this *via media* approach relates the epistemic status of unobservable entities such as, for instance, electrons. Here again, the critical realists are working on finding a path between positivists who are willing to recognize only what can be directly observed and instrumentalists who think that scientific theories are only useful fictions. Van den Brink briefly applies this stance to theology: "Now in the field of faith and theology a similar discussion is currently going on concerning non-observable entities which are important here, in particular of course the reality of God" (Van den Brink, *Philosophy of Science for Theologians*, 238). On this question, see also Le Poidevin, *Arguing for Atheism*, 107-110.

82 Alister E. McGrath, *A Scientific Theology (Volume 2): Reality* (London and New York: T&T Clark, 2006), 195. A recent introduction to a work of dogmatic theology provides an enlightening illustration of critical realism as applied to theology: "It has become quite common to encounter attempts to filter truth claims out of faith statements, done so on the supposition that statements of faith are merely expressions of experiences, demonstrations of trust, a moral commitment, a hopeful perspective on reality, and so forth. Certainly they do not constitute 'is statements,' that is, assertions about a really living God, let alone genuine knowledge of God. [...] It is correct to emphasize that faith statements are not detached propositions. The big problem is that faith statements cannot be reduced to the features so referred without destroying their

Critical realism is not a homogenous movement and one can find critical realist theologians at different places on the liberal-conservative theological spectrum. On the one side, one finds, for instance, Sallie McFague, whose critical realism seems to be close to liberal anti-realism.[83] On the other side, Alister McGrath proposes a much more realist and conservative understanding of critical realism.[84] In the United States, one can observe a theological school rooted at Princeton Seminary that develops a critical realist reading of Karl Barth.[85] The school of philosophical theology in Utrecht provides another example of a critical realist theological agenda.[86]

A closer study of this trend leads to the conclusion that there are in fact two tendencies in contemporary critical realism applied to theology.

---

character in an essential way. A statement such as 'The Lord is my light and my salvation' (Ps 27:1) is surely a statement of trust, but in addition it points to a particular situation, condition, or fact that is presupposed. It means more than simply, 'I look at the future with confidence.' Thus, statements of faith, whatever else they may be, are also factual statements about God and his relationship with us and with reality." Cornelis van der Kooi and Gijsbert van den Brink, *Christian Dogmatics. An Introduction* (Grand Rapids: Eerdmans Publishing Company, 2017), 120.

83 Sallie McFague deals explicitly with critical realism on pages 131ff of her *Metaphorical Theology. Models of God in Religious Language* (Philadelphia: Fortress Press, 1982). So does Janet Martin Soskice in *Metaphor and Religious Language* (Oxford: Oxford University Press, 1985), pages 106ff. See also Sue Patterson in *Realist Christian Theology in a Postmodern Age* (Cambridge: Cambridge University Press, 1999).

84 See the above-mentioned volume of his *Scientific Theology (Volume 2): Reality*, which is almost entirely devoted to the elaboration of a critical realist understanding of theology.

85 Bruce L. McCormack, *Karl Barth's Critically Realistic Dialectical Theology. Its Genesis and Development 1909-1936* (Oxford: Oxford University Press, 1995); Bruce L. McCormack, *Orthodox and Modern. Studies in the Theology of Karl Barth* (Grand Rapids: Baker Academic, 2008), especially chapters 5 and 6; La Montagne, *Barth and Rationality. Critical Realism in Theology*.

86 Vincent Brümmer, *The Model of Love. A Study in Philosophical Theology* (Cambridge: Cambridge University Press, 1993), chapter 1; Gijsbert van den Brink and Marcel Sarot (eds.), *Understanding the Attributes of God* (Frankfurt am Main: Peter Lang, 1999). On pages 21-22, van den Brink and Sarot describe in a programmatic way what critical theological realism is. Wentzel van Huyssteen also works from this perspective. He offers a good short synthesis of critical realism: "Critical realists—also in theology—take their theories to be representations of the world as a reality. They thus hold that their theories are valid and provisionally true as well as useful. To the critical realist science is discovery and exploration as well as construction and invention [...]. In this way critical realists try to acknowledge both the creativity of their thought and the existence of structures in reality not created by the human mind." *Theology and the Justification of Faith. Constructing Theories in Systematic Theology*, (Grand Rapids: Eerdmans Publishing Company, 1989), 157.

The first tendency can be labeled *methodological critical realism* and is represented by scholars who interpret critical realism as a synonym of scientific realism, and who insist on following a critical method while doing theology. The second tendency can be called *post-Kantian critical realism*, since its proponents insist on the indirect character of human knowledge.

The first tendency is best illustrated by the New Testament scholar N. T. Wright, who offers an important epistemological introduction to his work and defines critical realism as follows:

> This [critical realism] is a way of describing the process of "knowing" that acknowledges the *reality of the thing known, as something other than the knower* (hence "realism"), while also fully acknowledging that the only access we have to this reality lies along the spiraling path of *appropriate dialogue or conversation between the knower and the thing known* (hence "critical"). This path leads to critical reflection on the products of our enquiry into "reality," so that our assertions about "reality" acknowledge their own provisionality. Knowledge, in other words, although in principle concerning realities independent of the knower, is never itself independent of the knower.[87]

The critical dimension of Wright's realism is mainly methodological and can be understood as the process of adjusting human knowledge to reality. It does not seem to characterize a specific sort of knowledge produced by intellectual inquiry, but rather qualifies an appropriation of something close to the Socratic method.

The second tendency is *post-Kantian critical realism*, which applies the adjective "critical" to knowledge itself. Critical realists insist on the indirect character of human knowledge (against the so-called naïve realists who think they can know external reality in a direct way), arguing human beings always know external reality through the lens of concepts, models, symbols, etc. A representative example of this second form of critical realism can be seen in the following passage:

> In terms of a non-dualist understanding of knowledge, our bodies as well as our cultural framework, worldview, language etc. are not simply at the subject-side of the divide. They are the clothing in which people indwell

---

[87] N.T. Wright, *The New Testament and the People of God* (London: SPCK, 1992), 35.

this world; the lenses through which they see the world; the instruments with which they handle the world. Rather than being at the subject side of the divide, they are actually both the screen and the lens between the knowing subject and his world.[88]

Benno van den Toren claims to be a critical realist and struggles against what he calls a dualist approach to knowledge based on opposition between the knowing subject and the known, which is quite common in critical realist circles. The metaphor of the lens and the screen used to describe the *esse repraesentatum* that founds the indirect character of human knowledge is very significant. Realism in this form is "critical" because, unlike classical realism, it denies any direct access to external reality. I have called it *post-Kantian*, since it can be interpreted as a mild form of a philosophy of representation, and often develops into a constructivist understanding of human knowledge.

3.4.2 Classical and Radical Theological Realist Trends
The second contemporary realist ideal-type can be called *theological realism*.[89] This ideal-type can be used to group together a variety of theologians who work within the broad post-Barthian tradition.[90] Theological realists establish epistemological independence for theology by putting forward wholly theological concepts in their development of a realist conception of their discipline. They do not want to base their arguments on classical metaphysical, or more generally, philosophical concepts, but on a specifically theological frame. According to these thinkers, the *realism in theology* issues are not primarily pre-theological, philosophical, or scientific, but are theological from beginning to end.

---

88 Benno van den Toren, *Christian Apologetics as Cross-Cultural Dialogue* (London and New York: T&T Clark, 2011), 129.
89 Contemporary theologians have employed various concepts to characterize their particular take on a realist conception of theology: *theistic* realism, *eschatological* realism, *revelational* realism, *Christological* or *Christocentric* realism, etc. Theological realism is the most generic concept and therefore best fits this ideal-type.
90 Barth's main works in relation to the question of theological realism: *Church Dogmatics* II.1, chapter 5; "Fate and Idea," in *The Way of Theology in Karl Barth. Essays and Comments*, ed. H. Martin Rumscheidt (Eugene: Pickwick Publications, 1986); Karl Barth, *The Knowledge of God and the Service of God According to the Teaching of the Reformation* (London: Hodder and Stoughton Publishers, 1938); Emil Brunner and Karl Barth, *Natural Theology. Comprising "Nature and Grace" by Professor Dr. Emil Brunner and the reply "No!" by Dr. Karl Barth*, ed. John Baillie, trans. Peter Fraenkel (Eugene: Wipf and Stock, 2002).

They are thus opposed to modern epistemological models that lead to an increasing disregard for theology as a valuable truth-seeking discipline.

As for critical realism, there is reason to identify two main tendencies within the theological realism approaches. First, there is *classical theological realism*, and second, *radical theological realism*. The following paragraphs are given to the presentation of these tendencies.

Contemporary *classical theological realism* is an intellectual current mainly based on an interpretation of the work of Karl Barth, a twentieth century retrieval of classical Christian theology over and against modern theological liberalism. As an example, I offer the following lines of Thomas F. Torrance, a preeminent figure of this school of thought:

> In classical Christian theology, such as we find in the teaching of Athanasius and Cyril of Alexandria, it was held that God is open to knowledge in himself on the ground of his own self-evidencing and self-manifesting reality. Through his Word and Spirit God brings us face to face with himself so that through faith we may know him in the light of his own self-evidence and under the immediate compulsion of his own being.[91]

All the main themes of classical theological realism are present in these lines. One might first notice that this description of human knowledge of God is crossed by theological concepts from the first line to the last. Theological knowledge is not to be found in human natural faculties, nor does it have to follow philosophical or scientific standards in order to be valuable: it is based on God's revelation seized by faith. From this perspective, seeking to build theological realism on principles that could be accepted by secular philosophers or scientists would be a methodological capitulation on the part of the theologian. Secondly, and unlike the second tendency in critical realism, one can observe formulations that suggest a person can have direct knowledge of God: "God is open to knowledge in himself," "brings us face to face with himself," or "the immediate compulsion of his own being."[92] Yet, in contrast to common sense or positivist realism, this direct knowledge of God is never at the disposal of human beings, since it is generated by God's active revelation.

---

91 Torrance, "Theological Realism," 176.
92 This direct realism flows from a certain reading of the work of Karl Barth. Dietrich Bonhoeffer probably understood Barth in this way when he wrote the following famous formula, that Barth's thought is a "positivism of revelation." Dietrich Bonhoeffer, *Letters and Papers from Prison*, 3rd ed. (London: SCM Press, 1967), 153.

In the classical understanding of theological realism, this insistence on God's revelatory activity does not lead to the abandonment of serious philosophical or scientific reflection. These disciplines are simply to be understood from a theological point of view (rather than abandoned).[93] This is why a theologian like Thomas Torrance can be a theological realist passionately interested in the natural sciences without contradicting himself, even if this leads him to disagree with Barth on questions related to this topic.

A more *radical theological realism* can be found in the work of theologians who have read the work of Karl Barth, not as a retrieval of classical theology, but as a mainly modern or even postmodern reworking of the classical themes of Christian faith. The theologians who work from this perspective go beyond *classical theological realism*, since they not only honor the preeminence of theological concepts in the development of a realist conception of theology, but they generally reverse the traditional order between creation and redemption, and simultaneously reject any form of theology based on classical metaphysics. They insist on a Christocentric understanding of Christian theology, which stresses the impossibility of claiming any truth unless starting with God's dynamic revelation in Christ. When applied to the doctrine of creation, this stance leads to the rejection of metaphysical interpretations that are not rooted in Christology. These radical theological realists reject any ontology based on substances (for instance in an Aristotelian mode), and replace it with an ontology based on relations (for instance the believer's personal

---

93 John Webster also adopts contemporary classical theological realism in a typical way. The following passage illustrates how in this tradition one can accord preeminence to theological concepts without rejecting reason and metaphysics: "Christian theology is biblical reasoning. It is an activity of the created intellect, judged, reconciled, redeemed and sanctified through the works of the Son and the Spirit. More closely, Christian theology is part of reason's answer to the divine Word which addresses creatures through the intelligible service of the prophets and apostles. It has its origin in the Spirit-sustained hearing of the divine Word; it is rational contemplation and articulation of God's communicative presence." And a few pages further on: "By speaking of reason as a created reality, theology is committed to giving a metaphysical rather than a voluntaristic account: reason acts within an order of being grounded in God himself, and is not simply a tool of the will." John Webster, "Biblical Reasoning," in *The Domain of the Word. Scripture and Theological Reason* (London and New York: T&T Clark, 2012), 115 and 124. In the British context, Colin E. Gunton worked from a similar perspective. See for instance: "Trinity, Natural Theology, and a Theology of Nature," in *The Trinity in a Pluralistic Age*, ed. Kevin J. Vanhoozer (Grand Rapids: Eerdmans Publishing, 1997, 88-103) or *Revelation and Reason. Prolegomena to Systematic Theology* (London and New York: T&T Clark, 2008).

encounter with God in Christ).[94] While classical theological realism affirms the preeminence of theological categories without necessarily suppressing a metaphysical understanding of the doctrine of creation, radical theological realism goes one step further and promotes Christological concentration, which leads to the reinterpretation of all the main Christian theological themes.[95]

The work of Andrew Moore—*Realism and Christian Faith. God, Grammar, and Meaning*—is a contemporary illustration of this *radical theological realism*. Moore regularly insists that "Christian realism will be Christocentric."[96] He also rejects classical metaphysical realism, which he thinks "requires that we abandon creatureliness and become like Gods."[97] Finally, he affirms that "a Christocentric realism will also be a narrative realism," since "the realism that is appropriate to the Christian faith is one in which God's reality is shown under the narrative description offered in the Bible."[98]

4. The *Bavinck/Plantinga Model for a Realist Conception of Theology*

Having described the general background to, and the contextual relevance of this research, I devote the last section of this chapter to presenting the specific scope of this book. I first formulate the main research question, which leads to the development of an approach I call the *Bavinck/Plantinga Model for a Realist Conception of Theology* (4.1). Secondly, I put forward important methodological choices that have shaped this research (4.2). And finally, I briefly outline the content of the next three chapters (4.3).

---

94 For the wider context, see Mark A. Wrathall (ed.), *Religion after Metaphysics* (Cambridge: Cambridge University Press, 2003).
95 Here is Bruce McCormack's presentation of a modern or postmodern Barth: What Barth did "was to elaborate a nonmetaphysical, actualistic (divine and human) ontology which took the place of the classical metaphysics of being and the modern metaphysics of the religious a priori and which completed this language and made it meaningful in a new and different way" (*Orthodox and Modern. Studies in the Theology of Karl Barth*, 133). From the same perspective, see George Hunsinger's insistence on Barth's actualistic theological approach in *How to Read Karl Barth. The Shape of his Theology* (Oxford: Oxford University Press, 1991). Finally, Eberhard Jüngel has also interpreted Barth along these lines in *The Doctrine of the Trinity. God's Being is in Becoming* (Grand Rapids: Eerdmans Publishing, 1976).
96 Andrew Moore, *Realism and Christian Faith. God, Grammar, and Meaning* (Cambridge: Cambridge University Press, 2003), 214.
97 Moore, *Realism and Christian Faith. God, Grammar, and Meaning*, 215.
98 Moore, *Realism and Christian Faith. God, Grammar, and Meaning*, 219.

4.1 The Research Question

The fundamental intellectual motivation that has driven this research is the view that *realism in theology* questions are important for both intrinsic and contextual reasons. The intrinsic reason is that this issue concerns the very nature of theology and therefore deeply influences the understanding a theologian has of his or her own work. Even if it is possible to observe a consensus between realist and anti-realist theologians on specific theological formulations, a gap separates them when dealing with the deeper meaning of these theological assertions. While the former will formulate (even modest) truth-content propositions, the latter will stress the mainly metaphorical or sociological character of such theological formulations. For instance, realist and anti-realist may both adhere to the formulations of the Nicene Creed, but the theological interpretations of this adhesion will be totally different. Anti-realism potentially twists every single theological affirmation from the inside (even if these affirmations are consonant with the Christian tradition) and therefore has to be challenged.[99]

The contextual relevance of *realism in theology* questions flows from the two previous sections of this chapter. The vivid contemporary anti-realist trends and the responses proposed by critical and theological realists clearly show that the file is far from closed. On the contrary, there are still many research avenues that might be explored, and constructive work can be done to consolidate the general case in favor of a realist conception of theology. Thus, as indicated, the ambition driving this research is the wish to develop a synthesized realist model by relating aspects of the work of the twentieth century Dutch theologian Herman Bavinck (1854-1921) to that of contemporary American philosopher Alvin Plantinga (born in 1932).

Herman Bavinck was a Dutch Reformed theologian. He was a professor of systematic theology at the Free University of Amsterdam and worked between 1895 and 1911 on the publication of two editions of his four major volumes *Gereformeerde Dogmatiek*, which were translated

---

99 Roger Pouivet correctly describes theological anti-realism as a heresy since it deeply modifies the understanding of the constituent dogmas of the Christian faith: "Le glissement vers l'incroyance et le gauchissement des dogmes constitutifs du christianisme, celui de la résurrection du Christ par exemple, sont des caractéristiques de l'antiréalisme théologique dans son effort pour coller à certains « apports » de la philosophie contemporaine." Roger Pouivet, *Epistémologie des Croyances Religieuses* (Paris: Cerf, 2013), 160.

into English between 2003 and 2008.[100] This important theological work is characterized by a will to be faithful to the theology of the Calvinist Reformation and attentive to the philosophical and theological context of the Netherlands at the beginning of the twentieth century. In his *Reformed Dogmatics*, Bavinck manifests a vast historical and biblical erudition and a well-balanced approach to theological problems. He also constantly deals with the issues raised by the then dominant post-Kantian trends in theology. The first volume of this work is entirely devoted to the question of the *prolegomena* to theology, that is, a reflection on the status, scope, and method of theology. In this volume, Bavinck develops an important argument in favor of a realist conception of theology, which will be a cornerstone of this present research.

Alvin Plantinga is a well-known contemporary American analytic philosopher. He became famous in the 1980s when he worked on the philosophy of religion and laid the foundations for the *Reformed Epistemology* movement with his friend Nicholas Wolterstorff. Between 1993 and 2000 he published *Trilogy of Warrant*, an important epistemological work with the primary aim of developing an externalist theory of justification of knowledge: *Warrant: The Current Debates; Warrant and Proper Function; Warranted Christian Belief*.[101] Even if analytic philosophers do not consider Plantinga a major figure in the realism debates (the name of William P. Alston would undoubtedly come first),[102] Plantinga's work nevertheless contains unexplored potentialities which

---

100 The English translation is based on the second edition of the *Gereformeerde Dogmatiek* (1906-1911). The English editor suppressed a number of bibliographical references and slightly modified the nomenclature of the chapters. My relatively modest skills in Dutch allowed me to compare the general structure of the Dutch and English editions, and also to consider the bibliographical references in the original version, but not to evaluate the quality of the translation. Here follow references to the editions I refer to in this chapter. Herman Bavinck, *Gereformeerde Dogmatiek. Eerste Deel* (Kampen: J. H. Kok, 1928); Herman Bavinck, *Reformed Dogmatics. Prolegomena (Volume 1)* (Grand Rapids: Baker Academic, 2003); Herman Bavinck, *Reformed Dogmatics. God and Creation (Volume 2)* (Grand Rapids: Baker Academic, 2004); Herman Bavinck, *Reformed Dogmatics. Sin and Salvation in Christ (Volume 3)* (Grand Rapids: Baker Academic, 2006); Herman Bavinck, *Reformed Dogmatics. Holy Spirit, Church and New Creation (Volume 4)* (Grand Rapids: Baker Academic, 2008). The four volumes are edited by John Bolt and translated by John Vriend.
101 Alvin Plantinga: *Warrant: The Current Debate* (Oxford: Oxford University Press, 1993); *Warrant and Proper Function* (Oxford: Oxford University Press, 1993); *Warranted Christian Belief* (Oxford: Oxford University Press, 2000).
102 See among others: William P. Alston, "Realism and the Christian Faith," in *A Realist Conception of Truth* (Ithaca and London: Cornell University Press, 1996); *A Sensible Metaphysical Realism* (Milwaukee: Marquette University Press, 2007).

may contribute to the building of a strong model for a realist conception of theology.

The original aspect of this present research comes from relating relevant aspects of the works of these two thinkers and using them dialectically as it were, in order to move beyond them. This conjunction may seem surprising, since Bavinck is a theologian who worked in the early twentieth century European context, while Plantinga has been working contemporaneously in the American analytical philosophy context. I nevertheless consider this attempt cogent and promising. Plantinga was raised in an American Dutch Reformed family and has studied and taught at Calvin College (Grand Rapids), an important American Dutch Calvinist intellectual center. Historians have documented the influence of Abraham Kuyper and Herman Bavinck on this milieu,[103] and Plantinga himself recognizes this intellectual and spiritual heritage in several autobiographical articles.[104] I therefore hold and aim to show that there are sufficient similarities and differences between the works of these two thinkers to produce a fruitful and original interaction.

The main research question that underlies this book can now be formulated as follows:

> In what ways might the conjunction of Bavinck's prolegomena to dogmatic theology and Plantinga's theory of warrant (with its theistic

---

103 See for instance Richard J. Mouw, "Dutch Calvinist Philosophical Influences in North America," *Calvin Theological Journal* 1 (1989), 93-120.

104 Plantinga explicitly refers to Bavinck on pages 64-65, 71-73 and 92 of his seminal article "Reason and Belief," in *Faith and Rationality: Reason and Belief in God*, ed. Alvin Plantinga and Nicholas Wolterstorff (Notre Dame: University of Notre Dame Press, 1983), 16-93. He recognizes the influence on his work of Dutch Reformed theology more generally conceived in several autobiographical articles. See for instance, "Christian Life Partly Lived," in *Philosophers who Believe. The Spiritual Journey of 11 Leading Thinkers*, ed. Kelly James Clark (Downers Grove: InterVarsity Press, 1993), 45-82. On page 48, he describes the spiritual climate of the church he attended as a child: "Although most of the members of the church were rural folk who hadn't had the benefit of much formal education (my grandfather was lucky to finish the sixth grade), there was an astonishing amount of theological sophistication about. Many had read their Kuyper and Bavinck, and a few were considerably better at theology than some of the ministers in charge of the church." On page 53, he briefly describes the role played in his life by the Dutch Calvinist Calvin College: "Calvin College has been for me an enormously powerful spiritual influence and in some ways the center and focus of my intellectual life." Finally, his friend Nicholas Wolterstorff states: "Plantinga and I were both educated in the Dutch neo-Calvinist tradition of which Bavinck was a founder." Nicholas Wolterstorff, "Herman Bavinck – Proto Reformed Epistemologist," *Calvin Theological Journal* 45 (2010), 146.

extensions) strengthen the contemporary case in favor of a realist conception of theology?

There is indeed a high level of intellectual compatibility between Bavinck's defense of a realist conception of knowledge in general, and of theology in particular, and Plantinga's externalist theory of knowledge, which includes the knowledge of God and therefore theology. My aim is to show that the mutual improvement generated by the conjunction of the work of the Dutch Reformed theologian and the American analytic philosopher can strengthen the realist conception of theology in a way that has not been explored by contemporary critical or theological realists.

4.2 Methodological Clarifications

Four methodological clarifications can be brought to bear on the research question. First, it is helpful to interpret this research as part of a wider international movement in the contemporary analytical philosophy of religion, even if it is not an exercise in pure analytic philosophy or theology.[105] Without presenting this movement in detail, I will briefly describe how it has influenced my research. While sketching the history of this movement, Michael C. Rea stresses the resurgence of interest in religious epistemology and metaphysics which characterizes it:

> The wane of logical empiricism made room for more serious exploration of the epistemology of religious belief; the growth of speculative metaphysics made room for more serious theorizing about the nature of God and about the coherence of any systematic relations among various theological doctrines. Whereas non-analytic philosophy has largely pushed theological reflection in an apophatic direction, recent analytic philosophy has witnessed a great deal of substantive theoretical work on the epistemology of religious belief, on the metaphysical underpinnings of various traditional religious doctrines, and a lot else beside.[106]

---

105 This movement has now reached its academic maturity. For recent introductions, see William J. Wainwright (ed.), *The Oxford Handbook of Philosophy of Religion* (Oxford: Oxford University Press, 2005); Charles Taliaferro, Paul Draper, and Philip L. Quinn, *A Companion to Philosophy of Religion* (Oxford: Wiley-Blackwell, 2010); Chad Meister and Paul Copan, *The Routledge Companion to Philosophy of Religion* (London and New York: Routledge, 2013).
106 Michael C. Rea, "Introduction," in *Oxford Readings in Philosophical Theology, Volume 1*, ed. Thomas P. Flint and Michael C. Rea (Oxford: Oxford University Press, 2009), 1.

The phenomenon described in these lines (which can be related to the twentieth century epistemological revolution presented earlier in this chapter) deeply influenced this research. Indeed, it would not have been possible to work on the argument in this way had I been operating solely from the Continental perspective taught during my years spent studying philosophy at university. This contemporary movement in the philosophy of religion has created the possibility to do serious academic research on epistemological and metaphysical questions in relation to theistic beliefs.

The contemporary analytical philosophy of religion movement has influenced me in a second way, viz. by enabling me to break down the barrier that traditionally separates philosophy and theology. The perspective of *philosophical theology* represents a deeply interdisciplinary approach, since it uses philosophical tools to work on classical theological topics.[107] Nicholas Wolterstorff describes this perspective in a programmatic and crucial way as follows:

> But then why talk about philosophical theology? The term implies a distinction between theology as developed by philosophers and theology as developed by theologians—between philosophical theology and theological theology. Kant was carrying on the tradition of distinguishing the two by saying that philosophers appeal solely to reason whereas theologians appeal also to revelation. The now-current view among analytic philosophers concerning the epistemology of philosophy makes that way of distinguishing no longer applicable. The fact that someone views certain of his religious convictions as having their source in revelation does not imply that appealing to those convictions in the course of his reflections about God establishes that he is not engaged in philosophy. [...] I see no structural difference between philosophical and theological theology.[108]

---

107 See the following recent introductions to philosophical theology: Thomas P. Flint and Michael Rea (eds.), *Oxford Readings in Philosophical Theology* (2 vols.) (Oxford: Oxford University Press, 2009); Charles Taliaferro and Chad Meister (eds.), *The Cambridge Companion to Christian Philosophical Theology* (Cambridge: Cambridge University Press, 2009); Oliver D. Crisp (ed.), *A Reader in Contemporary Philosophical Theology* (London: T&T Clark, 2009); Oliver D. Crisp and Michael C. Rea (eds.), *Analytic Theology. New Essays in the Philosophy of Theology* (Oxford: Oxford University Press, 2009).

108 Nicholas Wolterstorff, "Introduction," in *Inquiring about God. Selected Essays, Volume 1*, ed. Terence Cueno (Cambridge: Cambridge University Press, 2010), 7.

It was by adopting such a perspective that I progressively developed the idea of bringing Bavinck and Plantinga together.[109] Without this insight, I would never have joined two such different works in order to build a coherent model for a realist conception of theology. An indirect consequence of this approach is that one can ignore older quarrels between philosophers and theologians over which discipline should be considered the most fundamental.

The second methodological clarification is also important. Given the fact that it is not my goal to propose an independent assessment of the realism vs. anti-realism debate in theology, I will not engage in weighing the pros and cons of both stances.[110] Thus, I will neither criticize anti-realism in a direct way, nor propose a straightforward plea in favor of realism. In that sense, I will not build an independent case for realism. My method is more indirect. I take up where Bavinck and Plantinga left off: I investigate what further gains there may be in synthesizing their insights into an encompassing realist model of theology. By presenting the work of Bavinck and Plantinga on the issue, and then having them interact, I seek to sketch what may be the best possible way to elaborate a cogent contemporary theological realist stance. One might therefore interpret this book as an exploration of realism in order to find out how it might best be substantiated.[111]

---

109 Here are the historical and methodological texts that exerted the greatest influence on the elaboration of my research question: Wolterstorff, "Introduction," "Analytic Philosophy of Religion: Retrospect and Prospect," "Is it Possible and Desirable for Theologians to Recover from Kant?" in *Inquiring about God*, 1-16, 17-34, 35-55; "Postscript: a Life in Philosophy," in *Practices of Belief. Selected Essays, Volume 2*, ed. Terence Cueno (Cambridge: Cambridge University Press, 2010), 409-425; "How Philosophical Theology Became Possible within the Analytic Tradition of Philosophy," in Oliver D. Crisp and Michael C. Rea (eds.), *Analytic Theology. New Essays in the Philosophy of Theology*, 155-168; "Then, Now, and Al," in Kelly James Clark and Michael Rea (eds.), *Reason, Metaphysics, and Mind. New Essays on the Philosophy of Alvin Plantinga* (Oxford: Oxford University Press, 2012), 203-216. See also Michael C. Rea and Oliver Crisp. Michael C. Rea, "Introduction," in Oliver D. Crisp and Michael C. Rea (eds.), *Analytic Theology. New Essays in the Philosophy of Theology*, 4-5. Michael Rea, "Introduction," in Michael Rea (ed.), *Oxford Readings in Philosophical Theology, vol. 1*, 2. Oliver D. Crisp, "Introduction," in Oliver D. Crisp (ed.), *A Reader in Contemporary Philosophical Theology*, 1.

110 Christopher Insole (among others) worked along these lines. See *The Realist Hope. A Critique of Anti-Realist Approaches in Contemporary Philosophical Theology*.

111 As it appears in the following chapters, my method resembles in a certain way that of Plantinga.

For clarity's sake, I will nevertheless briefly outline why I contest both *experiential-expressive* and *cultural-linguistic* forms of anti-realism. The main theological reason why I contest the *experiential-expressive* model is that it is based on a fundamental negation of the revelatory dimension of the Christian faith. The Kantian dualism between the phenomenal and the noumenal worlds is so well integrated in the core of this thought-system that no path can be found for any sort of truth-content revelation. I hold that this situation is lethal for Christian theology, since in the Christian faith God presents himself as a God who has spoken regularly to his people.[112] A fundamental Christian doctrine is that the climax of God's revelation is found in the incarnation of the second person of the Trinity, the Logos of God (to use the patristic vocabulary). Adopting Kantian dualism and affirming that nothing true can be said about God (since it is a noumenal reality) is a form of negation of the incarnation. For that reason, the *experiential-expressive* model cannot be considered a viable option in the *realism in theology* discussions.

The second anti-realist trend I contest is the *cultural-linguistic* model. I hold that this model is unable to adequately depict what Christian faith is. By keeping at a distance the question of the external reference of religious belief, and working mainly on the internal logic of faith and religious life, this model forgets that "the truth of the belief is a constitutive presupposition of the way of life, the latter would be incoherent if the former is denied."[113] Nicholas Wolterstorff sums up this main objection:

> The Wittgensteinians [who adopt the *cultural-linguistic* model] are right to call our attention to the fact that religious language is in good measure used to perform speech acts of other sorts than assertion, though surely

---

112 Two important recent philosophical theology books deal with the question: Richard Swinburne, *Revelation. From Metaphor to Analogy* (Oxford: Oxford University Press, 2007) and Nicholas Wolterstorff, *Divine Discourse. Philosophical Reflections on the Claim that God Speaks* (Cambridge: Cambridge University Press, 1995).

113 Vincent Brümmer, *The Model of Love* (Cambridge: Cambridge University Press, 1993), 18. While developing his thesis, Brümmer quotes Ronald W. Hepburn on page 18: "If I say 'the Lord is my strength and shield,' and if I am a believer, I may experience feelings of exultation and be confirmed in an attitude of quiet confidence. If, however, I tell myself that the arousal of such feelings and confirming of attitude is *the* function of the sentence, that despite appearances it does not refer to a state of affairs, then the more I reflect on this the less I shall exult and the less appropriate my attitude will seem. For there was no magic in the sentence by virtue of which it mediated feelings and confirmed attitudes: these were *responses* to the kind of Being to whom, I trusted, the sentence referred: and response is possible only so long as that exists to which or to whom the response is made."

they exaggerate when they suggest that none of it is used thus. But from the fact that the religious person is often doing something else with God-talk than making assertions, it does not follow that when she is praising, praying, expressing gratitude, and the like, she is not referring to God.[114]

Even if it often proposes interesting insights, the *cultural-linguistic* model relies on a misunderstanding of the object it studies and therefore cannot propose valuable solutions in the *realism in theology* debates.

The third methodological clarification is that my research question goes beyond the systematic presentation of the thought of Bavinck and Plantinga. It should be clear from the beginning that my aim is to propose a synthetic model for a realist conception of theology, and that I study the relevant works of these scholars for that reason. This means that even if the two central chapters of this book are written with the desire to be trustworthy and cogent in the presentation of these two authors, my intellectual agenda is not determined by the inner logic of their works. Thus, I restrict myself to examining relevant works of the two authors, without claiming to be exhaustive. And I will not enter debates that occupied those authors but do not stand in direct relation with my own research. For instance, many specific analytic philosophy debates will not even be mentioned in the Plantinga chapter. Yet, I hold that the two core chapters of this book can be understood as a specific contribution to the study of Bavinck and Plantinga, since they screen and connect their work from a specific angle. My working hypothesis is that bringing together the main insights on realism of these two authors will strengthen their individual cases.

The fourth and final methodological clarification (which actually follows from the previous ones) is that this work is done from a mainly appreciative and constructive perspective. The next two chapters are written in a way that puts forward the depth and the cogency of the studied works of Bavinck and Plantinga. This positive approach will not prevent me from formulating critical remarks here and there, or from raising sometimes difficult questions, since intellectual sympathy does not require thoughtless mimicry, but a mature and constructive dialogue.

---

114 Nicholas Wolterstorff, "Are Religious Believers Committed to the Existence of God?" in *Practices of Belief*, 371.

4.3 Structure and Content

As a conclusion to this introductory chapter, I will briefly outline the structure and the content of the following chapters. In chapter 2, I present Herman Bavinck's defense of a realist conception of theology as expounded in his *Reformed Dogmatics*. The function of this chapter in the context of this research is to analyze the basic canvas from which a synthesis will emerge. This study presents Bavinck's understanding of theology as a science and the way he closely relates this conception of theology to a general realist epistemology. I also consider the way he develops a realist conception of theology against the background of a metaphysical theological understanding of the world and humanity as created by the Logos of God. At the end of the chapter, I discuss some critical issues generated by Bavinck's proposal in relation to the scope of my research.

In chapter 3, I study Alvin Plantinga's work on warrant and proper function and show how this work can be understood as a development of a realist conception of knowledge in general, and of knowledge of God in particular. From this perspective, I pay attention to what Plantinga has called the *Aquinas/Calvin model* and the *Extended Aquinas/Calvin model*. While doing this, I explain how Plantinga's epistemological model fits within the broader frame of Bavinck's thought and how it strengthens it in an interesting way. At the end of the chapter, I also discuss some critical issues generated by Plantinga's proposal in relation to the scope of my research.

In the last chapter, I elaborate what I have been referring to throughout as my proposal, which is to synthesize the main findings of this research into a *Bavinck/Plantinga model for a realist conception of theology*. Having done this, I relate this model to the contemporary realist trends described in the introductory chapter and outline the specific contribution of this research to the *realism in theology* discussions. Finally, I broaden the scope of the reflection and present the significance of this research and the important questions it raises for the contemporary Western world.

Chapter 2

Herman Bavinck's Defense of a Realist Conception of Theology

1. Introduction

As noted in chapter one, the aim is to propose a cogent model for a realist conception of theology by presenting a synthesis of the works of the twentieth century Dutch Reformed theologian Herman Bavinck (1854-1921) and the contemporary American analytic philosopher of religion Alvin Plantinga (born in 1932). In this chapter, I describe and discuss what I consider as the Dutch theologian's contribution to this research.

Two interwoven aspects of Herman Bavinck's work led to his choice as a central figure for this research. First and most basically, one can find in his work a strong case in favor of a realist conception of theology. In and by itself, this fact can be viewed as a necessary but insufficient condition for his having such a central role in the context of this research. A second and more specific reason is that Bavinck belongs to a theological tradition that emerged in the context of the intellectual shift that occurred during the seventeenth century, and he worked on answering the numerous metaphysical, epistemological and semantic questions raised by the emergence of modernity. This interest in problems raised by the change of the status and epistemology of theology gave birth to a new section in dogmatic theologies, namely, the *prolegomena*.[1] The basic idea that underlies this attention to meta-theological questions is that since the emergence of modernity, it is no longer possible to start a dogmatic theology straight away with the doctrine of God, as did the sixteenth-century Reformers, for instance. On the contrary, numerous preliminary modern arguments that contest the possibility or cogency of theology

---

1 The modern *prolegomena* should not be confused with the medieval *praeambula fidei*, which are generally to be understood from the perspective of the Augustinian *fides quaerens intellectum* principle. Shortly before Bavinck, and also in Amsterdam, Abraham Kuyper published an entire prolegomena volume titled *Encyclopedia of Sacred Theology. Its Principles* (New York: Charles Scribner's Sons, 1898).

itself need to be discussed with care before embarking upon the properly dogmatic work.²

By publishing a nearly 600-page prolegomena volume to his *Reformed Dogmatics*,³ Bavinck made a major contribution to this field of studies. This book is of great interest from the perspective of this present research, since Bavinck develops a thorough defense of a realist conception of theology in a way that is very compatible with my own method of inquiry. For this reason I mainly focus on this "magnum opus."⁴ Both before and after his *Reformed Dogmatics* Bavinck penned some smaller writings for various occasions on the relation of philosophy and theology. Although I will at times refer to such occasional writings, I will not include these in my systematic analysis, since it is not my goal in this (or another) chapter to reconstruct Bavinck's *Werdegang* on the issue of realism in theology. I am interested instead in his most extensive, elaborate and internationally influential attempt to contribute to the discussion on the nature and foundation of theology as an academic discipline. Where possible, however, I triangulate my findings from the *Reformed Dogmatics* by comparing these to "the mature Bavinck on issues pertaining to revelation, philosophy, epistemology, and ontology."⁵ This "mature Bavinck" is to be found in his *Philosophy of Revelation* (hereafter *PoR*), the expanded version of the Stone Lectures that he presented at Princeton Theological Seminary in 1908.⁶ By explicitly relating what we would now call "philosophical theology" to "theological theology" as he does, and by discussing metaphysical, epistemological and semantic questions in relation to theology without being constrained by positivistic criteria,

---

2 A clear presentation of the emergence of this tradition in Reformed theology can be found in chapter 2 of Richard A. Muller, *Post-Reformation Reformed Dogmatics 1: Prolegomena to Theology* (Grand Rapids: Baker Book House, 2003). See also §4 of the first chapter of Wolfhart Pannenberg's *Systematic Theology (Volume 1)* (Grand Rapids: Eerdmans Publishing, 1991).
3 Herman Bavinck, *Reformed Dogmatics 1: Prolegomena* (Grand Rapids: Baker Academic, 2003). The first volume (out of four) of Bavinck's dogmatics was originally published in Dutch in 1895. This English translation is based on the second revised and expanded Dutch edition of 1906.
4 James Eglinton, *Bavinck. A Critical Biography* (Grand Rapids: Baker Academic, 2020), 144.
5 Herman Bavinck, *Philosophy of Revelation. A New Annotated Edition*, ed. Cory Brock and Nathaniel Gray Sutanto (Peabody, MA: Hendrickson Publishers, 2018), 2 (Preface to the Annotated Edition).
6 It was originally translated from the Dutch and published as *The Philosophy of Revelation. The Stone Lectures for 1908-1909* (New York etc.: Longman, Green and Co, 1909). In what follows I refer to the new annotated 2018 edition (the editors of which rightly dropped the definite article from the title).

Bavinck appears as a crucial discussion partner in the edification of a model for a realist conception of theology.

The second specific reason for choosing to analyze the work of Bavinck stems from the way he dealt with the intellectual and academic context of his time.[7] Shortly before he began to study theology, the Higher Education Act of 1876 redefined the academic status of theology in the Netherlands by proposing a sort of cohabitation between confessional Reformed theology and the new post-Kantian neutral and comparative "religious studies" approach.[8] Bavinck disapproved of this academic shift and became deeply involved in contesting it. He indeed interpreted this movement and the merely comparative approach to religion as potentially lethal for Christian theology, and was convinced that the cohabitation was impossible.[9] This led him to define with great care the specific scientific nature and scope of dogmatic theology in order to secure its position within the public universities. As James Eglinton briefly states, "[T]he significance of this movement [leading to the Dutch Higher Education Act] can scarcely be underemphasized in developing a reading of Bavinck's theology. Reasserting both the possibility and the place of theology forms a major emphasis in his *Prolegomena*."[10] This contextual

---

7 For detailed biographies of Bavinck, see Ron Gleason, *Herman Bavinck. Pastor, Churchman, Statesman and Theologian* (Phillipsburg: Presbyterian and Reformed Publishing, 2010) and James P. Eglinton, *Bavinck: A Critical Biography*. See also the first chapter of James Perman Eglinton, *Trinity and Organism. Towards a New Reading of Herman Bavinck's Organic Motif* (London and New York: T&T Clark, 2012).

8 For an insightful introduction to this post-Enlightenment European movement, see Thomas A. Howard, *Protestant Theology and the Making of the Modern German University* (New York: Oxford University Press, 2006). Pages 378 ff. are devoted to the emergence of religious studies in the 1860s and 1870s in Europe (and notably in the Netherlands). This issue is related to the question of realism and will be briefly addressed in the last chapter of this book.

9 The English reader has access to Bavinck's following texts on this question: "Theology and Religious Studies," in Herman Bavinck, *Essays on Religion, Science, and Society*, ed. John Bolt (Grand Rapids: Baker Academic, 2008), 49-60, and "Theology and Religious Studies in Nineteenth-Century Netherlands," in Herman Bavinck, *Essays on Religion, Science, and Society*, 281-288. On page 284, Bavinck boldly affirms: "Religious studies tries to find the true, pure religion by impartial, comparative research of all the religions of the world; this pure religion, as the basis of all historical religions, gradually emerges and comes to light. Actually, with this method Christianity is subjected to the abstract understanding of religion as conceived by the practitioner of religious studies. All of this is in direct opposition to the Christian faith." See also *Reformed Dogmatics* I, 50-54, and *Philosophy of Revelation*, 133-135.

10 Eglinton, *Trinity and Organism*, 18-19. From the same perspective, John Bolt further states: "What makes this prolegomena distinctive is the extent to which Bavinck confronts the profound epistemological crisis of post-Enlightenment modernity."

element is important from the perspective of this research, since it led Bavinck to develop in a thorough way his realist conception of theology in answer to what he perceived as a major institutional threat generated by antirealist approaches to religion.

The general aim of this chapter is to study and discuss Bavinck's argument in favor of a realist conception of theology as expounded in his *Reformed Dogmatics*.[11] This will simultaneously lay the first foundational element of my own model for such a conception of theology. The first section of this chapter presents Bavinck's own characterization of his theological project as a scientific enterprise (2). I then describe how Bavinck carefully develops his realist conception of theology in *Reformed Dogmatics 1: Prolegomena* (hereafter *RD 1*) (3). Thirdly, I complete the presentation of Bavinck's realism by working on specific questions developed in *Reformed Dogmatics 2: God and Creation* (hereafter *RD 2*) (4). Finally, I discuss Bavinck's argument in relation to the contemporary realist trends described in the first chapter of this book (5). While sections 2 to 4 entail listening to Bavinck as carefully as possible, quoting him extensively rather than approaching him through the lens of later interpreters, section 5 analyzes and discusses his proposal from a wider perspective, also taking into account the secondary literature.

2. Dogmatic Theology as a Science

Even if Bavinck is undoubtedly an irenic theologian, it would be difficult, in the highly post-Kantian context of late nineteenth century Europe, to find a more polemical theological project than that of *RD 1*: developing and defending, as it does, a scientific and realistic conception of dogmatic theology. The aim of this section is to study Bavinck's case in favor of such an understanding.

John Bolt, "Editor's Introduction," in Herman Bavinck, *Reformed Dogmatics. Prolegomena (Volume 1)*, 20.

11 In these pages, I mainly rely on *Reformed Dogmatics 1*, since, as indicated, this volume is specifically devoted to the type of questions dealt with in this book. Other relevant texts of Bavinck available in English (apart from his *Philosophy of Revelation*, henceforth *PoR*) include: "Foreword to the First Edition (Volume 1) of the *Gereformeerde Dogmatiek*," *Calvin Theological Journal* 45 (2010), 9-10; "The Catholicity of Christianity and the Church," *Calvin Theological Journal* 27 (1992), 220-251; *The Certainty of Faith* (Grand Rapids: Paideia Press, 1980); "Common Grace," *Calvin Theological Journal* 24 (1989), 35-65; "Calvin and Common Grace," in Emile Doumergue, August Lang, Herman Bavinck, Benjamin B. Warfield, *Calvin and Reformation. Four Studies* (London and Edinburgh: Fleming H. Revell Company, 1909), 99-130; *Christian Worldview* (Wheaton: Crossway, 2019). I occasionally refer to these writings (and especially to *PoR*) insofar as they clarify or complement aspects of Bavinck's argument in *RD*.

As shown in the previous chapter of this book, modernity (here in its Kantian form) has emptied theology of its traditional content. Bavinck's intellectual situation is determined by the following alternative: on the one side, one finds *faith*, perceived as a purely existential, ethical, or in any case non-cognitive, subjective reality; on the other, one finds the above-mentioned comparative *religious studies* method of inquiry (or "science of religion" as Bavinck also calls it).[12] Bavinck will reject both alternatives, writing an entire volume of prolegomena in order to explain why theology can neither retreat into a subjectivist or ethical faith, nor take refuge in a rationalistic science, but instead has to present itself as a science capable of formulating truth-content propositions: "The content of dogmatics is the knowledge of God as he has revealed it in Christ through his Word."[13] Theology doesn't only deal with the *fides qua creditur* (the faith by which one believes), but also with the *fides quae creditur* (the articles of faith that are believed). It is only when this affirmation has been carefully demonstrated in the *Prolegomena* that Bavinck begins to write, as did his eminent predecessors, on *God and Creation, Sin and Salvation in Christ*, and on *Holy Spirit, Church and New Creation*.

In *RD 1*, Bavinck refers repeatedly to dogmatic theology as a "science."[14] Since this concept has been defined in various ways in history, it is necessary to specify in which sense it is used. Generally speaking, one can say that Bavinck's conception of science is Aristotelian, and that on this question he largely follows the theological tradition of post-Reformation Reformed orthodoxy, even if this adhesion is not uncritical.

An Aristotelian conception of science implies not only one type of science (or one scientific method) determined by a specific structure of the human mind or the supposed mathematical structure of reality, but a multitude of sciences, considered as specifically organized bodies of systematically arranged information, all defined by their specific object, principles and method.[15] Bavinck thus considers theology one science among many others, with its own specific object, method and encyclopedic place.[16] In this section, I will show how Bavinck defines his view of a

---

12 See Bavinck, *PoR*, 166, 171. The Dutch original has *godsdienstwetenschap* for religious studies/science of religion.
13 Bavinck, *RD 1*, 110.
14 Bavinck defines theology as a science in the *PoR* also, viz. as "the science of the knowledge of God" (22).
15 For an introduction to Aristotle's conception of science, see Jonathan Barnes' commented edition of Aristotle, *Posterior Analytics* (Oxford: Clarendon Press, 1993).
16 Bavinck's understanding of science includes the humanities. It is thus different from the common Anglo-Saxon understanding that restricts *science* to the *empirical*

theological science through this Aristotelian lens. I start with the presentation of the object of theological science (2.1). I then study its specific method (2.2). Finally, I describe the place of theology in the field of all the sciences (2.3). This presentation is an attempt to synthesize the content of the introductory part of *RD 1* (Part I of the English translation).[17] It will nevertheless be enriched by some meaningful passages found in other writings of Bavinck.

Fortunately, the following analysis can build on recent studies that have been published in the wake of the so-called "Bavinck-renaissance" which is currently retrieving Bavinck's theology for the Anglophone world. In particular, one can profit from recent work on Bavinck's epistemology by Nathaniel Gray Sutanto.[18] Drawing on earlier attempts to this effect, in his monograph *God and Knowledge* (based on his Edinburgh doctoral dissertation) Sutanto convincingly synthesizes the variegated results of these previous studies, thus excavating the conceptual contours of Bavinck's theory of knowledge and reconstructing its historical background. Despite the subtitle of his monograph (which in this connection points to the strongly theological grounding of Bavinck's general epistemology), Sutanto is more interested in Bavinck's theory of human knowledge formation at large than in what we might call Bavinck's *theological* epistemology. That is, as he acknowledges himself, he does not discuss the specific question of how, according to Bavinck, human knowledge *of God* is actually possible with equal depth. It is this question in particular that is of concern in the present project. While making use of the way in which Sutanto sketches the historical connections between

---

sciences. As I will show in the next chapter, Plantinga proposes a typically Anglo-Saxon definition of science: "Science is a disciplined and systematic effort to discover [...] truths, an effort with a substantial empirical involvement. While it is difficult to give a precise account of this empirical component, it is absolutely crucial to science, and is what distinguishes science from philosophy." Alvin Plantinga, *Where the Conflict Really Lies. Science, Religion, and Naturalism* (New York: Oxford University Press, 2011), 268.

17 Before going further, one should notice that the English translation of *RD*, like that of *PoR*, though very trustworthy overall, is not entirely flawless. For example, it does not respect the nomenclature of the Dutch original. The beginnings and ends, as well as the titles of several chapters have been modified. Surprisingly, the English editor does not even mention this fact. My interpretation of these modifications is that the English editor has watered down the Aristotelian shape of the Dutch table of contents in order to make it look more *Reformed* to American readers. Even where I have worked on the English translation, I refer to the Dutch original version whenever such intentional changes seem relevant.

18 Nathaniel Gray Sutanto, *God and Knowledge. Herman Bavinck's Theological Epistemology* (London and New York: T&T Clark, 2020),

Bavinck and Plantinga,[19] the aim is to move beyond this by showing how the accounts of both can strengthen one other systematically.

2.1 The Object of Theological Science

In Bavinck's context, the question of the object of dogmatic theology was much debated. As presented in subsection 3.3 of the previous chapter devoted to anti-realist trends in theology, post-Kantian thinkers hold that knowing God is beyond the human cognitive faculties and that a religious discourse is an expression of an ethical or spiritual experience. Though the trends described in the first chapter gained traction in the course of the twentieth century, Bavinck's context was already deeply influenced by these post-Kantian developments. From this perspective, it is generally admitted that the object of theology is not God as he reveals himself, but rather human religious beliefs and experiences, and can thus ultimately be understood as a derived form of anthropology.

As stated above, Bavinck was perfectly informed of the nature of these post-Kantian systems and of their consequences for the theological undertaking. *RD 1* can be interpreted as a thorough effort to interact in a critical way with these trends. From the very beginning of this volume, Bavinck makes clear that he fundamentally disagrees with this understanding of theology by affirming that the object of dogmatic theology is God as he reveals himself. The following passage is so bold it can be read as a theological provocation in a post-Kantian anti-realist context:

> The truth and value of religion depend on the existence, the revelation and the knowability of God. Also the science of religion that incorporates metaphysics is in principle theology, and proceeds from the existence and knowability of God. If God is not knowable, did not reveal himself, or does not even exist, not only dogmatics or theology but religion itself collapses, for it is built on the knowledge of God. Thus dogmatics is, and can only exist as, the scientific system of the knowledge of God. More precisely and from a Christian viewpoint, dogmatics is the knowledge that God has revealed in his Word to the church concerning himself and all creatures as they stand in relation to him.[20]

---

19 Sutanto, *God and Knowledge*, 104-109.
20 Bavinck, *RD 1*, 38. See also *PoR*, 133: "(…) faith in the knowability of God is inseparable from the existence of God, which is presupposed in and with the truth of religion." In *RD I*, 53, Bavinck adds: "The word of God has an objective content that was established before, and persists apart from, our faith, just as much as the world of colors and sounds exists independently of the blind and the deaf. In that case, however, knowledge of the objective content of revelation has significance of and for itself. This

Bavinck's understanding of theology is based on a strong metaphysical and epistemological realism applied to God. The object of theology is a knowable external reality, God as he reveals himself. It would be difficult to be more opposed to representatives of the post-Kantian stance, their affirmation of an unknowable God and their understanding of theology as an expression of human ethical or spiritual experiences.

A couple of pages below, Bavinck pursues his argument and introduces an even more specific definition of the object of theology:

> The imperative task of the dogmatician is to think God's thoughts after him and to trace their unity. His work is not finished until he has mentally absorbed this unity and set it forth in a dogmatics. Accordingly, he does not come to God's revelation with a ready-made system in order, as best he can, to force its content into it. On the contrary, even in his system a theologian's sole responsibility is to think God's thoughts after him and to reproduce the unity that is objectively present in the thoughts of God and has been recorded for the eye of faith in Scripture.[21]

The famous Dutch neo-Calvinist statement that the theologian's responsibility is to "think God's thoughts after him" puts forward the understanding that theology is a cognitive discipline, like any other science. The object of theology is indeed not simply God, but "God's thoughts" as revealed in the Scriptures and seized by faith, since God has thoughts that can be grasped and adequately reproduced in a human language. In the *Philosophy of Revelation* Bavinck formulates the same stance when he claims that theology seeks "to ascertain by means of exegesis the content of revelation, [...] endeavoring to reduce to unity of thought this ascertained content [...]."[22] Although Bavinck is highly sensitive to the role of human consciousness in knowledge production, as will be seen, the object of theology he describes in both volumes leaves no room for the different forms of anti-realism presented in the first chapter. He proposes, on the contrary, a bold affirmation of a realist approach of theology.

2.2 The Method of Theological Science
To think God's thoughts after him and to reproduce their unity necessitates

---

is true of all science. All science has inherent value and purpose, apart from whether it has practical utility or yields benefits for life."
21 Bavinck, *RD 1*, 44.
22 Bavinck, *PoR*, 22.

a specific method, Bavinck affirms. He thus devotes an entire part of the introductory section of *RD 1* to this question.[23] He starts by defining and applying the concept of "method" to dogmatic theology:

> By method of dogmatics, broadly speaking, one must understand the manner in which the dogmatic material is acquired and treated. Three factors come into play in this acquisition: Holy Scripture, the church's confession, and Christian consciousness.[24]

These lines are important since they immediately locate Bavinck's approach in the context of his time. He is indeed opposed to two powerful modern epistemological trends. On the one hand, he rejects the post-Kantian subjectivism that denies the possibility of formulating any theological proposition with a truth-value. This is why he mentions Holy Scripture and the church's confession as two objective and external methodological factors. On the other hand, he rejects the positivistic objectivism which characterizes the natural sciences of his time by mentioning Christian consciousness as an internal (or subjective) methodological factor. He thus develops a theological method aimed at overcoming these modern oppositions.

Bavinck describes with clarity how the application of his theological method integrates the three above-mentioned factors:

> [Scripture] is a living whole, not abstract but organic. It nowhere contains a sketch of the doctrine of faith; this is something that has to be drawn from the entire organism of Scripture. Scripture is not designed so that we should parrot it but that as free children of God we should think his thoughts after him. But then all so-called presuppositionlessness and objectivity are impossible. So much study and reflection on the subject is bound up with it that no person can possibly do it alone. That takes centuries. To that end the church has been appointed and given the promise of the Spirit's guidance into all truth. Whoever isolates himself from the church, i.e., from Christianity as a whole, from the history of dogma in its entirety, loses the truth of the Christian faith.[25]

---

23 In the Dutch edition, Part 3 of the Inleiding section is titled "Methode der Dogmatiek."
24 Bavinck, *RD 1*, 61.
25 Bavinck, *RD 1*, 83. In *PoR* Bavinck highlights the organic connectedness of Scripture with God's revelation in nature (242), history (210), human conscience (167), and "the *sensus communis* of the whole of humanity" (243). Cf. RD 2, 353: "[...] special revelation should never be separated from its *organic* connection to history, the world, and humanity"—a point which Bavinck will elaborate *in extenso* in *PoR*.

Bavinck generally characterizes his method as "synthetic-genetic." The reasons he does so appear clearly in these lines, even if he doesn't mention this concept explicitly. First, it is "synthetic" because it does not oppose the objectivity of the Scriptures to the subjectivity of the theologian's conscience, but instead attempts to unify them in the practice of theology. Second, it is "genetic" since the tradition of the Christian church should play an important role in the work of the theologian. Another key word in this passage, which is closely related to that of "synthetic-genetic," is the adjective "organic," which allows the theologian to integrate in a harmonious way God's revelation, the theologian's subjectivity and the tradition of the Christian church. From Bavinck's point of view, these realities are perceived as complementary.

According to James Eglinton, who devotes an entire book to the organicism in the work of Bavinck, "the [organic] motif plays a crucial role in his approach to theology [...]. Even the most casual reading of Bavinck's work quickly reveals the regularity with which he uses organic language, imagery and concepts."[26] The context of the present presentation of Bavinck's theological method requires that the main function of his organic terminology be seen as opposition to any form of what he considers modern dualism.[27] Organicism is indeed the intellectual approach to God and the world that allows the theologian to bring together realities that modern thought tends to oppose, such as, for instance, the known object and the knowing subject, objectivity and subjectivity, facts and their interpretation, truth and meaning, faith and reason, general and particular revelation, etc. Eglinton summarizes this in a striking way: "Bavinck's theology of Creator as Trinity necessitates the conceptualization of creation as organism: Trinity *ad intra* leads to organism *ad extra*."[28] At the core of Bavinck's methodology "is the

---

26 Eglinton, *Trinity and Organism*, 51. In his third chapter Eglinton locates Bavinck's organicism within its wider intellectual context. In *God and Knowledge*, 17-73, Nathaniel Gray Sutanto, a former student of Eglinton, examines with great care the crucial role played by organicism in Bavinck's theological epistemology.

27 It is not my purpose here to draw the genealogy of Bavinck's organicism. It is nevertheless obvious that the strong Dutch neo-Calvinist opposition to modern mechanicism and dualism has influenced him. For a good introduction to nineteenth century's organicism, see Isaiah Berlin, *The Roots of Romanticism* (Princeton: Princeton University Press, 2001).

28 Eglinton, *Trinity and Organism*, 81. It seems to me that the word "necessitates" is actually too strong: God's Trinitarian being does not constrain God to constitute creation in an organic way, nor does Bavinck suggest this. Bavinck posits instead an *analogy* between the two (e.g. *RD* 2, 331). The same criticism applies to Daniel Ragusa, "The Trinity at the Center of Thought and Life: Herman Bavinck's Organic Apologetic," *Mid America Journal of Theology* 28 (2017), 149-175 (151).

principle that an essential coherence exists between Creator and creation."[29] This "coherence" is on the edge of the classical Christian tension between God's transcendence and immanence, and is therefore to be interpreted carefully. It nevertheless allows the theologian to constantly work with various concepts, as a "unity in diversity," a methodological approach inspired by Trinitarian theology.

This way of dealing with the theological material is a distinctive trait of Bavinck's *Reformed Dogmatics*. This is how he proceeds to "think God's thoughts after him and to trace their unity," as he writes. Since God is a lively intelligence, dualist or mechanistic approaches are doomed to fail: they may be fitted to the natural sciences, but not to theology. By contrast, an organic method will make possible the well-balanced presentation of the complexity of the different dogmas: "The synthetic-genetic method [...] gives the dogmatician the advantage that he can show the unity and organic interconnectedness of dogmatics. The different dogmas are not isolated propositions but constitute a unity."[30]

Since this question of Bavinck's organic theological method is important in the context of this research, it is useful to make a short *excursus* to illustrate the difference between this method and modern theological methods that build their arguments on oppositions rather than complementarities (in this book, I have labeled these methods as "dualistic"). The lowest common denominator of Protestant theology is to be found in its adherence to the five *solas* of the Reformation: *sola Scriptura*, *solus Christus*, *sola gratia*, *sola fide* and *soli Deo Gloria*. However, these five *solas* have been diversely interpreted through history. The organic interpretation of *sola Scriptura* has insisted on the complementary character of general and particular revelation, while the dualistic interpretation has understood it as the valorization of supernatural revelation (cf. the Barthian *Deus dixit!*) rather than any kind of natural knowledge of God (against *natural theology* and metaphysics in theology). The organic interpretation of the *solus Christus* has located this soteriological affirmation within the wider theological frame of salvation understood as a reordering of the creation, while the dualistic interpretation progressively culminated in a Christological concentration that gave precedence to the order of redemption over that of creation (creation must be read in the light of redemption—every theological locus is ultimately a part of Christology). The organic interpretation of the *sola gratia* stresses the impossibility of humans being saved apart from the

---

29 Eglinton, *Trinity and Organism*, 101.
30 Bavinck, *RD 1*, 94.

grace of God without denying the original goodness of the creation, while the dualistic interpretation has understood this as a sovereign divine intervention that occurs in a kind of metaphysical void. The organic interpretation of the *sola fide* has never opposed faith to the natural faculties of the human intellect, while dualistic interpretations have insisted that reason is definitively unable to seize any manifestation of the transcendence of God, and that paradoxically only faith allows us to face these realities. And finally, the organic interpretation of the *soli Deo Gloria* brings together God's natural and supernatural actions in unified praise, while dualistic interpretations only glorify God for his direct supernatural actions in a corrupt world.[31]

2.3 Dogmatic Theology and the Other Sciences

The last question raised by Bavinck's definition of dogmatic theology as a science is its location within the wider field of the sciences. As stated above, Bavinck holds that dogmatic theology should neither be the expression of a retreat into a self-sufficient expression of faith, nor a religiously neutral rational discipline. He therefore develops on the one hand a case against the merging of theology and religious studies at the

---

31 For obvious chronological reasons, I do not want to give the impression that Bavinck was struggling with Barth, even if the shadow of the Swiss theologian hangs over this short presentation of the dualistic interpretations of the *five solas* of the Reformation. However, from a contemporary systematic perspective, it makes sense to contrast different theological methods in a synthetic way. Barth developed his dialectical theological method a couple of decades after the publication of Bavinck's *Reformed Dogmatics*. But since this method first relies on the acceptance of a dualistic frame of thought before aiming to overcome it dialectically, it is worth mentioning here. The following quotations from "Fate and Idea in Theology" (1929), a work entirely devoted to the question of realism and idealism in theology, illustrates how Barth's dialectical method functions, and how it is opposed from a systematic point of view to Bavinck's organic method: "Certainly theology cannot pursue its calling without trying to think dialectically about how God is given and not given at the same time. We have seen that theology can be predominately [sic] realist or predominately idealist" (52). "The art of theology cannot be the art of synthesis. It may practice the art of including the opposite dialectically" (53). "Theology does not take pains to think dialectically about opposites because of the contradiction in human thought (which intimates a contradiction in human existence). This contradiction does not pose a riddle for which, as a technical discipline supposedly focused on humanity (say, humanity as it reflects on its own existence), it would more or less know how to give a clear and definite answer. On the contrary, theology thinks dialectically, because this contradiction has been placed into the world of thought and existence by God's Word as something it and only it resolves" (54). Karl Barth, "Fate and Idea in Theology," in *The Way of Theology in Karl Barth. Essays and Comments* (Eugene: Wipf and Stock Publishers, 1986), 25-61.

beginning of *RD 1*: "The Christian church cannot be satisfied with an objective account of the content of its faith but wishes that its faith be unfolded and set forth also as truth."³² And on the other hand, at the end of the same volume, he opposes the pietistic aversion to theology: "The Christian church, not content to limit itself to faith, almost from the beginning pursued knowledge of religious truth and gave birth to a special branch of science: theology."³³ An understanding of Bavinck's conception of dogmatic theology as a science can be deepened by exploring how, according to Bavinck, theology belongs to the common genus of science, while maintaining a specific character.

In order to understand why theology belongs to the sciences, one should have a clear idea of how Bavinck describes the relation between faith and reason. This issue is as old as Christian theology itself, quite complex, and important in the context of this research. At the end of *RD 1*, Bavinck states:

> In this context we must first of all and fundamentally reject the notion that regards faith and reason as two independent powers engaging in a life-and-death struggle with each other. [...] Faith, the faith by which we believe, is not an organ or faculty next to or above reason but a disposition or habit of reason itself. [...] Still reason is the recipient subject of faith, capable of faith. [...] In that sense faith is not a sacrifice of the intellect but mental health. Faith, therefore, does not relieve Christians of the desire to study and reflect; rather it spurs them on to the end. Nature is not destroyed by regeneration but restored.³⁴

Bavinck's organic method is at work in this passage. He avoids any modern dualistic opposition between faith and reason and adheres, by contrast, to the classical Christian stance according to which faith is a disposition of reason itself.³⁵ He also adopts the Thomistic principle

---

32 Bavinck, *RD 1*, 47. See pages 47 to 58.
33 Bavinck, *RD 1*, 603. See pages 603-621.
34 Bavinck, *RD 1*, 616-617. Bavinck further states: "Believers who want to devote themselves to the study of theology, accordingly, must prepare their minds for the task awaiting them. There is no admission to the temple of theology except by way of the study of the arts. Indispensable to the practitioner of the science of theology is philosophical, historical, and linguistic preparatory training."
35 As stated above, Bavinck's theology is influenced by Reformed orthodoxy, notably on this question of the relation between faith and reason. For an enlightening historical case study on this question, see Jeffrey Mallinson, *Faith, Reason, and Revelation in Theodore Beza (1519-1605)* (Oxford: Oxford University Press, 2003).

according to which "nature is not destroyed by regeneration but restored." This affirmation stresses the convergence between faith and reason. The conjunction of these two stances suggests that dogmatic theology clearly belongs to the field of sciences. Bavinck insists on the fact that it is impossible to practice theology without using the common tools of human rationality: theology is indeed not a sort of merely supernatural discipline. He states boldly in an organic way:

> In religion and theology we arrive at knowledge in no other way than in other sciences. Faith is not a new organ implanted in human beings, not a sixth sense, or "superadded gift." However much it disagrees with the "natural" [unscriptural] human, it is nevertheless completely natural, normal, and human. Both objectively and subjectively revelation connects with nature, re-creation with creation.[36]

Nevertheless, dogmatic theology as a science also has an irreducibly specific character, which directly flows from its object. In his rectorial address at Kampen in December 1894, Bavinck carefully develops his thought on this question. In the concluding section, he states:

> But here too re-creation is something different than creation. The arts and sciences have their *principium* not in the special grace of regeneration and conversion but in the natural gifts and talents that God in his common grace has also given to nonbelievers. [...]
> Theology itself as a science was not born apart from the gifts of the *gratia communis* [common grace]. She does of course hold a unique place among the sciences. She has her own principle, object, and goal and derives these exclusively from the *gratia specialis*. But she would still not be theology in the scientific sense had she not availed herself of the thinking consciousness of man sanctified by faith and used it to penetrate revelation and understand its content. Theology first came into existence in the body of Christ when *gratia communis* and *gratia specialis* flowed

---

36 Bavinck, *RD 1*, 566. On page 618, Bavinck states: "Theology operates like other sciences. Like these other sciences, it is bound to its object. In the process of thinking, it is subject to the laws that apply to this process. It too cannot violate the laws of logic with impunity. For theology, too, the supreme desideratum is the unity of truth, the system of the knowledge of God. Accordingly, however much theology may differ from the other sciences in principle, object, and goal, formally it agrees with them and may rightly claim the name of science. And since revelation does not per se clash with human reason but only 'on account of the accident of corruption and a depraved disposition,' theology may even in a sense be called 'natural' and 'rational.'"

together. Consequently, theology accords to the other sciences their full due. [...] Theology is ultimately nothing other than interpretation of the *gratia Dei* in the arena of science.[37]

Thus on the one hand, being rooted in God's general grace for all humanity, theology belongs to the sphere of the sciences, even giving them "their full due." On the other hand, because of its supernatural object (God's special grace or revelation), theology cannot be reduced to these other human sciences. Its *specific difference* has to be underlined; otherwise it will be swallowed by the anthropocentric approach of religious studies, or reduced to a specific form of philosophical thinking as is the case in post-Kantian approaches. It is this organic way of thinking, almost seamlessly weaving together general and special revelation, nature and grace, that is characteristic of Bavinck's theological method.

In his *Philosophy of Revelation* Bavinck again defends the status of theology as "an independent and genuine science," which comes with "its own method" (178). Theology is a science of its own because religion, however many other dimensions it may have, "always includes knowledge" (180). In the Christian religion in particular, the word *faith* includes "at the same time *cognitio* and *fiducia* (knowledge and trust)" and thus Christian faith cannot be reduced (as has been attempted "under the influence of Schleiermacher") to a feeling of trust in the heart (179). In short, religion's connection with matters of knowledge and truth requires that theology, as the study "of the revelation of God and of our knowledge concerning him" (22), is reckoned among the sciences.

But what about its method? Here, Bavinck goes beyond his earlier reflections by suggesting that, next to the critique of pure reason (Kant) and the critique of historical reason (Dilthey), which paved the way for the natural sciences and the humanities respectively, we also need a "critique of religious reason."[38] Appealing to the organic "richness and diversity" of the world and therefore of science (178), Bavinck rightly argues that the method of each science should be determined by its specific object. He then applies this to theology in the following way:

> Now, if the object of theology is no other than the true and pure religion, which appears to us in Christianity as the fruit of revelation, then the inquiry after method results in this one and very important question:

---

37 Bavinck, *Common Grace*, 64-65.
38 Bavinck, *PoR*, 180; the Dutch word "kritiek" should have been translated here as "critique" (as in Kant's *Critique of Pure Reason*), not as "criticism."

> How does the Christian religion itself represent that a human comes to her, acknowledges her truth, and by her becomes a true religious person—that is a Christian, a child of God? [...] The plan of salvation in the Christian religion determines the method of Christian theology.[39]

Thus, in this remarkable move, Bavinck situates the methodical starting point of theology not in the prolegomena or in the doctrines of God or Scripture, but in *soteriology*. In elaborating this point of view, Bavinck especially focuses on the phenomenon of conversion. For we come to the knowledge of God "not by science or art, not by good works or self-refinement, but by faith and conversion" (182). Therefore, Bavinck explores the process of conversion at some length (182-191). While acknowledging that "it is from the beginning to the end psychologically mediated" (190), he nevertheless concludes that a person's conversion is a revelation of the divine will, and that "if we are convinced in our deepest soul that God will save us personally" it is little wonder that we will see other traces of God's revelation "outside of us in history" (191).

Although this is a remarkable argument indeed, in that it seems to shift the rationale of Christian theology to the Christian's personal conversion experience, it is clear that in his *Philosophy of Revelation* also Bavinck upholds a realist understanding of theology, in that theology is methodically directed at the acquisition of reliable knowledge of the living God. Finally, the fact that this knowledge is not just of a theoretical nature is another reason why theology is not a science like any other. Without denying that other sciences can also lead the researcher to praise and adoration of God, in his *Reformed Dogmatics* Bavinck affirms that "dogmatics [...] is not a dull and arid science. It is a theodicy, a doxology to all God's virtues and perfections, a hymn of adoration and thanksgiving, a 'glory to God in the highest' (Luke 2:14)."[40]

3. Realism and the Principles of Theology

Having studied how Bavinck defines the object, the method and the place of dogmatic theology, I now present the way he deals with its principles. This section will progressively lead to the core of this research, since it is in the context of a sustained discussion of this topic that Bavinck develops his case in favor of a realist conception of theology. The presentation of the principles of theology is a common theme in the "prolegomena dogmatic tradition." It is generally, at least in post-Reformation Reformed

---

39 Bavinck, *PoR*, 180.
40 Bavinck, *RD 1*, 112.

dogmatics, determined by an Aristotelian understanding of science and goes together with the description of the object and method of theology, as displayed in the previous section of this chapter. In the Dutch edition of the *Gereformeerde Dogmatiek*, the entire *Prolegomena* volume is structured by the concept of *principia*.[41] This demonstrates the importance of this concept in Bavinck's thought. Without entering into details, the first chapter is titled "Principia in het algemeen." It has three sections: section 6 titled "Beteekenis der Principia," section 7 titled "Principia in de wetenschap," and section 8 titled "Principia in de Religie." In this section I first study the content of section 6 of the Dutch edition, which presents the principles of theology (3.1). Second, I pay attention to the first half of section 7 dealing with the question of realism in science (3.2). Third, I present the way Bavinck grounds his realism in a theology of the divine Logos in the second half of section 7 (3.3).

3.1 The Principles of Theological Science
In the Aristotelian definition of science, *principles* are of the greatest importance, since they represent the ultimately unprovable foundation of a particular science that govern its entire development.[42] For a theologian whose thinking is governed by an Aristotelian conception of science, the question of *principles* is also crucial. Richard A. Muller emphasizes this point:

> The identification of theological *principia* is the final and most truly foundational discussion presented within the prolegomena of theological system. Here the orthodox theologians penetrate still deeper into the substance of theology, deeper even than the identification of fundamental articles of the faith. Here they address the *sine qua non*, the necessary and irreducible ground of theology, apart from which not even the fundamental articles of the faith could be set forth and no articles of theology, fundamental or derivative, could be correctly stated.[43]

Bavinck, who adheres to the Aristotelian tradition, unsurprisingly develops a reflection on the principles of dogmatic theology. From his perspective, every science—even the more commonly acknowledged

---

41 Since, as its title indicates, the *Philosophy of Revelation* is focused on philosophy rather than theology, we do not find an exposition of the principles of theology therein.
42 Aristotle develops this question in the *Posterior Analytics* (Oxford: Clarendon Press, 1993) and at the beginning of book Delta of the *Metaphysics* (Oxford: Oxford University Press, 1924).
43 Muller, *Post-Reformation Reformed Dogmatics 1*, 295-296.

sciences, such as mathematics or physics—has its unprovable principles, and the goal of a science is not to prove its principles, but to deduce a structured body of knowledge from these original principles. This remark is important since it outlines Bavinck's strategy which aims to show that the theologian is ultimately no different from any other scientist when he is unable to prove in an independent way the principles of his science.[44]

Having formulated this general remark on the concept of principle, Bavinck applies it to the science of dogmatic theology in order to pursue his definition. He sums up the three principles of theology as follows:

> First, God as the essential foundation (*principium essendi*), the source, of theology; next, the external cognitive foundation (*principium cognoscendi externum*), viz., the self-revelation of God, which, insofar as it is recorded in Holy Scripture, bears an instrumental and temporary character; and finally, the internal principle of knowing (*principium cognoscendi internum*), the illumination of human beings by God's Spirit. The three are one in the respect that they have God as author and have as their content one identical knowledge of God.[45]

---

44 For Bavinck's specific Aristotelian definition of *principles*, see *Reformed Dogmatics 1: Prolegomena*, 211. Bavinck deals with the difficult question of the unprovable character of the principles of theology at pages 578ff of *RD 1*: "As soon as Christian theology started to reflect seriously on the final and deepest ground of faith, it came to the conclusion that no single intellectual or historical proof advanced for the truth of revelation can ultimately serve as such." (578) Henk van den Belt thoroughly develops this question in *The Authority of Scripture in Reformed Theology*. The way he compares Bavinck's position to that of B. B. Warfield is illuminating. In this perspective, it is interesting to read B. B. Warfield's appreciative but critical review of Bavinck's book *The Certainty of Faith*, in B. B. Warfield, "A Review of *De Zekerheid des Geloofs*" in *Selected Shorter Writings of Benjamin B. Warfield-II* (Nutley: Presbyterian and Reformed Publishing Co., 1973), 106-123. Cf. Gijsbert van den Brink, "On Certainty in Faith and Science: the Bavinck-Warfield Exchange," *The Bavinck Review* 8 (2017), 65-88.

45 Herman Bavinck, *RD 1*, 213. Let us notice here a translation problem. In the Dutch original, Bavinck doesn't translate the three Latin expressions. The English translation leads us to think that Bavinck makes a distinction between "essential" and "cognitive," but it is instead a distinction between the sphere of being and the sphere of knowing (in a more unified perspective). A better translation would thus have been: the "ontological foundation (or principle)" and the "external epistemological foundation (or principle)," without adding, as the English translator does, the explicative word "source."

The Aristotelian distinction between the principle of being and the principle of knowledge is recognizable in these lines. These Aristotelian principles became, in the context of medieval theology and later in that of Reformed orthodoxy, *principium essendi* (God's existence) and *principium cognoscendi* (God's self-revelation). Bavinck follows this tradition, but he is partly original in his introduction of a further distinction between the *principium cognoscendi externum* (the objective pole—revelation) and the *principium cognoscendi internum* (the subjective pole—faith).

In conformity with the Reformed scholastic tradition, Bavinck continues the presentation of the three principles of his theological science by introducing the fundamental distinction between archetypal and ectypal knowledge of God that he retrieves from the scholastic tradition:

> The archetypal knowledge of God in the divine consciousness; the ectypal knowledge of God granted in revelation and recorded in Holy Scripture; and the knowledge of God in the subject, insofar as it proceeds from revelation and enters into the human consciousness, are all three of them from God. It is God himself who discloses his self-knowledge, communicates it through revelation, and introduces it into human beings.

Bavinck further argues that these three are one not only *qua* source but also *qua* content: it is the very same knowledge of God that is involved in each of the three cases, even though Bavinck is well aware that the knowledge of God that is granted to humans has been accommodated to our finite consciousness.[46]

---

46 Bavinck, *RD 1*, 213-214. Muller shows how the study of principles is usually related to that of the *archetypal—ectypal* distinction in the context of Reformed orthodoxy: "[...] this final discussion of the *principia* must be viewed as the culmination of a process of reasoning begun in the distinction between archetypal and ectypal theology. [...] [T]he archetype is the higher science that supplies the principles used as the basis of conclusions in the ectypal, subalternate science. Granting the relation between archetype and ectype, the archetypal divine self-knowledge is one of the principles of ectypal theological knowing, that is, the *principium essendi*. The means by which the archetype definitively reveals itself, Scripture, must be the *principium cognoscendi* required by the subalternate science for its existence as a discipline." Muller, *Post-Reformation Reformed Dogmatics 1, 433*. See also Willem J. van Asselt, "The Fundamental Meaning of Theology: Archetypal and Ectypal Theology in Seventeenth-Century Reformed Thought," *Westminster Theological Journal* 64 (2002), 319-335, and Nathaniel Gray Sutanto, "Two Theological Accounts of Logic: Theistic Conceptual Realism and a Reformed Archetype-Ectype Model," *IJPR* 79 (2016), 239-260.

Therefore, the archetypal theology is God's knowledge of Himself and is the absolute principle, both *essendi* and *cognoscendi*, of theology; ectypal theology is the archetypal theology as revealed and adapted to creation and to the cognitive faculties of (notably) human beings (its ultimate principles are thus divided into the *principium cognoscendi externum* and *principium cognoscendi internum*).

At the end of his argument, Bavinck shows precisely how the Thomistic scholastic formula "the thing known is in the knower according to the mode of the knower" has to be applied to his understanding of theological science.[47] He specifies this idea by affirming that there are different forms of theology depending on the nature of the subject (i.e. Christ, the angels, the saints in heaven, believers on earth, etc.), which "is modified in each person's consciousness, depending on his or her capacity for it." He nevertheless insists on the fact that these theologies differ not in substance, but only in "degree and manner," concluding his argument by stating:

> Materially it is and remains identical knowledge, knowledge that proceeds from God and is transplanted by way of revelation to the consciousness of his rational creatures. These three principia, distinct yet essentially one, are rooted in the Trinitarian being of God. It is the Father who, through the Son as Logos, imparts himself to his creatures in the Spirit.[48]

These lines allow us to underline how, in Bavinck's thought, the method and principles of theology are deeply interwoven with its subject matter: the triune God. Bavinck sees a profound correspondence between the formal structure of theology and its material content. The three principles of theology are indeed interpreted as a *vestigium Trinitatis*, the first principle being connected with the Father, the second with the Son, and the third with the Holy Spirit. His organic method leads him to distinguish and simultaneously unify the principles and the content of theology in a striking way, as well as the different forms of knowledge of God.

3.2 Against Rationalism and Empiricism: Realism
Having presented the principles of dogmatic theology in the section titled "Betekenis der Principia," Bavinck broadens the scope of his work and

---

47 Here and there Bavinck quotes freely the famous scholastic principle formulated by Thomas Aquinas: "Cognitum est in cognoscente, secundum modum cognoscentis" (*Summa Theologiae*, 1a, q. 12, a. 4). For example, see footnote 50, below.
48 Bavinck, *RD 1*, 214.

devotes section 7 of *RD 1* ("Principia in de wetenschap") to the question of scientific knowledge in general:

> Science always consists in a logical relation between subject and object. Our view of science depends on the way we relate the two. At all times there have been two basic schools of thought that were diametrically opposed to each other in this respect: rationalism and empiricism.[49]

Because, in Bavinck's view, theology belongs fully to the arena of the sciences, it shares some crucial issues with other scientific disciplines, such as the relation between the knowing subject and the known object. Hence the theologian cannot avoid working on these kind of questions, for otherwise there will be important blind spots in his system. Bavinck's strategy in this section of his book is to first present what he perceives as the perennial epistemological dead-end opposition between rationalism and empiricism, and then to show how this opposition can be overcome by the appropriation of an Aristotelian and Thomist realist understanding of knowledge.

Bavinck starts defining rationalism by stating that "it was always marked by the same basic idea, namely that the origin of knowledge is to be found in the subject,"[50] and more precisely in the mind of the subject. Further, he defines empiricism by saying that it "totally subjects the human consciousness to the world outside of us" and it holds that "in the pursuit of knowledge, human beings bring with them nothing but the faculty of perception."[51] Thus, on the one hand (rationalism) the knowing subject is at the center and the external world plays a secondary role; on the other (empiricism), the opposite is true.

Bavinck criticizes both stances. He criticizes rationalism, and specifically Kantian idealism,[52] by first arguing that "it is contrary to all experience," and that "by nature we are all realists, including, in practice the idealists themselves."[53] Secondly, he holds that "idealism equates the

---

49 Bavinck, *RD 1*, 214.
50 Bavinck, *RD 1*, 215.
51 Bavinck, *RD 1*, 219.
52 Bavinck does not adhere to the generally acknowledged idea that Kant's philosophy proposes a sort of *via media* between Continental rationalism and Anglo-Saxon empiricism. He instead interprets Kant's idealism as a sort of rationalism, even if he concedes that "Kant admittedly did temper [...] rationalism insofar as he did not derive the content but only the forms of perception from the human mind (transcendental, critical idealism)" (*RD 1*, 215).
53 Bavinck, *RD 1*, 217.

organ of knowledge [i.e. the intellect] with the source of knowledge, as it were making the eye into the source of light."[54] In his *Philosophy of Revelation*, Bavinck emphatically repeats this point and elaborates it at quite some length. To be sure, Bavinck concedes that idealism is correct in seeing the human mind as "the basis and *principium* of all knowledge" (48). However, he accuses idealism of wrongly concluding from this "incontrovertible fact" that "therefore the object perceived must itself be immanent in the mind" (49). Instead,

> [...] there is a great difference between the view that subjective perception is the means and organ, and the other view that it is the principle and source of the knowledge of the object. The mistake of idealism lies in confounding the act with its content, the function with the object, the psychological with the logical nature of perception. [...] [P]erception as such terminates upon an object, and sensation and representation, logically considered, by their very nature are related to a reality distinct from themselves."[55]

Returning to the prolegomena of his *Reformed Dogmatics*, Bavinck also criticizes empiricism here, and its core idea that the human mind is a *tabula rasa*. The first objection is that "in its intellectual activity the human mind is never totally passive or even receptive but also always more or less active."[56] The second objection deals with the important metaphysical consequences of adopting an empiricist epistemology: "The inevitable result [of empiricism] is that science is then left, undefended and unarmed, to materialism. [...] If the content and, soon, the intellectual faculty of the soul as well proceed altogether from the external world, why then could not the soul itself be explained in terms of it as well?"[57]

Having briefly presented and criticized both rationalism/idealism and empiricism, Bavinck develops an Aristotelian-Thomistic form of moderate realism. He starts his argument by reversing the modern critical perspectives on epistemology. He indeed unequivocally affirms that knowledge precedes its critique. Therefore, epistemology is not an *a priori*, but an *a posteriori* discipline:

---

54 Bavinck, *RD 1*, 217.
55 Bavinck, *PoR*, 49. Bavinck actually expands on this point up until the end of the chapter (p. 69).
56 Bavinck, *RD 1*, 220. Cf. *PoR*, 55: "The mind of man is indeed no *tabula rasa*, no empty form (...)."
57 Bavinck, *RD 1*, 222.

> The starting point of the theory of knowledge ought to be ordinary daily experience, the universal and natural certainty of human beings concerning the objectivity and truth of their knowledge. After all, it is not philosophy that creates the cognitive faculty and cognition. Philosophy only finds it and then attempts to explain it. Any solution that does not explain the cognitive faculty but instead destroys it and, failing to understand cognition, turns it into an illusion, is judged by that fact. [...] Scientific knowledge is not a destruction but a purification, expansion, and completion of ordinary knowledge.[58]

This approach is important, since it characterizes all forms of common sense or moderate realism. The affirmation of continuity between ordinary and scientific knowledge also has far-reaching epistemological consequences and is strongly opposed to any form of post-Kantian criticism.

Having laid this foundation, Bavinck develops an Aristotelian empiricism (not to be confused with the modern positivist version of empiricism) that trusts and brings together both the senses and the intellect in the act of knowledge, in opposition to rationalism and empiricism:

> The intellect is bound to the body and thus to the cosmos and therefore cannot become active except by and on the basis of the senses. [...] But the moment the intellect is activated, it immediately and spontaneously works in its own way and according to its own nature. And the nature of the intellect is that it has the power (*vis*), ability (*facultas*), inclination (*inclinatio*), and fitness (*aptitudo*) to form certain basic concepts and principles.[59]

Both the senses and the intellect play an important role in the production of human knowledge of external reality. One should notice that even if he contests Kant's philosophy of representation, Bavinck does not deny that the intellect produces a mental image in order to grasp external reality.[60]

Having developed such a stance, Bavinck raises a question that is closely related to his post-Kantian context: "What is the relation between

---

58 Bavinck, *RD 1*, 223. As will be seen in the next chapter, this common sense understanding of scientific knowledge is shared by Plantinga.
59 Bavinck, *RD 1*, 225.
60 Thus, as Sutanto, *God and Knowledge*, 109-121, has shown, Bavinck remains firmly situated in the tradition of "representationalist epistemology"—a tradition that came to be contested in the course of the twentieth century (179).

the perceptual image in our consciousness and reality, the object outside us?"⁶¹ Bavinck's answer to this question shows that he clearly adheres to an Aristotelian-Thomistic form of realism:

> Objects [...] acquire an ideal existence in the soul by way of perception and thought. Scholasticism, adopting this position, said: "The thing known is in the knower by the mode of cognition, not by the mode of the thing known"; i.e., the things themselves do not pass into the soul but only their image or form (*eidos, forma, species, similitudo*). So on the one hand there is an essential difference between the thing and its representation, because the thing exists outside of us, has real existence there, while the second exists in us and merely has ideal existence. On the other hand, there is complete correspondence; the representation is an image, a faithful ideal reproduction of the object outside of us.⁶²

Bavinck continues to point out that modern philosophy created "an ever-growing gap" between the object and its image in the human mind. In his view, the human intellect does produce a mental image, but there is a correspondence between this representation and the external reality. It therefore does not lead to the production of an indirect knowledge of reality. On the contrary, Bavinck criticizes modern philosophy for having created a gap between external reality and its mental representation, which inescapably leads to various forms of anti-realism.

Having described the difficulties raised by rationalism and empiricism and having developed an Aristotelian-Thomistic realism in answer to these issues, Bavinck deals with another central debate in philosophy of knowledge in the last paragraph of the section [69]: the medieval *quarrel of the universals* between nominalists and realists in discussions related to intellectual knowledge. The basic question of this debate is close to that raised above concerning the relation between the mental image and the external reality. Bavinck formulates it as follows: "What is the relation between these intellectual concepts and the world of reality?"⁶³ In answering this question, he displays a total adhesion to the realist position.

Bavinck sums up the nominalist position by mentioning Roscellin: "Roscellin believed that universals were merely verbal (*flatus vocis*), conceptual things, for which there was no corresponding reality. In reality

---

61 Bavinck, *RD 1*, 227.
62 Bavinck, *RD 1*, 227-228.
63 Bavinck, *RD 1*, 230.

there are no universals, he said, but only particular, individual things."⁶⁴ He then states in a terse way: "If nominalism is correct, we can forget about science altogether."⁶⁵ Science indeed ultimately deals with universal truths, and not simply individual realities. If nominalism is true, efforts to formulate such truths are voided of all their content.

In opposition to nominalism, Bavinck proposes a typical Aristotelian realist stance:

> Concepts are not empty "things of thought" but the sum of the essential properties of things and therefore not names (*nomina*) but realities (*res*). Realism, accordingly, was doubtlessly correct in assuming the reality of universal concepts, not in a Platonic or ontological sense prior to the thing itself (*ante rem*), but in an Aristotelian sense in the thing itself (*in re*) and therefore also in the human mind subsequent to the thing itself (*in mente hominis post rem*).⁶⁶

He then concludes in a way that displays both the moderate character of his realism (as opposed to positivistic or non-philosophical naïve forms of realism) and his opposition to any form of a post-Kantian constructivist philosophy of representation:

> In entertaining concepts we are not distancing ourselves from reality but we increasingly approximate it. [...] It seems strange, even amazing, that, converting mental representations into concepts and processing these again in accordance with the laws of thought, we should obtain results that correspond to reality. Still, one who abandons this conviction is lost.⁶⁷

Human beings are never able to fully grasp or comprehend reality (and even more the reality of God), but whoever abandons the conviction that he is indeed capable of knowing something about the world "is lost."

---

64 Bavinck, *RD 1*, 230.
65 Bavinck, *RD 1*, 231. In *PoR*, 43-48, Bavinck argues that philosophical pragmatism (as represented by William James) is nominalist in character, and that as a result of this no knowledge of God (and other entities) is possible with pragmatism. Bavinck then objects to pragmatism, not on the grounds "that it strives to be empirical, but that it is not nearly sufficiently so," since it obscures from view "[r]eality, the whole, rich reality" (48).
66 Bavinck, *RD 1*, 231.
67 Bavinck, *RD 1*, 231.

In conclusion to this subsection, let us remember that in Bavinck's perspective, this development of a realist conception of knowledge is related to both human knowledge in general and theological knowledge in particular, since theology belongs fully in the arena of science.

3.3 A Form of Realism Sustained by a Classical Logos Theology
How does Bavinck explain this amazing correspondence between human cognitive concepts and reality? Arriving at this point in his argument in the prolegomena of *Reformed Dogmatics*, Bavinck unveils the keystone of his overall realist conception of knowledge:

> But that conviction [that "in entertaining concepts we are not distancing ourselves from reality but we increasingly approximate it"] can, therefore, rest only in the belief that it is the same Logos who created both the reality outside of us and the laws of thought within us and who produced an organic connection and correspondence between the two. Only in this way is science possible.[68]

The concept of the Logos introduced in this passage plays a central role in Bavinck's argument in favor of a realist conception of theology. It therefore deserves careful study. In this subsection, I show how Bavinck ends his reflection on the principles of science by introducing, in a way that is inspired by patristic readings of the Prologue of the Gospel of John, the metaphor of the light (of reason and of God) and the concept of the Logos.

An old theme of classical philosophy and patristic theology is the metaphor of *light* employed to evoke human knowledge of external reality. Since Plato, this metaphor is often interpreted in two ways.[69] There is indeed the light of God (or of the Idea of the Good) that enlightens the world, and there is the light of human reason that sees the world in God's light, while simultaneously projecting its own light in order to grasp external reality. Here is Bavinck's formulation of this classical idea:

> Just as with the physical eye we cannot see anything unless the sun sheds its rays over it, so neither can we see any truth except in the light of God, which is the sun of our knowledge. God is the light of reason in which, by

---

68 Bavinck, *RD 1*, 231.
69 Bavinck explicitly refers to Plato on pages 231-232. Plato develops this question in the *Republic*, 507a-509b. See Plato, "The Republic," in *The Collected Dialogues of Plato* (Princeton: Princeton University Press, 1961), 743.

which, and through which all things that shine so as to be intelligible, shine.[70]

Bavinck clarifies his use of the metaphor of the light of reason by referring to the Aristotelian (and Thomistic) concept of the active intellect and affirms that "the light of reason is […] identical with the active intellect, the faculty of abstraction, which shines its light on objects and brings to light the intelligible components of these objects."[71]

This clarification is important, since the active intellect is a fundamental concept that characterizes Bavinck's realism over and against both empiricism and rationalism (or critical idealism). While the empiricists are generally reluctant to put forward the activity of the knowing subject in knowledge (in order to preserve the objectivity of knowledge), the rationalists generally adopt a constructivist understanding of knowledge (the object of knowledge is constructed by the knowing subject). Bavinck's realism opposes both by proposing a model that confers an active role on human reason, but not in a constructivist way (since the world is given and enlightened by God).

Having developed the metaphor of the light of God and of human reason, Bavinck ends the section on the principles of science by developing the keystone concept of his entire case, the concept of the divine Logos. Here is the transitional passage:

---

70 Bavinck, *RD 1*, 232. A couple of lines below, Bavinck continues in an utterly patristic way: "Just as we look into the natural world, not by being in the sun ourselves, but by the light of the sun that shines on us, so neither do we see things in the divine being but by the light that, originating in God, shines in our own intellect. Reason in us is that divine light; it is not itself the divine logos, but it participates in it."

71 Bavinck, *RD 1*, 232. According to Aristotle, the active intellect abstracts the intelligible from particular beings: "And it is to the one intellect, which answers to this description because it becomes all things, corresponds the other because it makes all things, like a sort of definite quality such as light. For in a manner light, too, converts colours which are potential into actual colors. And it is this intellect which is separable and impassive and unmixed, being in its essential nature an activity." Aristotle, *De Anima* (430a), trans. R. D. Hicks (New York: Arno Press, 1976), 135. For a medieval perspective, see Thomas Aquinas's writings against Averroes, particularly *On the Unity of the Intellect against the Averroists* (Milwaukee: Marquette University Press, 1968). In these pages, Bavinck often refers to Augustine and Thomas Aquinas, but also to the Reformed orthodox theologians Polanus and Zanchius. In this context, David S. Sytsma's translation of Jerome Zanchius' "De actionibus intellectivae" in *De operibus Dei intra spacium sex dierum creatis* gives us access to an interesting historical source. David S. Sytsma, "Herman Bavinck's Thomistic Epistemology: The Argument and Sources of his *Principia* of Science," in John Bolt (ed.), *Five Studies in the Thought of Herman Bavinck, a Creator of Modern Dutch Theology* (Lewiston: The Edwin Mellen Press, 2011), 1-56.

> We owe that light [of reason] to God or, more specifically, to the Logos (Ps. 36:9; John 1:9). It is he who causes this light to arise in us and constantly maintains it. And so, when the truth discloses itself to our mind by the rays of that light, we owe it to God and not to human beings, who are merely the instruments.[72]

The means by which God enlightens the world and allows human beings to know something about him and external reality is his Logos. Logos theology is a prominent theme of patristic theology and Bavinck makes important use of it. I now present how he refers to this concept in *RD 1* in order to secure his realist conception of theology.[73]

As described above, Bavinck highly values historical theology, since he holds that dogmatic theology always has to be rooted in the Christian tradition of thought. His attention to the theology of the divine Logos is to be understood from this perspective.[74] In patristic theology, the Logos was one of the most central concepts and played a pivotal role in the elaboration of many theological topics. Without entering into details, the following passage of Jaroslav Pelikan sums up in a concise way the main functions of the Logos in Christian antiquity:

> The idea of the seminal Logos provided the apologists with a device for correlating Christian revelation not only with the message of the Old

---

72 Bavinck, *RD 1*, 232.
73 There are three places in *RD 1* where Logos theology plays an important role. First, pages 232-233, at the end of Bavinck's exposition on realism. Then on pages 278-279, at the end of the first major part of the volume devoted to the principles of dogmatic science ("Hoofdstuk I. Principia in het Algemeen"). Finally, pages 586-587, where Bavinck discusses the role played by faith in the act of knowledge (in the major part devoted to the principium internum of knowledge: "Hoofdstuk III. Principium internum"). Logos theology also appears in *RD 2*, in the section devoted to the Holy Trinity (Herman Bavinck, *RD 2*, 256ff). The perspective here is slightly different, since it deals more with Trinitarian and Christological questions than with metaphysical and epistemological ones. A connection can nevertheless be made, since, as seen above, Bavinck interprets the principles of theology from a Trinitarian perspective.
74 The study of the classical philosophical and theological theme of the Logos was strongly renewed at the Free University of Amsterdam by Jan Woltjer (1849-1917), a professor in the Faculty of Arts. His work exerted an important influence on both Abraham Kuyper and Herman Bavinck. See the following articles: John H. Kok, "Woltjer on Classical Antiquity," in Robert Sweetman (ed.), *In the Phrygian Mode. Neo-Calvinism, Antiquity, and the Lamentations of Reformed Philosophy* (Lanham: University Press of America, 2007), 41-64; Rob Nijhoff, "The World as Whodunit. Jan Woltjer and his Logo-Centric Philosophy in the Early Years of the VU, Amsterdam," *Calvin Theological Journal* 54 (2019), 353-382.

Testament, but also with the glimpses of the truth that had been granted to classical philosophers. As is evident from John 1:3 and its background in Proverbs 8:30, the doctrine of the preexistent Logos was also a means of correlating the redemption accomplished in Jesus Christ with the doctrine of creation. Creation, revelation both general and special, and redemption could all be ascribed to the Logos.[75]

As will become progressively apparent in the next pages and later in this book, all the theological themes mentioned by Pelikan play a central role in Bavinck's Logos theology. In the following paragraphs, given the research question, I mainly focus on the themes of creation and revelation.

Bavinck's use of Logos theology as the keystone of his argument in favor of a realist conception of science and of theology in particular is summed up in the very last paragraph of his entire discussion of realism:

> There just has to be correspondence or kinship between object and subject. The Logos who shines in the world must also let his light shine in our consciousness. That is the light of reason, the intellect, which, itself originating in the Logos, discovers and recognizes the Logos in things.[76]

The three-stage structure of Bavinck's thought is present in these lines and is to be understood in light of a theology of the divine Logos. First, there is the external reality, which is enlightened and structured by the Logos of God. Second, there is the knowing subject, who is also enlightened and structured by the Logos of God. Finally, there is a deep correspondence between object and subject, which is not due to chance, but which is secured by their common origin in the Logos of God. This tripartite structure has already been presented in my study of Bavinck's organic method and principles of theology. I now examine more closely how the Logos functions as the keystone of this theological proposal.[77]

---

75 Jaroslav Pelikan, *The Christian Tradition. A History of the Development of Doctrine. The Emergence of the Catholic Tradition (100-600)* (Chicago and London: The University of Chicago Press, 1971), 187-188. A major synthesis of the theology of the divine Logos and its development within the Christian tradition is found in the article "λεγω" in Gerhard Kittel (ed.), *Theological Dictionary of the New Testament (Volume IV)* (Grand Rapids: Eerdmans Publishing, 1967), 69-136.

76 Bavinck, *RD 1*, 233.

77 Nathaniel Gray Sutanto also recognizes the central role played by the Logos in Bavinck's theory of knowledge: "Bavinck affirms the ongoing work of the Logos in actively sustaining the subject-object relation. The revelatory work of the Logos that organically connects subject and object is indispensable. The Logos works with and through reason, enlightening it and guiding it in its attempts to apprehend the world,

First, Bavinck insists on the rationality of external reality, which is an "embodiment of the thoughts of God":

> The world is an embodiment of the thoughts of God: it is "a beautiful book in which all creatures, great and small, are as letters to make us ponder the invisible things of God" (art. 2, Belgic Confession). It is not a book of blank pages in which, as the idealists would have it, we human beings have to write down the words but a "reader" in which God makes known to us what he has recorded there for us.[78]

Secondly, he affirms that there is a perfect correspondence between the structure of external reality and the cognitive faculties of the knowing subject:

> Corresponding to the objective revelation of God, [...] there is in human beings a certain faculty or natural aptitude for perceiving the divine. God does not do half a job. He creates not only the light but also the eye to see it. Corresponding to the external reality there is an internal organ of perception. The ear is designed for the world of sounds. The "logos" implicit in creatures corresponds to the "logos" in human beings and makes science possible. [...] True and genuine religion can exist only in the complete correspondence of the internal to the external revelation.[79]

One should notice that this cognitive match is double-sided in Bavinck's thought, since it allows human beings to know not only external reality, but also God himself. The first sentence of this passage implicitly refers to the "sensus divinitatis"—the Calvinist concept that will play an important role in Plantinga's work.[80]

---

and is also the one who independently produces the contents into the creature's mind. In doing so, the [145] Logos further ensures that the ideal representation in the mind is a faithful rendering of the world outside" (*God and Knowledge. Herman Bavinck's Theological Epistemology*, 144-145). It is possible that Sutanto doesn't understand the role played by the Logos in Bavinck's thought exactly as I do. It seems that he reads Bavinck more along post-Hegelian "absolute idealist" lines. But since this potential difference has no direct impact on the scope of this research, I do not investigate it further.

78 Bavinck, *RD 1*, 233.
79 Bavinck, *RD 1*, 278-279. On page 505, Bavinck affirms: "Just as the eye answers to light, the ear to sound, the logos (reason) within us to the logos (rationality) outside of us, so there has to be in human beings a subjective organ that answers to the objective revelation of God."
80 Notice Bavinck's use in these lines of the concept of "design" that will also play a crucial role in Plantinga's system.

Bavinck's insistence on the "complete" correspondence between the object and the subject also deserves special attention in its relation to Logos theology. His classical realism indeed relies on a sort of triangle. The two lower apexes are the two forms of the "logos" (with lower case), that is, the logos or rationality in the external reality understood as the creation of God, and the logos in the knowing subject, that is, the cognitive structure of human beings, which fit both the reality of God and of nature. The higher apex is the "Logos" with a capital letter, understood not only as the second person of the Trinity, but also as God's Wisdom (Proverbs 8) or rationality. John Bolt clearly synthesizes Bavinck's argument in a metaphorical way:

> Cake batter has to be mixed in a bowl and baked in a pan. The bowl and pan that made it possible for Bavinck to mix his ingredients and provide a good shape to the cake as it baked in the oven was a *realist metaphysics* following the great tradition of Augustine and Thomas. Science was possible, he believed, because the universals that exist *in re* (not *ante rem*) are the creation of the eternal LOGOS who also created us in his image, with a lower case *l*, logos capable of discerning those universals in reality. Our mind forms true concepts of the external world because we are created by God for such understanding and service in his creation. Bavinck is a wonderful antidote to the pestilence of antirealism and the annoying flu of postmodernism that stalk our civilization.[81]

I end this presentation of Bavinck's use of Logos theology in his *Reformed Dogmatics* by quoting a passage that not only concludes his wide discourse on the principles of science, but that also introduces the convergence of the works of Bavinck and Plantinga. As already noticed in the previous quotations, the passages in which Bavinck relates Logos theology to his realist stance foreshadow in noteworthy ways important themes from Plantinga:

> All life and all knowledge is based on a kind of agreement between subject and object. Human beings are so richly endowed because they are linked with the objective world by a great many extremely diverse connections.

---

81 John Bolt, "The Bavinck Recipe for Theological Cake," *Calvin Theological Journal* 45 (2010), 17. In the same issue of the *Calvin Theological Journal*, a Roman Catholic thinker develops a similar idea: "[Bavinck] embraces a version of the Logos doctrine because the Logos overcomes the subject-object dualism, or egocentric predicament, of modernist epistemology." Eduardo J. Echeverria, "The Reformed Objection to Natural Theology: A Catholic Response to Herman Bavinck," 87.

They are related to the whole world. Physically, vegetatively, sensorily, intellectually, ethically, and religiously there is correspondence between them and the world. [...] Human beings have not put themselves in this relation to the world. They were adapted to the world from the beginning, and this world was reciprocally adapted to them. [...] It is the selfsame Logos who made all things in and outside human beings.[82]

If we finally briefly compare the results of this reading of Bavinck's *Dogmatics* concerning his Logos theology with his argument in the *Philosophy of Revelation*, we find that talk about the foundational epistemological role of the Logos has receded. To be sure, in the *Philosophy of Revelation* Bavinck also points to the classical Christian view (to be found "both in earlier and later times in the Christian Church") that any wisdom or truth to be found in non-Christian sources results from "the continuous illumination of the Logos."[83] The only other reference to the Logos, however, is intended to illustrate the organic connection between general and special revelation: "The Logos who became flesh is the same by whom all things were made. The firstborn from the dead is also the firstborn of every creature."[84] Bavinck does not apply this notion to the epistemological conundrum that concerns him in his *Reformed Dogmatics* and in other sources.[85]

Yet, in the *Philosophy of Revelation* Bavinck does restate his view that the correspondence between subject and object in the knowledge process is due to "the divine wisdom"—thus expressing his Logos-motif in slightly different (but still christologically charged) jargon. In particular, in a section on "Revelation and Philosophy" in which he zooms in on epistemology, he argues that "revelation is of the utmost importance [...] for epistemology," because:

> All cognition consists in a peculiar relation of subject and object and is built on the agreement of these two. The reliability of perception and thought is not assured unless the forms of thought and the forms of being correspond, in virtue of their origin in the same creative wisdom. Philosophy itself has not failed to perceive the necessity of this, but by taking a wrong start it has strayed either to the right or to the left.[86]

---

82 Bavinck, *RD 1*, 586.
83 Bavinck, *PoR*, 142-143.
84 Bavinck, *PoR*, 24-25.
85 See e.g. his *Christelijke wereldbeschouwing* (Kampen: Kok, 1904), 32-33, as quoted by Sutanto, *God and Knowledge*, 142 n.82.
86 Bavinck, *PoR*, 66.

Bavinck then considers Hegel and Kant as examples of such errors, and concludes with von Hartmann[87] that "there is no other way of doing justice to both subject and object except by recognizing that it is one and the same Reason" that is active in both.[88] To Bavinck, it is clear that this Reason is to be identified with "the divine wisdom."[89] In this way we can justify the certainty we intuitively have of the reality of both our ego and the external world. "Whosoever here does not believe [viz. in the reality of both] shall not be established," Bavinck writes in a playful allusion to the practical impossibility of skepticism.[90] It is the idea of divine wisdom as displayed in general revelation, however, that accounts for this certainty. It is because of this "firm theistic foundation" of the epistemic process that we may even believe in "the progress of science." In this way, the *Philosophy of Revelation* strengthens and expands on Bavinck's epistemological use of classical Logos theology.

4. Realism in *Reformed Dogmatics 2: God and Creation*

The two previous sections of this chapter have been devoted to the presentation of Bavinck's argument in favor of a realist conception of theology as developed in *RD 1*. But even if the scope of Bavinck's argument in this first volume is very broad, it is not complete. Two other questions in relation to the *realism in theology* debates are indeed discussed in *RD 2*. The aim of this section, then, is to complete the description of Bavinck's realist conception of theology by presenting these two questions. The first subsection will study how Bavinck relates a realist conception of theology to the classical Christian dogma of the transcendence of God (4.1). The second subsection will be devoted to the presentation of an important dimension of Bavinck's realism that was not developed in *RD 1* either: semantic realism (4.2).

---

87 As Sutanto, *God and Knowledge*, 119-149, has made plausible, Bavinck indeed derives his crucial insight for the pivotal epistemological role of the Logos from the work of (the now almost-forgotten) German philosopher Eduard von Hartmann (1842-1906), who posited "the Absolute Unconscious" as the bridge between subject and object. All Bavinck had to do was to replace this notion with that of the personal Absolute of Christian theology, viz. God the Creator of the world and of every human being.

88 Bavinck, *PoR*, 66-67. The editors of *PoR* suggest (in fn. 68) that when using "Reason" (with a capital) Bavinck is referring to "the *Logos* of God," but it seems that since obviously he cannot ascribe that concept to von Hartmann, he deliberately uses this more general and neutral term.

89 Bavinck, *PoR*, 67.

90 Bavinck, *PoR*, 59. The biblical allusion is obviously to Isa. 7:9 and not to John 3:18, as Brock & Sutanto (fn. 51) suggest.

4.1 Realism and the Transcendence of God

Subsection 2.3 of the first chapter of this book notes the classical Christian theological tension between the affirmation that God is altogether incomprehensible and yet also knowable. Bavinck is perfectly aware of this issue. The first sentence of *RD 2*, devoted to the doctrine of God, affirms that "mystery is the lifeblood of dogmatics," since God is transcendent. A couple of lines below, he nevertheless and paradoxically states that "the knowledge of God is the only dogma, the exclusive content, of the entire field of dogmatics."[91]

Bavinck's solution to this difficulty is to be found in the distinction he introduced when dealing with the principles of theology: the distinction between archetypal and ectypal theologies. This distinction indeed allows him to distinguish between *comprehension* and *knowledge* of God. Archetypal theology is comprehension of God in the fullest sense of the term; ectypal theology is an imperfect but nevertheless real knowledge of God.[92] Since there is an organic (or analogical) relation between these forms of theology, human knowledge of God is not merely arbitrary. Ectypal theology is made possible by God's revelation (both general and special), which is seized by human faith and reason:

> What we know of God we know only of his revelation and therefore only as much as he is pleased to make known to us concerning himself and as much as finite humans can absorb. Knowledge of God, accordingly, can be true and pure, but it is always most relative and does not include but excludes comprehension. Basil was right in telling Eunomius that "the knowledge of God consists in the perception of his incomprehensibility."[93]

In the pages devoted to the question of the knowledge of God in the context of the doctrine of God, Bavinck struggles against both rationalist realists who tend to underestimate God's transcendence and develop a

---

91 Bavinck, *RD 2*, 29.
92 In *RD 1*, Bavinck indirectly deals with the question of the incomprehensibility and the knowability of God before elaborating the question in *RD 2*. For instance, in the context of the presentation of the principles of theology, he states: "The relation of God's own self-knowledge to our knowledge of God used to be expressed by saying that the former was archetypal of the latter and the latter ectypal of the former. Our knowledge of God is the imprint of the knowledge God has of himself but always on a creaturely level and in a creaturely way. The knowledge of God present in his creatures is only a weak likeness, a finite, limited sketch, of the absolute self-consciousness of God accommodated to the capacities of the human or creaturely consciousness." Bavinck, *RD 1*, 212.
93 Bavinck, *RD 2*, 104.

too self-secured and anthropomorphic theology, and idealist theologians who infer from God's transcendence a merely symbolic understanding of theology.[94]

In conclusion to his epistemological analysis of God's incomprehensibility and knowability, Bavinck proposes a five-point solution:

> Theology must be called ectypal or analogical, not symbolic. Implied in this is the following:
> 1. All our knowledge of God is from and through God, grounded in his revelation, that is, in objective reason.
> 2. In order to convey the knowledge of him to his creatures, God has to come down to the level of his creatures and accommodate himself to their powers of comprehension.
> 3. The possibility of this condescension cannot be denied since it is given with creation, that is, with the existence of finite being.
> 4. Our knowledge of God is always only analogical in character, that is, shaped by analogy to what can be discerned of God in his creatures, having as its object not God himself in his knowable essence, but God in his revelation, his relation to us [...]. Accordingly, this knowledge is only a finite image, a faint likeness and creaturely impression of the perfect knowledge that God has of himself.
> 5. Finally, our knowledge of God is nevertheless true, pure, and trustworthy because it has for its foundation God's self-consciousness, its archetype, and his self-revelation in the cosmos.[95]

The cautious and well-balanced character of Bavinck's solution is obvious and displays the subtle character of his defense of a realist conception of theology. It is transposed in a philosophical key in Bavinck's later acknowledgement that "[n]o philosophy of revelation [...] shall ever be able to exhaust its subject or thoroughly master its material. All knowledge here on earth remains partial [...]. But nevertheless, it lives and works in the assurance that the ground of all things is not blind will or incalculable accident, but mind, intelligence, wisdom."[96] Such lines are a theological *tour de force* in the context of modern thought and will contribute to the elaboration of my proposal.

---

94 Bavinck, *RD 2*, 109: "[The] "symbolic" character of theology turns that names of God into a reflex of one's own inner life, deprives them of all objective reality, and looks for their ground in ever-changing subjective reason. Humanity then becomes the standard of religion: as humans are, so is their God."
95 Bavinck, *RD 2*, 110.
96 Bavinck, *PoR*, 24.

4.2 Semantic Realism

As noted, while working on the doctrine of God in *RD 2*, Bavinck pays attention to the classical theological problem of the names of God. In this exposition, he raises the question of the possibility that human language can name God in an adequate way (and formulate truth-content propositions about God):

> Now the names by which God calls himself in his revelation present a peculiar intellectual difficulty. In an earlier chapter we learned that God is incomprehensible and far superior to all finite creatures. In his names, however, he descends to the level of the finite and becomes like his creatures. What we encounter here is an antinomy that seems insoluble.[97]

If we remember the wider presentation of the realism debates in the previous chapter of this book, we will recognize a typical semantic realism issue here. As *RD 1* mainly develops the question of metaphysical and epistemological realism, this semantic addendum completes Bavinck's argument in favor of a realist conception of theology.[98]

Bavinck's semantic realism is based on the Calvinist doctrine of the *accommodatio Dei*. This doctrine is double-sided. First, influenced as it is by the classical rules of rhetoric, it insists on the idea that the speaker must accommodate himself to the aptitude of his audience. Applied to theology, this means that God cannot reveal himself in his infinite nature, but only in a way that accommodates the weakness of human beings. Bavinck's organic theological method (accompanied by the distinction between archetypal and ectypal theology) leads him to affirm that there is no opposition or gap between God as he is, and God as he reveals himself:

> The name of God in Scripture does not describe God as he exists within himself but God in his revelation and multiple relations to his creatures. This name, however, is not arbitrary: God reveals himself in the way he does because he is who he is.[99]

---

97 Bavinck, *RD 2*, 104.
98 As stated in the first chapter of this book, the question of semantic realism was debated increasingly during the twentieth century. This is probably the reason why Bavinck does not discuss this question in *RD 1*.
99 Bavinck, *RD 2*, 99. Not everyone in the Calvinist tradition shares this organic interpretation of the *accommodatio Dei*. Nominalist, dualistic or dialectical readings of this doctrine sharpen the distinction between God as he exists in himself and God as revealed to us.

This theology of the divine accommodation fully acknowledges natural human language as an adequate means of revelation. Even the anthropomorphisms contained in Scripture to name and describe God are recognized as bearing authentic witness to the truth:

> And inasmuch as the revelation of God in nature and in Scripture is specifically addressed to humanity, it is a human language in which God speaks to us of himself. For that reason the words he employs are human words; for the same reason he manifests himself in human forms. From this it follows that Scripture does not just contain a few scattered anthropomorphisms but is anthropomorphic through and through.[100]

Bavinck's semantic realism is thus in opposition to all the *experiential-expressive* anti-realist interpretations that consider the language of revelation as merely symbolic (that is, deprived of any direct truth content).

The second facet of the semantic realism that flows from the doctrine of the *accommodatio Dei* is that since God has revealed himself by using human language, the theologian may properly use this same human language while doing his work: "We have the right to use anthropomorphic language because God himself came down to the level of his creatures and revealed his name in and through his creatures."[101]

Bavinck's semantic realism is also based on his understanding of the world as God's creation. From this perspective, human language is suited to ascribing names to God since it has been created, as with the rest of the world, by God himself:

> On what ground do we ascribe [names] to God, who is infinitely superior to all his creatures and cannot be contained by the finite?
> The reason can only be this: the whole creation, though as creature it is infinitely removed from God, is still God's handiwork and related to him. The world is not an independent entity on a par with, and antithetically related to, God.[102]

---

100 Bavinck, *RD 2*, 99. The ultimate theological foundation of this affirmation is the incarnation of the divine Logos: "The whole revelation of God is concentrated in the Logos, who became 'flesh' and is, as it were, one single act of self-humanization, the incarnation of God. If God were to speak to us in a divine language, not a creature would understand him." (100)
101 Bavinck, *RD 2*, 104.
102 Bavinck, *RD 2*, 104.

Bavinck's organic theological method is once more recognizable in these lines and continues to play an important role in the elaboration of his argument in favor of a realist conception of theology.

5. Bavinck's Realism Synthesized and Interpreted
In the last section of this chapter, I synthesize and discuss Bavinck's argument in favor of a realist conception of theology. First, I analyze the content of this chapter from the perspective of the overview of the realism debates proposed in the second section of chapter one (5.1). I then bring Bavinck's realism into a conversation with the two main contemporary realist conceptions of theology, the *critical realism* and *theological realism* trends presented in the third section of chapter one (5.2). This process improves our understanding of Bavinck's work, as it is confronted with critical remarks and located within the range of contemporary realism discussions.

5.1 Synthetic Remarks on Bavinck's Realism
There are three synthetic remarks to be made about Bavinck's realism before specifying its metaphysical, epistemological and semantic dimensions.

First of all, one should notice the deep influence exercised by Bavinck's organic method on his entire proposal. It is indeed striking to observe that he never opposes philosophy and theology, or scientific knowledge in general and dogmatic theological science in particular, as many modern thinkers do. While working on Bavinck's defense of a realist conception of theology, one has to show sufficient intellectual flexibility to move from theology to philosophy and back, without any significant editorial flagging. The distinctions between the passages that deal with human knowledge in general and theological knowledge in particular are also not very sharp. It seems obvious that in Bavinck's thought, these elements are to be distinguished but not opposed. The theologian feels thus authorized to move from one to the other with great flexibility, since the realities studied are intimately interconnected. This flexibility may be somehow disconcerting for the modern reader, but if one misses the imprint of Bavinck's organic method on his work, one loses the global coherency and a facet of the originality of his argument.

Secondly, one should notice the "catholicity" of Bavinck's argument. In the presentation of his theological method, Bavinck affirms that the history of Christian doctrine plays an important role in the elaboration of a dogmatic theology. The theologian should not seek novelty or intellectual originality, but rather a faithful application of the theological tradition to a specific cultural context. While struggling with modern thought in the elaboration of a realist conception of theology, Bavinck builds his argument on classical Christian doctrines. He thus refers to the patristic Logos theology as the ultimate metaphysical foundation of his system, and unashamedly refers to Aristotelian Thomism while developing his general theory of knowledge. He develops the semantic facet of his realism by using the Calvinist *accommodatio Dei* theological concept. Finally, his central reflection on the principles of dogmatic science relies deeply on the work of post-Reformation Reformed orthodoxy.

Thirdly, by developing a Logos theology as he does, Bavinck opposes the modern decision to start dealing with epistemology rather than metaphysics. The way he builds his entire argument shows that he is indeed convinced that metaphysics comes first, and that stances in epistemology and semantics flow from prior metaphysical affirmations. In his thought, the ontological principle comes before epistemological principles, both external and internal, and the divine Logos is put forward as the metaphysical foundation. Even if such a stance is highly controversial in a post-Kantian context, it is nevertheless the main source of the insightfulness and coherency of Bavinck's argument.

I now explore how Bavinck's case in favor of a realist conception of theology can be characterized as a thoroughly classical metaphysical, epistemological and semantic realism in light of the typology proposed in the first chapter. First, Bavinck's work can be interpreted as a classical form of *metaphysical* realism. The reference to the theology of the Logos indeed has important metaphysical consequences. First, the world has to be understood as a cosmos, which means that it is a rational and intelligible reality. One can indeed affirm that since the divine Logos has created the world, it is structured in a "logical" or rational way. Further, as human beings are understood as having been created in the image of God, they are also the bearers, in a derivate way, of the divine Logos. As noted above, this implies that there is a fundamental metaphysical correspondence between external reality and human beings.[103]

---

103 Bavinck's metaphysical use of the doctrine of the divine Logos is inspired by patristic Christian theology and is therefore close to Stoicism and Middle Platonism. For further details, read among others, Henry Chadwick "Philo and the Beginnings of Christian Thought," in *The Cambridge History of Later Greek and Early Medieval Philosophy*, ed. A. H. Armstrong (Cambridge: Cambridge University Press, 1967), 137-193. It is of course also deeply influenced by Johannine Christology (see e.g. John 1:9).

A second metaphysical consequence of Bavinck's use of Logos theology is that the world and human beings are metaphysically open to God's intervention or manifestation. There is indeed an ontological correlation (but no identification) between the divine Logos and its creaturely reflection within external reality and human beings. This metaphysical correlation functions in Bavinck's thought as the foundation of his theology of revelation (both general and special) and of faith (which is a faculty of the rational soul). From this Logos-based perspective, these supernatural realities are understood as almost "natural" developments of a Christian metaphysics of creation (see the above-mentioned Thomistic adage: *Gratia non tollit naturam, sed perficit*—better translated as "Nature is not destroyed/removed by grace but perfected/fulfilled").[104]

Bavinck's *epistemological* realism relies deeply on his metaphysical realism. The affirmation of an ontological correspondence between external reality and human beings indeed has crucial epistemological consequences. Thus, human cognitive faculties (both sensory and intellectual) are fitted to the structure of reality and this match makes a direct (even though imperfect) knowledge of the world possible. Human perception and production of concepts can be adequate and allow human beings to *really* know something about the world.

The metaphysical openness to God's action or manifestation also has important epistemological consequences, since it allows Bavinck to develop a realist epistemology of revelation and faith. These two crucial theological concepts are not understood as contrary to the natural functioning of human cognitive faculties. They instead allow human beings to gain adequate (albeit imperfect) knowledge (although not comprehension!) of God. According to Bavinck, it is thus reasonable to develop a realist understanding of dogmatic theology based on these epistemological concepts.

These elements lead to the conclusion that Bavinck adopts a classical moderate-realist epistemology, which is characterized by an altogether modest and confident attitude towards the human ability to know something about external reality. The knowing subject plays an active role, but not in a constructivist way. Metaphysical entities can be known and human knowledge does not limit itself to brute facts.

Finally, Bavinck's *semantic* realism also relies on his metaphysics of the divine Logos. The Greek meaning of Logos is indeed not only "reason"

---

104 I quoted Bavinck's use of this formula in section 2.3 of this chapter. He probably quotes it from memory, since his translation is not very precise. The original formulation can be found in Thomas Aquinas, *Summa Theologiae*, I.1.8, ad 2.

(or proportion, harmony, structure), but also, as translated in most English Bibles, "Word." Logos theology thus makes possible the development of a semantic realist understanding of theology. God uses human language to address humanity in his revelation and this language fits its object, since it is spoken by the Logos of God (the second person of the Trinity), who has also created the world and human beings. The language of revelation is thus not arbitrary, but corresponds to the being of God, to the intelligibility of the world, and to the cognitive structure of human beings.

The second facet of Bavinck's semantic realism is that the language used by the theologian to describe theological truths is also adequate. Even if the truth of God can never be expressed in a perfect way (God is transcendent and incomprehensible), the concepts developed by Christian theologians through the centuries allow them to formulate truth-content propositions. Here again, this affirmation has its foundation in the metaphysics of the divine Logos as developed above.

Bavinck's semantic realism is thus philosophically based on a correspondence theory of truth (truth as the *adequatio intellectus ad rem*), since it relies on the basic idea that there is a correspondence between the theologian's words and the world. It is also close to the classical Christian semantic theories that have been developed in order to describe how human beings can effectively talk about God without denying his transcendence.

5.2 Is Bavinck a Critical Realist?
It may appear anachronistic to bring Bavinck into a conversation with the contemporary critical realist trends in theology, since the spread of critical realism in the field of theological studies only dates back to the 1970s. Nevertheless, some contemporary thinkers claim that the work of Bavinck on realism is close to what I termed post-Kantian critical realism. By contrast, I have proposed an interpretation of Bavinck developing a thoroughly classical realist understanding of theology. The aim of this subsection is thus to justify this interpretation of Bavinck's defense of a realist conception of theology.

There is a tradition of reading Bavinck as if he were a sort of "bipolar" theological figure "who vacillates between moments of 'orthodoxy' and 'modernity' without ever resolving his own basic crisis of theological identity."[105] More interestingly, from the perspective of the present

---

105 James P. Eglinton, *Trinity and Organism*, 28. A whole chapter of this book (viz. chapter 2, "How many Herman Bavincks?" 27-50) is devoted to this interpretative

research, even thinkers who recognize the internal coherence of Bavinck's work ask if he was perhaps not more influenced than he would have admitted by the post-Kantian idealist context in which he was working. Henk van den Belt has recently raised this question in an interesting way, for instance. He defends, as I do, a unified understanding of Bavinck's work, but he is also sensitive to potential Kantian influences that can be found in his theology. By presenting and discussing van den Belt's interpretation of Bavinck's realism, I aim to sharpen my own understanding of some contemporary issues in Bavinck studies and defend the cogency of my proposal.[106]

In *The Authority of Scripture in Reformed Theology*, van den Belt develops the question of Bavinck's conception of theological knowledge. He compares it with historic Reformed orthodoxy as well as with that of his colleague from Princeton, B. B. Warfield. In his book, van den Belt advances the idea that the Dutch theologian may not be quite as realistic a theologian as one might think, and that he may well have been influenced by German idealism. In the last subsection of chapter 6 of his book (significantly titled "Achilles' Heel or Cornerstone?") he questions "whether Bavinck succeeds in his attempt to avoid subjectivism."[107] His answer is cautious:

---

question, even if Eglinton doesn't adhere to this hypothesis. I suggest that this interpretation is based more on biographical factors than on a careful study of the *Reformed Dogmatics*.

106 In an unpublished document, Eglinton raises a similar issue: "However, the question arises; could it be that in bringing Bavinck's system together—whereby human perception (which itself is not the reality) interprets something (i.e. reality) that is, in itself, an analogous, anthropomorphic representation of something else (i.e. God, who is wholly other)—Bavinck's understanding of reality and perception is actually slightly closer to modern philosophy than he admits? To be fair, Bavinck's critique of modern philosophy on this point does emphasize the 'ever-growing' nature of the gap it posits between reality and representation. This leaves room for any gap asserted by Bavinck, for example, to be fixed (rather than ever-increasing)." James Eglinton, *Response to "Working with the Grain of Nature: Epistemic Underpinnings for Christian Witness in the Theology of Herman Bavinck" by Steve Duby*, Unpublished Document. For Duby's article see: "Working with the Grain of Nature: Epistemic Underpinnings for Christian Witness in the Theology of Herman Bavinck," *The Bavinck Review* 3 (2012): 62-74. Since, as far as I know, Eglinton does not develop this interrogation in any published document, I refrain from discussing it further in this book. Sutanto also works along these interpretative lines and substantiates the case in favor of a "partially post-Kantian Bavinck": see pages 101-109 of *God and Knowledge. Herman Bavinck's Theological Epistemology*. Finally, see also Arvin Vos, "Knowledge According to Bavinck and Aquinas," *The Bavinck Review* 6 (2015): 9-36.

107 Van den Belt, *The Authority of Scripture in Reformed Theology. Truth and Trust*, 290.

> [Bavinck] rejects subjectivism and tries to avoid it by stressing the evidences [apologetic arguments for the faith] or by pointing to the universal Christian witness regarding Scripture. In the meantime, his position remains subjectivistic because Bavinck's epistemology is dominated by the subject-object dichotomy. Something within us must necessarily correspond to the truth outside of us. The predominance of this dichotomy in the *principia* causes the shift of faith from soteriology to prolegomena. A subjective element is introduced in the foundational structure of systematic theology, next to the objective revelation in Scripture.[108]

Indeed, the previous analysis of Bavinck's elaboration of the specific method of theology in his *Philosophy of Revelation* revealed the prominent role he ascribes to the concept of faith (and the concomitant notion of conversion). In the following paragraphs, I examine and discuss the idea that there may well be sufficient elements in the *Reformed Dogmatics* to justify the hypothesis of a more-or-less subjectivist Bavinck, which would undoubtedly lead one to relate his work to post-Kantian critical realist trends.

In defense of this interpretation, van den Belt puts forward two inescapable observations. First, Bavinck departs from classical orthodox Reformed dogmatics by introducing—via the partial displacement of faith from soteriology to the prolegomena[109]—the knowing subject in the *principia* (the very foundation) of theology.[110] Far from being inconsequential, this innovation would bear the mark of a subjectivist

---

108 Van den Belt, *The Authority of Scripture in Reformed Theology. Truth and Trust*, 294. He pursues his answer by stressing the relevance of the issue: "This may have had an influence on the development of Neo-Calvinism and the acceptance of liberalism in the Reformed Churches in the Netherlands. The way in which Bavinck struggles with this dichotomy evokes the theological question how to deal with the relationship between objective truth and subjective certainty in a postmodern context. This is one of the most foundational questions for Christian theology at this moment."

109 The displacement is only partial because Bavinck also deals with faith in the soteriological volume 3 of the *Reformed Dogmatics*.

110 Without going back to the content of subsection 3.1, the beginning of Muller's definition of the principles of theology confirms van den Belt's affirmation: "Principia theologiae: *fundamental principles or foundations of theology*. According to the Protestant scholastics, theology has two *principia*, Scripture and God, i.e., the revelation and the one who reveals himself. The scholastic systems frequently begin with a definition of theology followed by a statement of its *principia*, viz., a *locus* on Scripture and a *locus* on God." Richard A. Muller, *Dictionary of Latin and Greek Theological Terms* (Grand Rapids: Baker Books, 1985), 245.

and modern sensibility. Second, one should notice that Bavinck quite repeatedly makes use of strongly subjectivist formulations in the *Reformed Dogmatics*.[111] Such expressions, while foreign to the traditional Reformed theological language, are familiar to post-Kantian thought. These observations lead van den Belt to the conclusion that Bavinck is influenced by Kantian subjectivism.

Without contesting the pertinence of these observations, they may nevertheless be interpreted in a way that is compatible with the classical realist Bavinck argued for in this present work. I agree with van der Kooi, another Bavinck scholar, when he states that "it may appear ungracious to say that Bavinck cooperates in the turning towards the subject, and thereby (probably more than he likes) pays tribute to the anthropocentrism of modernity."[112] I therefore propose in the following paragraphs four ways of taking account of Bavinck's subjectivist formulas without abandoning an interpretation of his work as a defense of a classical realist understanding of theology.

The first way of integrating Bavinck's subjectivist formulations in a classical realist interpretative frame is well formulated by Carl E. Trueman:

> Bavinck takes seriously the need to articulate the faith in a manner which respects the historic doctrinal trajectories yet which addresses contemporary intellectual and social patterns of behavior. This is most important, since there is a difference between a biblical defense of the

---

[111] For instance and among many others: "Christian theology indeed takes its starting point in the human subject." Bavinck, *RD 1*, 564.

[112] Cornelius van der Kooi, "The Appeal to the Inner Testimony of the Spirit, especially in H. Bavinck," *Journal of Reformed Theology* 2 (2008), 107. Van der Kooi justifies this statement in a well-balanced paragraph that synthesizes many elements developed in the previous subsections of this chapter: "One can undoubtedly object that Bavinck's epistemology is found instead in a realistic tradition, and his epistemology follows the tracks of the Aristotelian tradition. Truth consists in the agreement between the thought and the object. (…). However, Bavinck's epistemology is not just a repetition of realism, or reduced to a form of logos speculation. In his thought, a central place is assigned to the knowing subject. 'All that is objective can be approached only from the vantage point of the subject; the *Ding an sich* is unknowable and does not exist for us.' [*Reformed Dogmatics. Prolegomena*, 586] Such expression betrays, in a high degree, a post-Kantian situation, and could never really have been uttered by someone like Calvin. Bavinck's expression can nourish the thought that the existence of things can be acknowledged only as they appear to the mind's eye. That would be a modern Cartesian point of departure. One can (…) not accuse Bavinck of such a position. It is true, however, that his focus is strongly directed to the religious subject to whose mind's eye the things of revelation must appear if he or she wants to find them worthy or true" (107-108).

faith once delivered to the saints and a mindless reaction against anything new. That difference is clear in the work of all great theologians, and Bavinck is no exception.[113]

These lines stress the importance of the context in which a dogmatician works. As studied above, historical sensitivity is a part of Bavinck's theological synthetic-genetic method. Without doubt, this sensitivity includes an understanding of the context in which a dogmatic theology is written. It is therefore probable that Bavinck worked on formulating the content of the "faith once delivered to the saints" in a way likely to interest and hopefully convince readers who work in a post-Kantian intellectual context. From this perspective, Bavinck's subjectivist assertions may be interpreted as an effort at contextualization, which very much resembles that of the apostle Paul as he spoke on the Areopagus.

A second reason for defending an interpretation of Bavinck as a classical realist theologian may be found in the wider context of late nineteenth-century Calvinist thought. The Dutch neo-Calvinists had close and brotherly contacts with their American colleagues at Princeton. They all worked on developing a realist conception of theological discourse, but their defense of realism differed. On the one hand, the Princeton theologians were indeed mainly influenced by the Anglo-Saxon Bacon-Reid *common sense* tradition. This tradition insisted strongly on facts and objective knowledge, and proposed a theological method directly inspired by that of the natural sciences.[114] Bavinck, on the other hand, was deeply influenced by an Aristotelian-Thomistic realism that included the activity of the knowing subject in the act of knowledge (cf. the active intellect). As seen above, from this perspective, emphasizing the activity of the knowing subject is not necessarily a sign of post-Kantian idealism or subjectivism. It may be interpreted as a specific part of what I have called moderate realism, as opposed to the mere objectivism of positivist or naïve realism. The opposition between

---

113 Carl E. Trueman, "Editorial: Some Advantages of Going Dutch," *Themelios* 3 (2000), 3.
114 See chapters 3, 6 and 7 of Harriet A. Harris, *Fundamentalism and Evangelicals* (Oxford: Oxford University Press, 1998). An illustration of this can be found in Charles Hodge's *Systematic Theology*. The first chapter, titled "On Method," section "A. *The Inductive Method as applied to Theology*" begins as follows: "The Bible is to the theologian what nature is to the man of science. It is his store-house of facts; and his method of ascertaining what the Bible teaches, is the same as that which the natural philosopher adopts or ascertain what nature teaches." Charles Hodge, *Systematic Theology 1* (Grand Rapids: Eerdmans Publishing Company, 1982), 10 (or. ed. New York: Scribner's, 1872).

these two methodological approaches is explicit, and I hold that Bavinck gave a slightly subjectivist coloration to his work in order to make clear that he did not share all the views of his American colleagues.[115]

The third reason to argue in favor of a classical realist Bavinck, even if he happens to be interpreted as a critical realist, lies in his declared philosophical eclecticism:

> Theology is not in need of a specific philosophy. It is not per se hostile to any philosophical system and does not, a priori and without criticism, give priority to the philosophy of Plato or of Kant, or vice versa. But it brings along its own criteria, tests all philosophy by them, and takes over what it deems true and useful. What is needed is philosophy in general. In other words, it arrives at scientific theology only by thinking. The only internal principle of knowledge, therefore, is not faith as such, but believing thought, Christian rationality.[116]

---

115 In the presentation of his theological method in the *Prolegomena* volume of the *Reformed Dogmatics*, Bavinck explicitly criticizes Charles Hodge: "This synthetic-genetic method must not be confused with the empirical or experimental method, as this happens in Charles Hodge and R. Mc. Ch. Edgar of Dublin" (93-94). In his context, he criticizes the influence of Bacon's experimental method on Princeton theologians, but he doesn't mention Thomas Reid. This observation raises an interesting historiographical question which is related to this study but cannot be deepened here: is Thomas Reid's common sense realism best understood from the perspective of the philosophy of Aristotle or that of the modern Anglo-Saxon experimental method? If the latter is correct, as I believe, there is a potential historical argument in favor of bringing together Bavinck and Plantinga, since Bavinck's realism presents similarities with Reid's common sense realism and Plantinga openly refers to the Scottish philosopher's work. Sutanto, however, rightly points out that there is also an important difference between Bavinck and Reid, in that the former affirms the existence of a gap between subjective representations and objective reality, which the latter denies; see *God and Knowledge*, 119 (in the context of 109-121).

116 Bavinck, *RD 1*, 609. From a more historical perspective, Bavinck states on page 607: "Theology first arose in the Christian community after the naiveté of childhood lay behind it and the adult thinking mind had awakened. Gradually a need arose to think through the ideas of revelation, to link it with other knowledge and to defend it against various forms of attack. For this purpose people needed philosophy. Scientific theology was born with its help. [...] [The church fathers] did not utilize the whole of Greek philosophy but made a choice; they only utilized the philosophy that was most suited to help them think through and defend the truth of God. They went to work eclectically and did not take over any single philosophical system."

It is not surprising to find various philosophical elements in the work of a theologian who claims such a philosophical eclecticism.[117] It is indeed possible to find Kantian sequences in Bavinck's work, as does van den Belt. But one may also identify Hegelian influences, such as the importance given to the organic method or the way the opposition between the object and the subject is overtaken by the theology of the divine Logos.[118] Eglinton has studied the question of a Hegelian influence on Bavinck's work with care in his *Trinity and Organism*, and his conclusion is that Bavinck does effectively use Hegelian terminology, but that he gives it a largely Christian content. Taking this philosophical eclecticism into account may prevent us from over-interpreting Bavinck's post-Kantian elements of thought.

Lastly, taking every subjectivist affirmation contained in the *Reformed Dogmatics* at face value raises a major interpretative problem. By denying the fact that the Logos perspective succeeds in bringing together in a synthetic way external reality and its representation in human consciousness, one questions *de facto* the cogency of Bavinck's theological method itself. Affirming, as van den Belt does, that "Bavinck's epistemology is dominated by the subject-object dichotomy," constitutes a serious attack against *RD 1* as a whole. First, because it is precisely the point of Bavinck's organic method to overcome the subject-object dichotomy, one may ask about the purpose of practicing a science whilst at the same time contesting one of its core elements. Secondly, Eglinton has correctly affirmed that in Bavinck's thought "Trinity *ad intra* leads to organism *ad extra*." If "organism *ad extra*" is a methodological failure, one is entitled to ask whether "Trinity *ad intra*" is still a viable stance, and what would be the impact of this methodological failure on Bavinck's Trinitarian theology.

In conclusion, Bavinck's realism cannot be assimilated to any form of what I have labeled post-Kantian critical realism.[119] On the contrary,

---

117 Bavinck's eclecticism plays a crucial role in Nathaniel Gray Sutanto's *God and Knowledge*. Sutanto's whole argument is built on the presentation of the tension between Bavinck's eclecticism and its overcoming by his organic method.

118 See for instance the references to the words "Organism," "Subject," "Object," or "Logos" in the indexes of Michael Inwood's *A Hegel Dictionary* (Oxford: Blackwell Publishers, 1992). Here and there, Bavinck has written astonishingly Hegelian paragraphs. See for instance page 68 of his *Philosophy of Revelation*: "In the knowledge of the truth lies the end of its revelation; reality is an instrument to enable us to find the truth; reality is intended to become truth in our consciousness and in our experience. Reality, therefore, does not offer us in the truth a mere copy of itself, so that the world, as pragmatism objects, would be duplicated. In the truth, reality rises to a higher mode of existence […]."

119 At the end of his book devoted to Bavinck's epistemology, Nathaniel Gray Sutanto

though he cannot be considered a proponent of so-called "naïve realism," he proposes a classical Christian defense of a realist conception of theology, even when he interacts in a lively way with his intellectual context.

5.3 Is Bavinck a Theological Realist?
Having discussed whether the work of Bavinck can be interpreted as post-Kantian critical realism, this subsection explores whether it is cogent to understand it as a precursor of radical theological realism, as described in the first chapter of this book. First, I discuss whether Bavinck's realism is first of all a philosophical or a theological stance. I then concentrate on important debates that have been generated throughout the twentieth century by his reference to the theology of the divine Logos as a foundation of his system.

As presented in the first chapter, a constant concern of what I have called contemporary *radical theological realism* is that we should resist the temptation to use philosophical or scientific concepts as a foundation of theology. From this perspective, the theologian has to unashamedly develop specific theological concepts (such as revelation, faith, eschatology, etc.) as a foundation for the entire dogmatic edifice. Referring to other types of concepts is interpreted, in this context, as a methodological capitulation to the influence of a wider cultural frame (for instance that of the Western academic world). While dealing with the question of realism in theology, Karl Barth, the most inspiring figure of contemporary theological realism, raised a programmatic question: "We have to ask, in short, whether we are really doing theology or merely realistic philosophy."[120] This opposition between philosophy and theology has become commonplace in contemporary theological realist circles.

Henk van den Belt applies this programmatic question to Bavinck's defense of a realist conception of theology with a high degree of theological accuracy:

> Bavinck places theology in the general philosophical context, but wants to keep it free from philosophical influences. He keeps science, general revelation, and special revelation together in his concept of the *principia*

---

shares this conclusion: "The term 'critical realism' can hardly be adequate to capture the theological and philosophical depth of Bavinck's conception of the epistemic process." (*God and Knowledge. Herman Bavinck's Theological Epistemology*, 145).
120 Barth, "Fate and Idea in Theology," in *The Way of Theology in Karl Barth*, 41.

and at the same time distinguishes them in different levels. Bavinck says that theology has its own epistemology and is independent of all philosophical systems. [...] Bavinck fits his general epistemology into his theological framework via the concept of the divine *Logos*. It seems as if he approaches philosophy from a theological perspective, but his prolegomena are so influenced by his philosophical epistemology, that in reality he approaches theology from a philosophical perspective.[121]

Van den Belt's last sentence constitutes an important critique of Bavinck's work when considered from the standpoint of radical theological realism (which is not van den Belt's perspective). Nevertheless, Bavinck is not interested in answering this sort of question. Instead, he explicitly refers to his classical Reformed heritage to defend his synthetic-organic theological method as developed previously in this chapter.

The following lines can be interpreted as Bavinck's anticipated answer to the concern formulated by van den Belt:

> The relation of faith and knowledge, of theology and philosophy, of authority and reason, of head and heart, of Christianity and humanity, of religion and culture, of heavenly and earthly vocation, of religion and morality, of the contemplative and the active life, of Sabbath and workday, of church and state—all these and many other questions are determined by the problem of the relation between creation and re-creation, between the work of the Father and the work of the Son.[122]

In Bavinck's mind, creation and re-creation, the work of the Father and the work of the Son, are not to be opposed to each other but are to be understood in an organic (or complementary) way. Therefore, one should not work from a perspective that tends to oppose theological and philosophical concepts. Bavinck's defense of a realist conception of theology has to be understood in this way. The main question is not whether the intellectual tools employed are philosophical or theological, but rather if they allow the theologian to develop a cogent and coherent system of truth. Bavinck's method is, on this question, close to that adopted by the contemporary analytic philosophy of religion movement mentioned at the end of chapter one, which refuses to oppose what

---

121 Van den Belt, *The Authority of Scripture in Reformed Theology. Truth and Trust*, 266. At page 282, van den Belt continues: "It is difficult to determine whether his [Bavinck's] epistemology rests on his theology or whether his theological epistemology is based on philosophy."
122 Bavinck, *Common Grace*, 56.

Wolterstorff has named "philosophical theology" with "theological theology."[123]

Bavinck's theological method is not only synthetic, but also genetic, which means that the Christian tradition plays an important role in the elaboration of his dogmatic theology. It is therefore interesting to briefly present here how he refers to article 2 of the *Belgic Confession* (one of the three most important Confessional standards of the Dutch Reformed churches of his time) in order to defend his approach against the forerunners of contemporary theological realisms. Here is the complete article 2 of the *Belgic Confession*:

> We know him by two means: first, by the creation, preservation and government of the universe; which is before our eyes as a most elegant book, wherein all creatures, great and small, are as so many characters leading us to contemplate the invisible things of God, namely, his eternal power and Godhead, as the Apostle Paul saith (Rom 1:20). All these things are enough to convict men and to leave them without excuse.
> Secondly, he makes himself more clearly and fully known to us by his holy and divine Word, that is to say, as far as is necessary for us to know in this life, to his glory and our salvation.[124]

This article has been widely commented upon within Reformed circles. The content of the first paragraph, and the fact that it is not opposed to that of the second (see the use of the comparative instead of an antithetic transition) indeed raises great theological difficulties for the tenets of theologies that are methodologically based on oppositions, as is the case with radical theological realism.[125] Bavinck is aware of this and thus affirms in an openly polemical tone:

> Admittedly, article 2 of the Belgic Confession states that God is known by two means—nature and Scripture—and natural theology is upheld in its truth and value by all Reformed theologians. But in that first period,

---

123 This is Nicholas Wolterstorff's formula. See chapter 1, subsection 4.2.
124 Arthur C. Cochrane (ed.), *Reformed Confessions of the 16th Century* (Louisville: Westminster John Knox, 2003), 189-190. For a historical introduction to the elaboration and the reception of the *Belgic Confession*, see Nicolaas H. Gootjes, *The Belgic Confession. Its History and Sources* (Grand Rapids: Baker Academic, 2007).
125 As van den Brink has shown in "A Most Elegant Book: The Natural World in Article 2 of the Belgic Confession," *Westminster Theological Journal* 73 (2011), 273-291, article 2 strongly resists modern attempts to read it in a dualistic anti-metaphysical way.

before rationalism infected Reformed theology, it was clearly seen that nature and Scripture are not detached and independent entities, any more than natural and revealed theology are. Calvin incorporated natural theology into the body of Christian dogmatics, saying that Scripture was the spectacles by which believers see God more distinctly also in the works of nature.[126]

"Before rationalism infected Reformed theology," Bavinck affirms, with the support of a major sixteenth century Confessional standard, there was no dualism in the articulation of creation and redemption, reason and faith, natural knowledge and divine revelation, but rather a harmonious organic organization.[127] Rationalism has indeed led to the radical separation of the rational natural world on the one side, and the irrational supernatural world on the other. According to Bavinck, this alternative has to be rejected in itself. The question of the theological

---

126 Bavinck, *RD 1*, 87. This reference to Calvin's metaphor of the book of creation read through the spectacles of Scriptures (see the *Institutes of Christian Religion*, I.vi.1) is crucial but problematic within the field of Reformed theology. The problem discussed in this subsection is indeed probably due to the fact that a part of the Reformed tradition has insisted on the book, while the other on the spectacles. See Paul Helm's contribution to this debate in parts 1 and 8 of *Faith and Understanding* (Grand Rapids: William B. Eerdmans Publishing, 1997).

127 Bavinck could have quoted two other major Confessional standards. The first is article 2 of the *French Confession of Faith* (1559) (one of the main sources of De Brès in his redaction of the *Belgic Confession*): "As such this God reveals himself to men; firstly, in his works in their creation, as well as in their preservation and control. Secondly, and more clearly, in his Word, which was in the beginning revealed through oracles, and which was afterward committed to writing in the books which we call the Holy Scriptures." Arthur C. Cochrane (ed.), *Reformed Confessions of the Sixteenth Century*, 144. The second text comes from the second most important Confessional standard of the Dutch Reformed churches, *The Canons of Dort*, a text not particularly known for its underestimation of the fall and its consequences: "There remain, however, in man since the fall, the glimmerings of natural light, whereby he retains some knowledge of God, of natural things, and of the difference between good and evil, and discovers some regard for virtue, good order in society, and for maintaining an orderly external deportment." Philip Schaff (ed.), *The Creeds of Christendom With a History and Critical Notes (Volume 3: The Evangelical Protestant Creeds with Translations)*, (Grand Rapids: Baker Book House, 1983), 588. In *Reformed Dogmatics 3: Sin and Salvation in Christ*, Bavinck follows the same theological line on page 121: "The doctrine of the total corruption of human nature by no means implies, therefore, that the sinful disposition that lies at the bottom of the human heart always erupts in the kind of deeds that betray clear hostility and hatred towards God and neighbor."

"purity" of the premises of theology is the result of modern dualistic thought and may be ignored without damage.

I end this subsection with two debates connected to Bavinck's use of the theology of the divine Logos in relation to theological realism. This will help in locating the work of Bavinck within the context of contemporary theological realism with greater precision. First, I sketch an indirect but nevertheless important discussion between B. B. Warfield and Geerhardus Vos on the interpretation of a theology of the divine Logos. Second, I present the disagreement between two contemporary scholars, K. Scott Oliphint and John Bolt, on the question at hand. I conclude these brief surveys with a couple of telling quotes bearing on the issue from Bavinck's *Philosophy of Revelation*.

In 1905-1906 (the same year as the publication of the first volume of the Dutch second edition of Bavinck's *Reformed Dogmatics*), B. B. Warfield published a series of three articles titled "Tertullian and the Beginnings of the Doctrine of the Trinity" in the *Princeton Theological Review*.[128] The general scope of these articles is historical (retracing the early history of the Trinitarian dogma), and Bavinck is not mentioned. Nevertheless, if one remembers the interest in the Logos motif manifest by the Dutch neo-Calvinists, and if one also takes into account the close relations maintained between the Princeton and the Amsterdam theologians, it is difficult to read these articles as mere historical exercises. On the contrary, I think that by publishing this thorough study, Warfield did not only contribute to Tertullian studies, but also initiated an indirect polemic against the interest of the Amsterdam theologians in reintroducing a theology of the divine Logos in Reformed theology.

Warfield begins his study with an appreciative historical interpretation of the use of the Logos theology in the church of the first centuries: "The value of the Logos speculation to the first age of Christianity was that it enabled Christian thinkers to preserve the unity of God while yet guarding His transcendence."[129] He nevertheless quickly moves towards a critique of the patristic use of this theological concept, because of its subordinationist tendency. From this perspective, Tertullian is praised as the first to distance himself from Logos theology in order "to do full justice to the true deity of Christ."[130] For this reason, Tertullian's theology has "the

---

128 The three articles were republished later in a book: Benjamin B. Warfield, *Studies in Tertullian and Augustine* (New York: Oxford University Press, 1930). The following quotations are drawn from this publication.
129 Warfield, *Studies in Tertullian and Augustine*, 20-21.
130 Warfield, *Studies in Tertullian and Augustine*, 73.

promise and potency of the better things to come,"[131] which are the Nicene and Chalcedonian Trinitarian theologies.

While developing his argument in a careful way, Warfield slips in a remark that is of great interest in the context of this present research:

> Perhaps it is not too much to say that the supplanting among Christian thinkers of the Logos speculation by a doctrine of immanent Trinity was largely mediated by the shifting of interest from the cosmological to the soteriological aspect of Christian truth.[132]

Warfield praises this theological shift. Apart from its historical cogency, I hold that such a way of framing soteriological categories as standing over and against cosmological or ontological ones is fully compatible with major themes of the forthcoming twentieth century radical theological realism.

Geerhardus Vos, who like Warfield was a professor at Princeton, responded indirectly to his colleague's articles devoted to Tertullian. In 1913, and also in the *Princeton Theological Review*, Vos published a pair of articles titled "The Range of the Logos-Title in the Prologue to the Fourth Gospel."[133] The aim of these articles was to defend the authenticity and theological significance of John's use of the Logos-motif in the Prologue to his gospel against the modernizing trends of biblical scholarship. The articles are very detailed, and so I refrain from summarizing them, and instead devote my full attention to their general conclusion:

> [The Prologue] links together creation and redemption as both mediated by the same Logos. Vs. 4, 5 and 10 taken together are preeminently the *sedes* for the church-doctrine of natural revelation in its relation to God's redemptive disclosure in Christ. While it is plainly taught that mankind subjectively fails to appropriate this revelation of nature, it is likewise implied that it nevertheless remains objectively valid. Moreover we receive the guarantee of the inner harmony and mutual interdependence of the two realms of truth in which the one Logos rules. Especially in our days, when a potent current of thought seeks to banish all natural theology from religion and void the Christian mind of all antecedent rational knowledge of God, the principle just formulated assumes more than

---

131 Warfield, *Studies in Tertullian and Augustine*, 99.
132 Warfield, *Studies in Tertullian and Augustine*, 88.
133 Geerhardus Vos, "The Range of the Logos-Title in the Prologue to the Fourth Gospel," *Princeton Theological Review* 11 (1913), 365-419 and 557-602.

ordinary importance, and the old exegesis of the Prologue, in which it finds classical expression, becomes invested with a new apologetic interest.[134]

When read in light of the present discussion, these lines clearly extend beyond their immediate application. Vos explicitly takes a position in favor of the development of a theology of the divine Logos, and this in the manner of Bavinck (the Logos motif "links together creation and redemption" and unites the principles of theological science: "we receive the guarantee of the inner harmony and mutual interdependence of the two realms of truth in which the one Logos rules"). Further, he does not hesitate at the end of the passage to attack frontally numerous postulates on which twentieth century radical theological realism is built, especially the opposition between natural and supernatural knowledge of God.[135]

A second interesting debate that falls within the scope of this research in relation to theological realism occurred in America during the first decade of the twenty-first century between Calvin Seminary professor John Bolt and Westminster Seminary professor K. Scott Oliphint. As the editor of the English translation of Bavinck's *Reformed Dogmatics*, John Bolt has written several articles devoted to Bavinck and to the role of Dutch Calvinism in America. In 2008, he published a text titled "*Sola Scriptura* as an Evangelical Theological Method?"[136] In this article, he defends the following thesis:

---

134 Vos, "The Range of the Logos-Title in the Prologue to the Fourth Gospel," 601-602.
135 In the 1930s, a series of critiques emerged from Reformed circles against the revival of theologies of the divine Logos. In the Netherlands, Herman Dooyeweerd and his colleague Dirk H. Vollenhoven insisted on the gap that separates God from his creation: see Albert Wolters, "Dutch Neo-Calvinism: Worldview, Philosophy and Rationality," in Hendrik Hart, Johan van der Hoeven and Nicholas Wolterstorff (eds.), *Rationality in the Calvinian Tradition* (Lanham: University Press of America, 1983), 126-127. John Bolt proposed another summary of this critique in "Grand Rapids Between Kampen and Amsterdam: Herman Bavinck's Reception and Influence in North America," *Calvin Theological Journal* 38 (2003), 270. In the 1930s American context, while formulating a globally very positive appreciation of the *Reformed Dogmatics*, Reformed theologian Cornelius Van Til also explicitly criticized Bavinck's *Prolegomena* for its appeal to Aristotelian realism and its reference to Logos theology. Van Til's conclusion is that Bavinck is not consistent with his own Protestant presuppositions (i.e., the modern reading of the five *solas*) in referring to a general realist epistemology and a "Pagan ontological motif": see Cornelius Van Til, *Introduction to Systematic Theology* (Phillipsburg: Presbyterian and Reformed Publishing Co., 1974), 48.
136 John Bolt, "*Sola Scriptura* as an Evangelical Theological Method?" in Gary L. W. Johnson and Ronald N. Gleason (eds.), *Reforming or Conforming? Post-Conservative Evangelicals and the Emerging Church* (Wheaton: Crossway Books, 2008), 62-92.

> In fact evangelical theology has been insufficiently metaphysical instead of too much so. The accusations laid against so-called evangelical rationalism—too much philosophy; not enough relationality based on mystery and faith—are precisely the Achilles' heel of the postmodern enthusiasts.[137]

In defense of this thesis, Bolt explicitly refers to the work of Bavinck. Here follows a synthesis paragraph presenting the theological use he makes of the work of the Dutch theologian:

> As an alternative [to Evangelical post-modern anti-metaphysical thought], I appealed to Herman Bavinck's Christian realism, the epistemology that is rooted in the creation of all things, including the human logos, by the divine Logos. All truth is from God; we participate in the truth to the degree that our intellects adequately form concepts that correspond to the things of this world including our experience of God. We attempted to show, in broad strokes, that this view is characteristic of all the great theologians including Augustine, Thomas Aquinas, and Francis Turretin, as well as Herman Bavinck. Concretely this means that while the Bible is the final source and norm for Christian theology, the knowledge of God obtained by natural reason, reflected in the religions of the world, as well as legitimate, reasonable inferences from biblical truth, are all part of the theologian's thesaurus of truth.[138]

In the context of this research, it is interesting to notice that Bolt explicitly refers to Bavinck to oppose contemporary trends that base their theology on "relationality," mystery, and faith over and against rationality and metaphysics.

This article generated a sharp reaction from K. Scott Oliphint, who published in response a wide-ranging article entitled "Bavinck's Realism, The Logos Principle, and *Sola Scriptura*."[139] In this article, Scott Oliphint notably responds to Bolt's above-quoted appeal to Bavinck's realism as an epistemology "rooted in the creation of all things." He contests this formula and states that "it does not give us an adequate account of the knowledge situation itself." He then concludes:

---

137 Bolt, "*Sola Scriptura* as an Evangelical Theological Method?" 92.
138 Bolt, "*Sola Scriptura* as an Evangelical Theological Method?" 89.
139 K. Scott Oliphint, "Bavinck's Realism, The Logos Principle, and *Sola Scriptura*," *Westminster Theological Journal* 72 (2010), 360-390.

It is a revelational epistemology including as it must the Logos principle, and not a realistic epistemology, that alone is able to account for any universality of knowledge, and, more importantly, that alone is able to bring the gospel to bear on the church and on the world.[140]

K. Scott Oliphint's answer to John Bolt crystallizes the theological oppositions between a Bavinck-style Logos realism and a radical theological realism. Revelational epistemology is opposed to classical realistic epistemology as part of a strong effort to maintain the theological method in a state of perfect theological purity.

In conclusion, Bavinck's realism cannot be assimilated to any form of radical theological realism. On the contrary, his use of the theology of the divine Logos leads one to think that he belongs instead to the family of classical theological realism. The way in which, according to Bavinck, the philosophy of revelation "seeks to correlate the wisdom […] in revelation with that [wisdom] which is furnished by the world at large," offers further confirmation of this view.[141] In his *Philosophy of Revelation* Bavinck even argues that Christian theology "never wholly thought through the notion of general revelation, nor fully made clear its rich significance for the whole of human life."[142] In this connection, he explicitly criticizes "not a few theologians" who abandon the entire world to modern science and retreat to either the Person of Christ or the human soul as the sole locus of divine revelation.[143] He could hardly have distanced himself more clearly from what I have called radical theological realism.

Thus, Bavinck helps to strengthen the case for classical theological realism in an interesting way. This view will be developed in the last chapter of this book, which will expound upon the Bavinck/Plantinga model and the issues it raises.

---

140 Scott Oliphint, "Bavinck's Realism, The Logos Principle, and *Sola Scriptura*," 389-390.
141 Bavinck, *PoR*, 24.
142 Bavinck, *PoR*, 24. Unfortunately, the English translation is mistaken here (a mistake that even made its way into the new 2018-edition), since it says that Christian theology never fully unpacked "this distinction" (viz. between general and special revelation). The Dutch original unambiguously states that it did not fully think through "general revelation" (*algemeene openbaring*).
143 Bavinck, *PoR*, 24.

Chapter 3

Alvin Plantinga's Theory of Warrant and Realist Theology

1. Introduction

Having presented Bavinck's realist understanding of theology in the previous chapter, I move now to the work of Alvin Plantinga. It is a combined reading of these two thinkers that makes possible the elaboration of a synthesized model for a realist conception of theology.

Alvin Plantinga is a leader of the contemporary analytic philosophy of religion movement. His work is careful and original, and even thinkers who do not share his convictions acknowledge its intrinsic value. During the 1990s, Plantinga wrote a couple of programmatic articles that enlighten his overall philosophical program: in these articles, he works on describing the specific responsibility of the Christian philosopher and proposes four main working fields: philosophical theology, apologetics (both positive and negative), Christian cultural criticism, and positive (or constructive) Christian philosophy.[1]

Plantinga affirms that the first two fields of study are common to the entire Christian tradition. From the very beginning, Christian theologians and philosophers have indeed worked on thinking "about the central doctrines of the Christian faith from a philosophical perspective" employing the resources of philosophy to do so,[2] and have defended the basic claims of Christian faith against opposing philosophical or

---

1 Alvin Plantinga, "Advice to Christian Philosophers," *Faith and Philosophy* 3 (1984): 253-271; "The Twin Pillars of Christian Scholarship," in *Seeking Understanding. The Stob Lectures, 1986-1998,* ed. Calvin College and Calvin Theological Seminary (Grand Rapids: Eerdmans Publishing, 2001), 117-161; "Augustinian Christian Philosophy," *The Monist* 3 (1992): 291-320; "Christian Philosophy at the End of the 20th Century," in *Christian Philosophy at the Close of the Twentieth Century. Assessment and Perspective,* ed. Sander Griffioen and Bert M. Balk (Kampen: Uitgeverij Kok, 1995), 29-53.
2 Plantinga, "Augustinian Christian Philosophy," 291.

theological systems.³ The third and the fourth working fields characterize in a more specific way the work of Plantinga and pertain to the scope of this research. They therefore deserve a more careful description.

The third field of study Plantinga calls *Christian cultural criticism* and is explicitly inspired by the work of both Augustine and Abraham Kuyper. The basic idea is that there is no absolute spiritual and intellectual neutrality, even in the academic world: the *Civitas Dei* and the *Civitas Mundi* are the two parts of "an antithesis that in one way or another cuts across and manifests itself in every important area of human life."⁴ The function of cultural criticism is to identify the intellectual strands that are in conflict in a given culture. Thus, Plantinga identifies three major strands in Western culture that are in mutual conflict: *perennial naturalism*,⁵ *Enlightenment humanism (or creative antirealism)*,⁶ and finally *(Christian) theism*. *Christian cultural criticism* consists in clarifying the basic assumptions of these approaches and in putting forward how they affect one's practice of philosophy, psychology, sociology, natural sciences, etc.

The fourth working field of the Christian philosopher is called *positive (or constructive) Christian philosophy*. Plantinga defines this as "thinking about the sorts of questions philosophers ask and answer from an explicitly Christian point of view," or as "thinking about philosophical

---

3 "First, there is negative apologetics, where the aim is to defend Christianity against attacks from its detractors. This enterprise, of course, has gone on from the very beginnings of Christianity. […] There is also positive apologetics. […] The efforts of the positive apologete are directed first of all towards giving theistic proofs or arguments: proof or arguments for the existence of God." Plantinga, "Augustinian Christian Philosophy," 291.
4 Plantinga, "Augustinian Christian Philosophy," 295.
5 Plantinga's definition of "naturalism": "There is no God, nor anything else beyond nature; and we human beings are insignificant parts of a vast cosmic machine that proceeds in majestic indifference to us, our hopes and aspirations, our needs and desires, our sense of fairness or fittingness." Plantinga, "Augustinian Christian Philosophy," 296. Since Plantinga deals a lot with naturalism in his work, this concept will appear many times in this chapter.
6 Plantinga's definition of "creative antirealism": "It is we ourselves—we human beings—who are responsible for the basic structure of the world." Plantinga, "Augustinian Christian Philosophy," 296. From this perspective, "the whole idea of an objective truth, the same for all of us, […] is an illusion, or a bourgeois plot, or a sexist imposition, or a silly mistake. Thus does anti-realism breed relativism and nihilism." Plantinga, "Augustinian Christian Philosophy," 303. Plantinga assimilates creative anti-realism mainly to twentieth century Continental philosophy and does not focus his work on this trend.

questions, taking for granted or starting from theism."⁷ He admits that this facet is "clearly the most difficult of the four; it requires more creativity and intellectual suppleness, more insight and discernment than we can easily muster. But it is also in some ways the most important."⁸

The part of Plantinga's work that is the focus of this chapter—the "Trilogy of Warrant"⁹ and some science and religion publications¹⁰—represents a sustained attempt to develop these third and fourth dimensions of the work of the Christian philosopher in debates related to the theory of knowledge. This observation leads to the hypothesis that there are important meeting points between Plantinga's work and the scope of the present research.

The general aim of this chapter is therefore to study and discuss Plantinga's important work on warrant (and some of its related adjunctions) in relation to the realism debates described in the first chapter of this book. In so doing, following up on the Bavinck chapter, I will lay the second stepping stone towards a synthetic model for a realist conception of theology. In order to achieve this, I first describe Plantinga's realist theory of knowledge based on the concept of "warrant" step-by-step (2). I then study how Plantinga extends his general theory of knowledge to the question of human knowledge of God, and more specifically to Christian theistic beliefs (3). Finally, I discuss two meaningful critical issues in Plantinga studies that are related to the scope of this research (4).

2. Plantinga's Theory of Warrant

During the second part of the twentieth century, Anglo-Saxon analytic philosophy was widely preoccupied with epistemological questions. One of the most important debates was generated by the reemergence, shortly after the Second World War, of an old definition of knowledge that can be found in Plato's *Theaetetus* (201c). In this dialogue, Plato writes: "True

---

7 Plantinga, "Augustinian Christian Philosophy," 308-309.
8 Plantinga, "Christian Philosophy at the End of the 20th Century," 45.
9 Alvin Plantinga, *Warrant: The Current Debate* (Oxford: Oxford University Press, 1993); *Warrant and Proper Function* (Oxford: Oxford University Press, 1993); *Warranted Christian Belief* (Oxford: Oxford University Press, 2000).
10 See among others: Alvin Plantinga, "Evolution and Design," in *For Faith and Clarity. Philosophical Contributions to Christian Theology*, ed. James K. Beilby (Grand Rapids: Baker Academic, 2006), 201-217; *Where the Conflict Really Lies. Science, Religion, and Naturalism* (New York: Oxford University Press, 2011); Daniel C. Dennett and Alvin Plantinga, *Science and Religion. Are they Compatible?* (Oxford: Oxford University Press, 2011).

judgment with an account is knowledge."[11] American analytic philosophers have generally reformulated this by saying that knowledge is *justified true belief* and have started to discuss with great care each word of this definition.[12]

This discussion gave birth to the following question: what does it mean for a true belief to be "justified"? For several decades the dominant position was to affirm, after Descartes, Locke, and Kant, that a true belief can be justified when we admit that the knowing subject has inner access to the criteria of knowledge, and adjusts his or her belief to the available evidence. This position has been called *internalism*, since knowing subjects have inner access to their cognitive faculties. Internalist thinkers generally adhere to epistemic *deontologism*, since they hold that we have a moral duty not to believe things that are beyond the evidence at our disposal.

In the 1980s, several philosophers started to strongly oppose internalism and denied the possibility of inner access to the criteria for justification of our knowledge. They developed instead a position that came be known as *externalism*. In this view the justification of true beliefs relies mainly on the way the cognitive faculties of the knower function in a given external context. If the cognitive faculties work well in an appropriate context, knowledge is then *reliable*.[13] This trend led to the rediscovery in the United States of the epistemological work of the Scottish Common Sense philosopher, Thomas Reid, as an antidote to the modern internalist tradition.[14]

Plantinga develops an externalist view of knowledge in his "Trilogy of Warrant." The aim of the first volume, *Warrant: The Current Debate*, is to show in detail why internalism is wrong and why reliabilist externalism is

---

11 Plato, *Theaetetus* (Oxford: Clarendon Press, 1973), 94.
12 The modern seminal article on this question is that of Edmund Gettier: "Is Justified True Belief Knowledge?" *Analysis* 23 (1963), 121-123.
13 Externalists are therefore often *reliabilists* like Plantinga, but they can also be deontologists. This stance is for example defended by Roger Pouivet in *L'éthique intellectuelle, une* épistémologie *des vertus* (Paris: Vrin, 2020). For convenient access to the main sources of this debate, *pro* and *contra*, see Part V ("Theories of Epistemic Justification") of *Epistemology. An Anthology*, ed. Ernest Sosa, Jaegwon Kim, Jeremy Fantl, and Matthew McGrath (Oxford: Blackwell Publishing, 2008).
14 Thomas Reid, *Inquiry and Essays*, ed. Ronald E. Beanblossom and Keith Lehrer (Indianapolis: Hackett Publishing, 1983). As an example of this rediscovery, see Nicholas Wolterstorff, *Thomas Reid and the Story of Epistemology* (Cambridge: Cambridge University Press, 2001) and cf. Terence Cuneo and René van Woudenberg (eds.), *The Cambridge Companion to Thomas Reid* (Cambridge: Cambridge University Press, 2004).

correct, even if incomplete. The goal of the second volume, *Warrant and Proper Function*, is then to improve externalist reliabilism by developing a positive concept of warrant, whose function is, among others, to replace the internalist concept of *justification*.[15] The philosophical richness of this trilogy cannot be reduced to the analytic justification debates, however, and Plantinga develops in this major part of his work a coherent and cogent realist conception of knowledge worthy of study for its own sake. Even if this aspect of the trilogy of warrant has been neglected in the context of analytic philosophy, it opens rewarding philosophical perspectives that may come to the aid of the ensuing attempt to construe a viable realist conception of theology.

The aim of this section is therefore to study Plantinga's theory of warrant and to show how it contributes to the development of a philosophical model for a realist conception of knowledge. In order to do this, I first work on three key concepts upon which Plantinga's theory relies (2.1). I then put forward Plantinga's argumentative strategy, which invites the reader to move progressively from a naturalistic epistemology to a supernaturalist metaphysics (2.2). Finally, I devote attention to Plantinga's more recent work, *Where the Conflict Really Lies*, and show how this book develops important theistic metaphysical themes in the perspective of the theory of warrant (2.3).

2.1 Warrant, Proper Function, and Design Plan
In the Preface to *Warrant and Proper Function*, Plantinga explicitly refers to the definition of knowledge found in Plato's *Theaetetus* while formulating his introductory statement: "What is this elusive quality or quantity enough of which, together with truth and belief, is sufficient for knowledge? Call that quantity, whatever it is, 'warrant.'"[16] The overall aim of *Warrant and Proper Function* is to reach a description that is as precise as possible of what "warrant" is.[17] Plantinga starts with two important

---

15 For a good presentation of Plantinga's work on warrant in the context of the post-Gettier epistemological debates, see chapters 3 and 5 of James Beilby, *Epistemology as Theology. An Evaluation of Alvin Plantinga's Religious Epistemology* (Burlington: Ashgate, 2005).

16 Plantinga, *Warrant and Proper Function*, v. Since the scope of the first book of the trilogy, *Warrant: The Current Debate*, is beyond this present research, I have concentrated attention on the second book, in which Plantinga develops in a positive way his theory of knowledge.

17 Much has been published on Plantinga's definition of warrant and its related concepts. See, among others, these valuable contributions: "Book Symposium on *Warrant: The Current Debate* and *Warrant and Proper Function*," *Noûs* 1 (1993), 34-82; "Book Symposium on *Warrant: The Current Debate* and *Warrant and Proper Function*,"

introductory chapters, in which he works on defining the following three concepts: *warrant, proper function* and *design plan*. While doing this, he draws the main lines of his theory of warrant. He then devotes the next eight chapters to a precise description and discussion of how we can effectively form warranted beliefs, that is, how human beings concretely know things about themselves and the world. Finally, the last two chapters of this book invite the reader to move from a mere epistemological description to the deeper metaphysical structure that underlies the theory of warrant.

I start by presenting the three above-mentioned concepts. Even if Plantinga acknowledges that it is probably not possible to give a univocal definition of *warrant*—reality is too complex for this[18]—he devotes numerous pages to describing the main components of warrant and explaining why they are important. At the end of the book, we find the most complete definition:

> According to the central and paradigmatic core of our notion of warrant (so I say) a belief B has warrant for you if and only if (1) the cognitive faculties involved in the production of B are functioning properly [...]; (2) your cognitive environment is sufficiently similar to the one for which your cognitive faculties are designed; (3) the triple of the design plan governing the production of the belief in question involves, as purpose or function, the production of true beliefs (and the same goes for elements of the design plan governing the production of input beliefs to the system in question); and (4) the design plan is a good one: that is, there is a high statistical or objective probability that a belief produced in accordance with the relevant segment of the design plan in that sort of environment is true. Under these conditions, furthermore, the degree of warrant is given by some monotonically increasing function of the strength of S's belief that B. This account of warrant, therefore, depends essentially upon the notion of proper function.[19]

Philosophy and Phenomenological Research 2 (1995), 393-464; *Warrant in Contemporary Epistemology. Essays in Honor of Plantinga's Theory of Knowledge*, ed. Jonathan L. Kvanvig (Lanham: Rowman and Littlefield Publishers, 1996).

18 Plantinga interestingly states in *Warrant and Proper Function* (ix) that it is hard to break down the concept of warrant into a clearly defined number of necessary and sufficient conditions that must apply. Yet it is possible to distinguish unambiguous cases of warranted true belief from borderline cases, where we may just have something analogically related to warrant. Like Bavinck, Plantinga seems to employ an organic or synthetic method of reasoning here.

19 Plantinga, *Warrant and Proper Function*, 194.

This definition encapsulates all the significant elements of Plantinga's theory of knowledge. The first part of the definition is focused on the knowing subject, the second on the cognitive environment, and the last two delineate the general structure of human cognition. The fact that only the first criterion is devoted to the knowing subject shows how distant Plantinga's externalism is from any form of internalism, epistemological subjectivism, or idealism. These epistemological traditions indeed devote the most attention to the cognitive structure of the subject. Furthermore, the realist character of knowledge which flows from this definition is obvious: if one indeed tried to interpret these four criteria from an anti-realist perspective, one would immediately fall into irrelevancy.

Plantinga's definition also introduces two central and deeply interconnected concepts: *proper function* and *design plan*. He devotes the very first section of *Warrant and Proper Function* to defining the concept of *proper function*. He notices that this concept is frequently and unambiguously used while talking about technical devices ("my TV is functioning properly"), or about bodily organs ("my heart is functioning properly"). Plantinga's thesis, which is more original and risky in the field of epistemological studies, is that this concept of proper function may also be employed in a cogent way while dealing with human knowledge:

> A necessary condition of a belief's having warrant for me is that my cognitive equipment, my belief-forming and belief-maintaining apparatus or powers, be free of [...] malfunction. A belief has warrant for you only if your cognitive apparatus is functioning properly, working the way it ought to work, in producing or sustaining it.[20]

Plantinga recognizes that proper function is necessary but not sufficient for human beings to develop warranted beliefs. Therefore, he goes further and notices that proper function can be understood only from the perspective of a *design plan*. A device or an organ can function properly only if it has been designed to function in such a way (otherwise the concepts of proper function and dysfunction are void). He states:

> Human beings are constructed according to a certain design plan. This terminology does not commit us to supposing that human beings have

---

20 Plantinga, *Warrant and Proper Function*, 4. This concept of proper function is so important that Plantinga has sometimes named his theory "the theory of proper function." See *Warrant: The Current Debate*, viii.

been literally designed—by God, for example. Here I use "design" the way Daniel Dennett (not ordinarily thought unsound on theism) does in speaking of a given organism as possessing a certain design, and of evolution as producing optimal design.[21]

According to Plantinga, a part of this design plan, when applied to human beings, is aimed at the production of true beliefs about ourselves and the external world.[22] Major sections of *Warrant and Proper Function* are devoted to the illustration and the defense of this much-debated idea.[23]

I finally stress Plantinga's insistence on the naturalistic character of his epistemological theory. The reference to naturalism is obvious in the previous quotation and appears frequently in *Warrant and Proper Function*. Since the concept of "naturalism" is highly polysemic, Plantinga proposes a definition that clarifies how he employs it here:

> The account of warrant I propose is an example of *naturalistic* epistemology: it invokes no kind of normativity not to be found in the natural sciences; the only kind of normativity it invokes figures in such sciences as biology and psychology.[24]

---

21 Plantinga, *Warrant and Proper Function*, 13.
22 Plantinga states on page 14 of *Warrant and Proper Function*: "The purpose of the heart is to pump blood; that of our cognitive faculties (overall) is to supply us with reliable information: about our environment, about the past, about the thoughts and feeling of others, and so on."
23 Plantinga is far from being naïve and he is fully aware of the difficulties raised by such a thesis. Many scholarly critics of Plantinga's theory have strongly attacked this facet of his argument. Plantinga nevertheless defends his use of the concept of design plan: "While the notions of proper function and design plan are clear enough when it is artifacts of which we speak, they do not apply as clearly to natural organisms and their parts. [...] Now it must be conceded that the notions of purpose, design plan, proper function, damage, and their colleagues are most at home in thought about artifacts, machines, and other devices that have been designed and constructed by such conscious, purposeful agents as human beings. [...] Still, we certainly do apply this whole family of concepts to the natural world. [...] The notions of proper function, disease, and damage apply here and in a thousand other contexts; thinking in these terms is natural and apparently unavoidable for human beings." (Plantinga, *Warrant and Proper Function*, 195-196).
24 Plantinga, *Warrant and Proper Function*, 194. This definition of naturalism is quite common nowadays and close to that found in contemporary dictionaries of philosophy. I nevertheless think that Plantinga employs this concept in a more Aristotelian way than he seems to admit here. In *Warrant: The Current Debate* (134ff.) and in *Warranted Christian Belief* (109ff.), he develops the concept of "Aristotelian Rationality." I hold that this concept enlightens his reference to "naturalistic epistemology" as well as "supernatural metaphysics" (see the next subsection of this

The way Plantinga refers to the concept of naturalism in this context is limited to its epistemological or methodological dimension. Contrary to what will be presented in the next subsection, it is not to be understood from a metaphysical or "worldview" perspective.[25]

Plantinga's insistence on the naturalistic character of his epistemological work may surprise at first sight, or be perceived as slightly insincere, but it is of great interest in the perspective of this present research. Like Bavinck, who explicitly refers to Aristotelian realism in his *Reformed Dogmatics*, Plantinga does not understand his epistemological work as acceptable to theistic thinkers only. He even provokes his theistic readers by affirming that "the most plausible way to think of warrant, from a theistic perspective, is in terms of naturalistic epistemology."[26] This methodological approach will influence the elaboration of my overall argument.

2.2 From Naturalistic Epistemology to Supernatural Metaphysics

Having devoted the core of *Warrant and Proper Function* to the careful description of a naturalistic theory of warrant based on concepts such as proper function and design plan, Plantinga enlarges the scope of his thought in the last two chapters. In these pages, he seeks to discover which metaphysical conception of the world fits best with his epistemological theory of warrant. This transition is due to the fact that Plantinga does not consider epistemology as an absolutely independent discipline. In a classical way, he thinks that there is an "intimate connection between epistemology and metaphysics,"[27] since basic epistemological

---

chapter) in a very interesting way. Plantinga indeed seems to employ the concept of naturalism against the background of the Aristotelian "nature." From this perspective, Plantinga's naturalism is based on a human nature characterized by a rationality that is able "to form concepts, grasp propositions, see relationships between them, think about objects both near and far" (*Warrant: The Current Debate*, 134). This understanding of naturalism has very little to do with the modern one based on undifferentiated laws known by the physical sciences, which apply to all things, including humans in their cognitive activity.

25 Plantinga refers to the metaphysical or worldview dimension of naturalism (everything is composed of natural entities) in the already quoted programmatic articles, especially when he deals with cultural criticism. He then speaks of *perennial naturalism*. He also uses the term in a metaphysical way on page ix of *Where the Conflict Really Lies*: "I take naturalism to be the thought that there is no such person as God, or anything like God. [...] Naturalism is what we could call a worldview, a sort of total way of looking at ourselves and our world."
26 Plantinga, *Warrant and Proper Function*, 46.
27 Plantinga, *Warrant and Proper Function*, 183.

affirmations depend directly on metaphysical assertions about human beings and external reality.

Plantinga sums up his core thesis on the metaphysics of warrant in a striking way: "The right way to be a naturalist in epistemology is to be a supernaturalist in metaphysics."[28] The paradoxical and provocative character of this thesis is typical of Plantinga, and has to be interpreted as a part of a wider strategy that starts with doing serious academic philosophical work before showing that the conclusions of this work are probably far more compatible with a theistic worldview rather than with rival worldviews (and particularly naturalism).[29] In this subsection, I first show how Plantinga argues that his theory of warrant is probably incompatible with metaphysical naturalism. I then show his argument that it is, on the contrary, much more congruent with a theistic worldview.

While introducing the question of the relation between the proposed theory of warrant and metaphysical naturalism in chapter 11 of *Warrant of Proper Function*, Plantinga raises the following issue: "The real question is whether there is a satisfactory *naturalistic* explanation or analysis of the notion of proper function."[30] His answer, which is the result of two decades' work, is negative.[31] The name of the argument that justifies the negative answer is *The Evolutionary Argument Against Naturalism* (EAAN) and is summed up as follows in *Warrant and Proper Function*:

---

28 Plantinga, *Warrant and Proper Function*, 211.
29 As we have seen, in his programmatic articles Plantinga mentions three main rival worldviews: theism, naturalism, and creative anti-realism. In *Warrant and Proper Function*, he does not seem very interested in anti-realism. He devotes a couple of pages to fictionalist interpretations of proper function and design plan and concludes: "These antirealist stances are refined and highly sophisticated—in fact a bit contorted. And, like all unnatural stances, they become awkward and uncomfortable if held for any length of time. If in one way a fiction can help you understand a phenomenon, in another it can harm your understanding of it" (Plantinga, *Warrant and Proper Function*, 213-214).
30 Plantinga, *Warrant and Proper Function*, 198.
31 The "definitive" version of the argument can be found in *Where the Conflict Really Lies* (chapter 10, pages 307ff). The following articles are more or less contemporary with the redaction of *Warrant and Proper Function* and bring us back to the genesis of the argument: "Justification and Theism," *Faith and Philosophy* 4 (1987), 403-426; "Positive Epistemic Status and Proper Function," in *Philosophical Perspectives 2: Epistemology*, ed. James E. Tomberlin (Atascadero: Ridgeview Publishing, 1988); "Justification in the 20th Century," *Philosophy and Phenomenological Research*, Supplement (Fall 1990), 45-71; "An Evolutionary Argument Against Naturalism," *Logos* 12 (1991), 27-49; "Warrant and Designing Agents: A Reply to James Taylor," *Philosophical Studies* 2 (1991), 203-215.

If metaphysical naturalism and this evolutionary account are both true, then our cognitive faculties will have resulted from blind mechanisms like natural selection, working on such sources of genetic variation as random genetic mutation. Evolution is interested, not in true belief, but in survival or fitness. It is therefore unlikely that our cognitive faculties have the production of true belief as a proximate or any other function, and the probability of our faculties' being reliable (given naturalistic evolution) would be fairly low.[32]

Stated differently, the conclusion of the argument is that "if, as it looks, it is in fact impossible to give an account of proper function in naturalistic terms, then metaphysical naturalism and naturalistic epistemology are at best uneasy bedfellows."[33] The metaphysical naturalist is thus in a philosophically weak position, since he is unable to propose a cogent account of how he gains knowledge of himself and of external reality.

One might notice here Plantinga's probabilistic or conditional strategy, which is part of his philosophical method. He does not suggest that it is logically wrong to adhere simultaneously to the theory of warrant and to metaphysical naturalism. Instead he states that the probability that both are true is "fairly low" (probabilistic argument), or that "if" the theory of warrant is true, "then" metaphysical naturalism is very likely false (conditional or modal argument).[34] In one of his programmatic articles, he carefully develops why he thinks that this method is a core element of the work of the philosopher.[35] As this method also appears in *Warranted*

---

32 Plantinga, *Warrant and Proper Function*, 219.
33 Plantinga, *Warrant and Proper Function*, 211.
34 Plantinga's strategy is not without tension. By adopting a probabilistic or conditional argument, he gives his reader the ultimate freedom to adhere to the proposed argument or not. Nevertheless, it is easy to find in *Warrant and Proper Function* affirmations that show that Plantinga is convinced, beyond probability or conditionality, of the *truth* of theistic metaphysics. For instance, one can read in the very conclusion of *Warrant and Proper Function*, on page 237: "Naturalistic epistemology conjoined with naturalistic metaphysics leads *via* evolution to skepticism or to violation of canons of rationality; conjoined with theism it does not." One can also observe behind Plantinga's strategy the adoption of a theistic understanding of evolution, which allows him to combine naturalist epistemology and theistic metaphysics. See *Where the Conflict Really Lies*, Part III.
35 In a long treatise on faith and reason in the Thomistic and Augustinian traditions, Plantinga develops his thinking on what he calls "knowledge of the conditionals." Beyond the contextual character of these paragraphs, I believe that he unveils a crucial component of his method and how he perceives his work as a philosopher. Alvin Plantinga, "Augustinian Christian Philosophy," *The Monist* 3 (1992), 316-317. In this article, he calls the deliverances of faith "F," and their rational consequences "FS." After

Christian Belief and raises an important question in relation to realism issues, I will address it in the last section of this chapter.

Having shown that metaphysical naturalism does not fit with his naturalistic epistemological theory of warrant, Plantinga develops the apparently paradoxical idea that a supernaturalist theistic metaphysics can give a much better account of the way human beings know things about themselves and external reality: "Naturalism in epistemology can flourish only in the context of supernaturalism in metaphysics."[36] As in Socratic dialogues, it is not always the most obvious solution to a problem that is true, and it is precisely the task of the philosopher to help the reader move from *doxa* to *episteme*.

The core of Plantinga's argument in favor of a theistic supernaturalist metaphysics is that, unlike naturalism, it is perfectly able to give a sensible account of the way one gains knowledge. Plantinga doesn't try to prove directly the veracity of theism, as is often done in traditional apologetics, and neither does he attempt to prove the falsity of naturalism. He argues instead that if the naturalist theory of warrant he has developed all through *Warrant and Proper Function* is correct, it is then highly probable that a theistic metaphysical worldview is also. Plantinga here uses the same probabilistic or conditional method, but in a reverse way.

The first step in Plantinga's argument in favor of metaphysical theism is to highlight why theists are familiar with the application of concepts such as proper function or design plan to natural beings (and not only to specific organs or technological devices):

> The bulk of mankind [...] has applied the notions of purpose and proper function to natural organisms, and has done so without any confusion or incoherence at all: for most human beings have thought that natural organisms and their parts *are*, in fact, designed. Most human beings *now* think so; certainly theists of all stripes do. And from a theistic point of view, of course, there is no problem here at all. From a theistic perspective there is no problem in applying these notions to natural organisms, for (from that perspective) natural organisms have indeed been designed by a conscious and intentional designer: God. From a theistic point of view,

---

insisting that working on "FS" is not doing theology, but philosophy, sociology, or any discipline for which the deliverances of faith may have consequences, he concludes as follows: "Perhaps it doesn't greatly matter whether we say that asserting those consequents is theology, on the one hand, or philosophy, psychology or economics or whatever on the other. What *is* of great importance, at present, is that we work at discovering and developing our knowledge of the conditionals" (317).

36 Plantinga, *Warrant and Proper Function*, 194.

human beings, like cathedrals and Boeing 747s, have been designed; we might say that they are divine artifacts.[37]

The argument is based on an analogy: just as a technical device is designed by a human rational agent, so human beings (as well as other natural organisms) can be considered designed by a divine intelligence. If the theory of warrant is true—if concepts such as proper function or design plan contribute to a cogent account of human knowledge—then one is naturally invited to complete the analogical square and admit the idea of a divine intelligence within the field of thought.[38]

The second step of Plantinga's argument in favor of a theistic foundation for his theory of warrant consists in the idea that human beings are designed by a divine intelligence to be *knowing beings*. From this perspective, the capacity of human beings to know something about themselves and the world is not an accident but a part of a wider design plan. In order to develop this idea, Plantinga introduces the classical theological concept of the *imago Dei* and explains how it fits in with his overall project:

> In setting out to create human beings in his image, then, God set out to create *rational* creatures: creatures with reason or *ratio*; creatures who reflect his capacity to grasp concepts, entertain propositions, hold beliefs, envisage ends, and act to accomplish them. Furthermore, he proposed to create creatures who reflect his ability to hold *true* beliefs. [...] From this perspective it is easy enough to say what it is for our faculties to be working properly: they are working properly when they are working in the way they were intended to work by the being who designed and created both them and us.[39]

---

37 Plantinga, *Warrant and Proper Function*, 196-197.
38 On page 214 of *Warrant and Proper Function*, Plantinga formulates this invitation to move from his theory of warrant to theism as follows: "Suppose [...] you are convinced (as most of us are) that there really is such a thing as warrant and really are (for natural organisms) such things as proper function, damage, design, dysfunction, and all the rest. [...] Then if you also think there is no naturalistic analysis of these notions, what you have is a powerful argument against naturalism. Given the plausible alternatives, what you have, more specifically, is a powerful theistic argument; indeed, what you have is a version of Thomas Aquinas's Fifth Way." Aquinas' Fifth Way is based on Aristotle's final cause and its conclusion is formulated as follows: "Everything in nature, therefore, is directed to its goal by someone with intelligence, and this we call 'God.'" Thomas Aquinas, *Summa Theologiae* Ia.I.2, trans. T. McDermott (Garden City: Image Books/Doubleday, 1969), 70.
39 Plantinga, *Warrant and Proper Function*, 197.

The understanding of human beings as created in God's image is a classical theme of theological anthropology.[40] The introduction of the concept of the *imago Dei* in *Warrant and Proper Function* may surprise the reader and requires some comment. First, one should notice that the introduction of this concept does not interfere with Plantinga's core epistemological work, since it appears in the last two chapters of the book, where he compares the compatibility of his theory of warrant with different wider worldviews. It is therefore not surprising to see Plantinga working with a theological concept while elaborating a theistic metaphysical perspective. Second, one should notice that Plantinga's use of the concept is influenced by classical philosophy and theology in putting forward the rational, intellectual capacities of the human being as a key element of what it means to be created in the image of God.[41] Human beings can acquire

40 For recent theological studies on the question of the *imago Dei*, see: Richard Middleton, *The Liberating Image. The Imago Dei in Genesis 1* (Grand Rapids: Brazos Press, 2005); J. Wentzel van Huyssteen, *Alone in the World? Human Uniqueness in Science and Theology* (Göttingen: Vandenhoeck & Ruprecht, 2006), 111-162. It is interesting to notice that Plantinga's reference to the *imago Dei* is much less discussed in the scholarly literature than his reference to another theological concept developed in *Warrant and Christian Belief*, the *sensus divinitatis*. This is probably due to the fact that these concepts are mainly discussed by theologians and philosophers of religion, who are more interested in the specific question of the knowledge of God (made possible by the *sensus divinitatis*) than in human knowledge in general (the *imago Dei*). From the perspective of current biblical scholarship (Middleton et al.), however, Plantinga's view of the *imago* as mainly consisting in our cognitive faculties can be questioned for not being in line with the intentions of the biblical writers.

41 While developing his argument on page 229 of *Warrant and Proper Function*, Plantinga interestingly quotes Thomas Aquinas: "Since human beings are said to be in the image of God in virtue of their having a nature that includes an intellect, such a nature is most in the image of God in virtue of being most able to imitate God" (*Summa Theologiae*, Ia, q. 93, a. 4). "Only in rational creatures is there found a likeness of God which counts as an image. [...] As far as a likeness of the divine nature is concerned, rational creatures seem somehow to attain a representation of [that] type in virtue of imitating God not only in this, that he is and lives, but especially in this, that he understands" (*Summa Theologiae*, Ia, q. 93, a. 6). These quotations can easily be read from the perspective of what has been said about Plantinga's "Aristotelian naturalism." From an Aristotelian-Thomistic point of view, human beings, created in the image of God, are *by nature* able to know him. This sort of naturalism is thus fully compatible with the affirmation of supernaturalist metaphysics. Plantinga's proposal is thus apparently paradoxical (naturalistic epistemology—supernaturalist metaphysics), but it is coherent when understood from the perspective I propose here. Fiona Ellis works along similar lines (even if it is from a perspective that includes Continental philosophers) when she proposes an "expanded naturalism." This sort of naturalism is aimed at overcoming the opposition between (scientific) naturalism and supernaturalism by including the humanities and even theology. See Fiona Ellis, *God, Value, and Nature* (Oxford: Oxford University Press, 2014).

real knowledge about themselves and external reality because they have been designed for this. And when our cognitive structure functions properly, it produces concepts and propositions that describe in an accurate way such an external reality.[42]

2.3 Where the Conflict Really Lies

Plantinga's main epistemological texts on warrant and proper function were published around 1990. He then gave a more explicitly Christian direction to his work in *Warranted Christian Belief* (2000), a book that will be studied in the next section of this chapter. Since the beginning of the twenty-first century, Plantinga has been increasingly involved in the American science and religion debate. This debate has become an important issue in the United States during this period, notably in terms of the educational question about the legitimacy of teaching literalist creationism, intelligent design theories, or naturalist evolution in natural science classes. Several important public pleas for a naturalist conception of science that would definitively put an end to any theistic belief sharpened the confrontation.[43] Plantinga has been strongly involved in this debate and is now considered an important spokesman within that field.[44]

This debate is not directly related to the scope of this research, but Plantinga's main science and religion book, *Where the Conflict Really Lies. Science, Religion, and Naturalism*, nevertheless contains ideas that are of great interest here. While *Warrant and Proper Function* is mainly research in academic epistemology with a transition towards metaphysical questions in the last two chapters, *Where the Conflict Really Lies* is a book

---

42 Yet Plantinga does not have a reductionist understanding of the image of God, since he does not limit it to intellectual faculties. On page 209 of *Warrant and Proper Function*, he states: "More generally, from a theistic perspective it could be true that many subsystems of our cognitive and affective systems have functions, and function properly, not because their functioning in that way promotes survival, but because it serves other ends; the possibility of a certain sort of knowledge, or of morality, or loyalty, or love, or a grasp of beauty, or something else." Even if Plantinga does not explicitly mention the image of God in these lines, it is quite easy to connect the content of this quotation to that concept.

43 See notably the books of Richard Dawkins, Daniel Dennett, Christopher Hitchens and Sam Harris.

44 Beside *Where the Conflict Really Lies*, see e.g. Alvin Plantinga, "Evolution and Design," in *For Faith and Clarity. Philosophical Contributions to Christian Theology*, ed. James K. Beilby (Grand Rapids: Baker Academic, 2006), 201-217; Daniel C. Dennett and Alvin Plantinga, *Science and Religion. Are they Compatible?* (Oxford: Oxford University Press, 2011).

that was written in a polemical context. The harsh nature of the debates led Plantinga to make his theistic metaphysical convictions even more explicit. The aim of this subsection is first to briefly clarify Plantinga's interpretation of modern science, and second, to study three important metaphysical stances he develops in the context of his wider argument—stances that are highly relevant from the perspective of the present research goal, viz. the elaboration of a viable realist conception of theology.

Plantinga presents his thesis in one sentence at the very beginning of *Where the Conflict Really Lies*: "My overall claim in this book: *there is superficial conflict but deep concord between science and theistic religion, but superficial concord and deep conflict between science and naturalism.*"[45] The book is structured in such a way that it subsequently discusses the four different facets of this overall claim. Here I devote attention to the *deep concord between science and theistic religion* part of the book (this topic is treated in Chapter 9). Plantinga's method is close to that employed in the last two chapters of *Warrant and Proper Function*. His use of concepts such as "theism" and "naturalism," as well as the premises and conclusions of his argument, are similar. The most important difference lies in the fact that Plantinga does not deal here with human knowledge in general, but with the natural sciences in particular. I shall now briefly present how he understands this specific area of human knowledge named "science."

From the very beginning of his book, Plantinga makes it clear how much he appreciates the development of modern science: "Modern science is certainly the most striking and impressive intellectual phenomenon of the last half millennium."[46] He further states that the "conflict between religion and science, from that perspective [of Christian theism], is initially anomalous, disturbing, perplexing."[47]

Plantinga's definition of science can be understood as a specification of his conception of knowledge developed by his theory of warrant. First, the aim of science is to gain knowledge of ourselves and of external reality:

> How shall we think of science? There are many opinions here. Realists think science is an effort to learn something of the sober truth about our

---

45 Plantinga, *Where the Conflict Really Lies. Science, Religion, and Naturalism*, ix.
46 Plantinga, *Where the Conflict Really Lies. Science, Religion, and Naturalism*, xi.
47 Plantinga, *Where the Conflict Really Lies. Science, Religion, and Naturalism*, 5.

world; instrumentalists think its value lies in its ability to help us get on in the world; constructive empiricists claim that its point is to produce empirically adequate theories, the question of the truth of these theories being secondary. Initially (and perhaps naïvely) the realists are right: science is a search for truth about ourselves and our world.[48]

Second, Plantinga perceives science as an extension of human common-sense knowledge. Unlike numerous Continental philosophers of science, he does not think that there is an epistemological break between these two forms of knowledge:

> Science, clearly, is an extension of our ordinary ways of learning about the world. As such, it obviously involves the faculties and processes by which we ordinarily do achieve knowledge. [...] What is involved in science is these basic ways of knowing; of course it is also true that by use of these basic ways we can construct devices and instruments (telescopes, electron microscopes, and accelerators, not to mention opera glasses) that vastly extend the reach of our ordinary cognitive faculties.[49]

These observations are important since they lead one to relate what has been studied in the previous subsection to the argument he develops in *Where the Conflict Really Lies*. There is indeed a mutually strengthening relation between these two parts of Plantinga's work. From an epistemological perspective, science does not provide us with some special access to knowledge, but is based on an extension of the normal ways in which humans acquire everyday knowledge. Thus, the epistemological conclusions Plantinga reaches in his Warrant trilogy also pertain to those most elevated means of human knowledge production: the natural sciences. Conversely, knowledge that is acquired through the sciences should be warranted in similar ways as everyday knowledge. In both cases, according to Plantinga, a couple of underlying metaphysical

---

48 Plantinga, *Where the Conflict Really Lies. Science, Religion, and Naturalism*, 266-267.
49 Plantinga, *Where the Conflict Really Lies. Science, Religion, and Naturalism*, 270. At this stage, one can observe the similarity between Bavinck and Plantinga's definition of science. Indeed, both defend a realistic and common-sense approach to science based on a sort of organic conception of knowledge. The main difference is largely cultural. Bavinck defines science in a broad Continental way that includes the *humanities*. In an Anglo-Saxon style, Plantinga affirms that science is an "effort with substantial empirical involvement" (*Where the Conflict Really Lies*, 268), a definition which leads to the identification of science with the *natural sciences*. Therefore, unlike Bavinck, he never speaks of theology as a science.

principles suffice to explain how knowledge can actually get off the ground. It is to an exploration of these principles that I turn in the following paragraphs.

In chapter 9 of *Where the Conflict Really Lies* (titled "Deep Concord: Christian Theism and the Deep Roots of Science"), Plantinga develops and proposes a theistic metaphysical justification of the following central thesis formulated in his preface: "[God has] created us and our world in such a way that there is a *match* between our cognitive powers and the world. To use the medieval phrase, there is an *adequatio intellectus ad rem* (an adequation of the intellect to reality)."[50] Human knowledge in general and science in particular are made possible, according to Plantinga, by the adhesion to three metaphysical stances that will be studied in the following paragraphs. The first idea has already been briefly presented in the previous subsection: human beings are in a position to know significant things about themselves and external reality since they are created in the image of God. The second idea is that the world is structured in an orderly way. The third and most basic idea is that there is a *match*, or an *adequatio*, between the cognitive structure of human beings and the structure of the world.[51] The reader will recognize in these three metaphysical stances important similarities with classical forms of metaphysical and epistemological realism as described in the introductory chapter of this book.

The first metaphysical (or anthropological) affirmation—that humans are created in the image of God (*imago Dei*)—has been presented in the previous subsection. I will nevertheless briefly quote a synthetic presentation of the theme, since it plays an important role in Plantinga's thought:

> This doctrine of the *imago dei*, the thought that we human beings have been created in the image of God has several sides and facets; but there is

---

50 Plantinga, *Where the Conflict Really Lies. Science, Religion, and Naturalism*, xiv.
51 In presenting these theistic metaphysical underpinnings, Plantinga is swimming in typical *natural theology* waters. The issue of natural theology has interested Plantinga all through his philosophical career. See among others: "The Prospects for Natural Theology," in *Philosophical Perspectives 5: Philosophy of Religion*, ed. James E. Tomberlin (Atascadero: Ridgeview Publishing, 1991), 287-316; "Appendix: Two Dozen (or so) Theistic Arguments," in *Alvin Plantinga*, ed. Deane-Peter Baker (Cambridge: Cambridge University Press, 2007), 203-227. For a discussion of the question of natural theology within the Reformed tradition, see Michael Sudduth, *The Reformed Objection to Natural Theology* (Farnham: Ashgate, 2009).

one aspect of it that is crucially relevant to the present context. This is the thought that God is a knower, and indeed the supreme knower. God is omniscient, that is, such that he knows everything, knows for any proposition p, whether p is true. We human beings, therefore, in being created in his image, can also know much about our world, ourselves, and God himself. No doubt what we know pales into insignificance beside what God knows; still we know much that is worthwhile and important.[52]

The formulation of this central idea is close to that found in *Warrant and Proper Function*. It is nevertheless more detailed in the way it insists on the propositional and realist character of human knowledge, including human knowledge of God. From Plantinga's perspective, far from being an obstacle to a metaphysical, epistemological and semantic realism, theism and its anthropology of the *imago Dei* is a solid foundation for such a view.[53]

The second important theistic metaphysical stance developed in *Where the Conflict Really Lies* is that God has created the world in a structured way, with order and regularity:

> The idea is that the basic structure of the world is due to a creative intelligence: a person, who aimed and intended that the world manifest a certain character. The world was created in such a way that it displays order and regularity; it isn't unpredictable, chancy or random. And of course this conviction is what enables and undergirds science.[54]

Plantinga holds that it is strange for a theist to be opposed to science. Indeed, "for science to be successful, the world must display a high degree of regularity and predictability,"[55] and theism is the worldview that probably proposes the most cogent explanation for this regularity. One might notice that Plantinga distinguishes between regularity on the one hand, and necessity and determinism on the other. Since the world is not an emanation of the divine but a free creation, it is open to God's action

---

52 Plantinga, *Where the Conflict Really Lies. Science, Religion, and Naturalism*, 268.
53 In *Where the Conflict Really Lies*, Plantinga refers again to Aquinas' *Summa Theologiae*. On page 5, he also develops a more specifically Reformed distinction between a broad and a narrow image of God: "Some Reformed thinkers distinguish a broad image of God (as with Aquinas, including personhood, rational faculties, knowledge of right and wrong) from a narrow image (righteousness, knowledge of God, and holiness)."
54 Plantinga, *Where the Conflict Really Lies. Science, Religion, and Naturalism*, 272.
55 Plantinga, *Where the Conflict Really Lies. Science, Religion, and Naturalism*, 271.

and is contingent. This contingency forces us to examine how the natural world is actually structured—we cannot come to know it just by correct thinking (as various forms of rationalism hold).

While developing the concept of regularity, Plantinga makes an important excursion into medieval philosophy. He indeed presents the classical opposition between Ockham's voluntarist and Thomas' intellectualist understanding of God. Against Thomistic intellectualism, Ockham emphasizes God's freedom in such a way that it becomes completely unpredictable. Yet if God is primarily characterized by an absolutely free will, "there is no guarantee that the world at some deep level is governed, or lawful; there is no guarantee that God's world is such that by rational, intellectual activity, we will be able to learn something about its deep structure."[56] Plantinga therefore adheres to Thomistic intellectualism and directly relates this to his understanding of an ordered world. He therefore does not seem to hesitate to do theology in the strictest sense of the term in order to justify the theistic worldview as an understanding of reality that is most compatible with the practice of science.

The third important theistic metaphysical stance developed in *Where the Conflict Really Lies* is that there is a match between human cognitive faculties and the structure of the world:

> God created both us and our world in such a way that there is a certain fit or match between the world and our cognitive faculties. The medieval had a phrase for it: *adequatio intellectus ad rem* (the adequation of the intellect to reality). The basic idea, here, is simply that there is a match between our cognitive or intellectual faculties and reality, thought of as including whatever exists, a match that enables us to know something, indeed a great deal, about the world—and also about ourselves and God himself.[57]

Plantinga refers to the classical definition of truth mentioned in the first chapter of this book to present his thoroughly realist conception of knowledge and science. Interestingly, from the perspective of this present

---

56 Plantinga, *Where the Conflict Really Lies. Science, Religion, and Naturalism*, 273-274.
57 Plantinga, *Where the Conflict Really Lies. Science, Religion, and Naturalism*, 269. Plantinga also applies this general idea to the specific question of scientific knowledge: "Part of the job of science is to discover the laws of nature; but then of course science will be successful only if it is possible for us human beings to do that. Science will be successful only if these laws are not too complex, or deep, or otherwise beyond us" (Plantinga, *Where the Conflict Really Lies*, 277).

research, he explicitly includes the knowledge of God in this overall metaphysical stance. This fact will play an important role in the elaboration of my proposal in the next chapter.

I conclude this section by stressing the fundamental similarities between the content of *Warrant and Proper Function* and that of *Where the Conflict Really Lies*. The three metaphysical stances of the latter can easily be related to the above-studied definition of warrant (§3.2.1). The first metaphysical affirmation is a reformulation of the first criterion of this definition (pertaining to our cognitive faculties); the second affirmation is a reformulation of the second criterion (pertaining to our cognitive environment); and the third affirmation is a reformulation of the third and fourth criteria of the definition of warrant (pertaining to the production of true beliefs as the purpose of a well-functioning design plan). What changes between the two works is their basic scope: in *Warrant and Proper Function*, Plantinga mainly describes the empirical manifestation of his proposal (in a naturalistic epistemological way), while in *Where the Conflict Really Lies* he develops a much more metaphysical approach.

This observation supports the coherency of Plantinga's work. There is indeed a deep complementarity between the content of *Warrant and Proper Function* and that of *Where the Conflict Really Lies*. On the one hand, it seems obvious that Plantinga's strong theistic metaphysical affirmations are rooted in his naturalistic epistemological theory of warrant. And on the other hand, these metaphysical stances extend in a consistent way the metaphysical content of the last two chapters of *Warrant and Proper Function*.

By way of conclusion, in Plantinga's view, what is going on in the sciences can best be understood as a special case of the "normal" functioning of our cognitive mechanisms directed at the acquisition of warrant: both the epistemological structure and the metaphysical underpinnings are the same. I now move on to Plantinga's exploration of another special case of human knowledge, viz. human knowledge of God.

3. Human Knowledge of God
The coherency of Plantinga's proposal is not limited to *Warrant and Proper Function* and *Where the Conflict Really Lies*. It also includes the third volume of the trilogy of warrant, *Warranted Christian Belief*, which is devoted to the question of human knowledge of God and the legitimacy

of the major affirmations of the Christian faith.[58] As Plantinga himself states at the very beginning of *Warrant: The Current Debate*, "the projected (but so far unwritten) third volume of this series, *Warranted Christian Belief*, will be an application of the theory developed in *Warrant and Proper Function* to Christian and theistic belief."[59] Seventeen years later, he reminds his reader, in the *Preface* of *Warranted Christian Belief*, that he has not forgotten this initial project:

> I go on [...] to offer a model, the Aquinas/Calvin (A/C) model, for theistic belief's having warrant [...]. Next [...], I propose the extended A/C model; according to this model, Christian belief is warranted because it meets the conditions of warrant spelled out in *Warrant and Proper Function*.[60]

The overall movement of the warrant-trilogy is thus made clear. First, Plantinga proposes a general theory of knowledge, the theory of warrant. He then provides a first development of the theory that includes theistic beliefs.[61] Finally, he goes further and presents a final extension of the theory of warrant which applies the entire system to specifically Christian beliefs. The whole theory is obviously characterized by continuity between its three main steps. There is no opposition in Plantinga's project between the "natural" content of *Warrant and Proper Function* and the "supernatural" content of *Warranted Christian Belief*.

---

58 On *Warranted Christian Belief*, see two book symposia: *Analytic Philosophy* 2 (2002), 81-135, and *Philosophia Christi* 2 (2001), 327-402. See also among others the following book reviews: Paul Helm in *Mind* 440 (2001), 1110-1115; K. Scott Oliphint, "Epistemology and Christian Belief," *Westminster Theological Journal* 63 (2001), 151-182; Richard Swinburne, "Plantinga on Warrant," *Religious Studies* 37 (2001), 203-214.
59 Plantinga, *Warrant: The Current Debate*, viii.
60 Plantinga, *Warranted Christian Belief*, xii.
61 Plantinga mentions in passing the knowledge of God in the context of his general theory of knowledge: "We should pause for a moment to marvel at the enormously articulate, subtle, and complex nature of our cognitive faculties. These faculties produce beliefs on an enormously wide variety of topics—our everyday external environment, the thoughts of others, our own internal lives (someone's internal musings and soliloquies can be complex and interesting enough both to him and others to be worth an entire novel), the past, mathematics and logic, what is probable and improbable, what is necessary and possible, beauty, right and wrong, *our relationships to God*, and a host of other topics" (Plantinga, *Warrant and Proper Function*, 42). The possibility of human knowledge of God is also occasionally mentioned in the science and religion works. Its full elaboration and substantiation, however, is to be found in *Warranted Christian Belief*.

In *Warranted Christian Belief*, Plantinga addresses what he identifies as *de jure* objections to Christian theistic beliefs. Plantinga observes that many of its critics do not attempt to falsify the Christian faith by demonstrating that it is untrue, but nevertheless hold that for some reason it is intellectually untenable. *De jure* objections are common ideas that lead people to think that Christian faith is epistemologically deficient, even though its falsity cannot be demonstrated.[62] In his answer to these objections, Plantinga's strategy is not to prove directly the effective truth of Christian belief. Unlike classical Christian apologetic works, he even leaves the truth question largely unaddressed: "What I officially claim for the extended A/C model is not that it is *true* but, rather, that it is *epistemologically possible* (i.e. nothing we know commits us to its falsehood)."[63] Thus, the conditional method studied above leads him to focus on the warrant of Christian belief rather than on its truth. His aim is to demonstrate, or at least to make plausible, that if Christian belief is true, it is also warranted—epistemologically there is nothing wrong with it. There is nothing irresponsible or intellectually substandard in adhering to it.

Even though questions of the *truth* and *warrant* of Christian belief are distinct, they are not totally separated: "If Christian belief is true, it very likely does have warrant; hence any objection to its having warrant will have to be an objection to its being true."[64] Therefore, if Plantinga's approach is successful, the critics of Christian belief should come up with *de facto* objections, objections against its factual truth, since *de jure* objections won't work. Plantinga devotes the first two parts of *Warranted*

---

62 Here is Plantinga's definition of *de jure* objections: "These are arguments or claims to the effect that Christian belief, whether or not true, is at any rate unjustifiable, or rationally unjustified, or irrational, or not intellectually respectable, or contrary to sound morality, or without sufficient evidence, or in some other way rationally unacceptable, not up to snuff from an intellectual point of view" (Plantinga, *Warranted Christian Belief*, ix). Plantinga distinguishes such *de jure* objections from *de facto* objections. The *de facto* objections directly address the truth-claim of the Christian faith.

63 Plantinga, *Warranted Christian Belief*, xii. Dewey J. Hoitenga interestingly states on page 227 of "Christian Theism: Ultimate Reality and Meaning in the Philosophy of Alvin Plantinga," in *American Philosopher's Ideas of Ultimate Reality and Meaning*, ed. Tibor Horvath (Toronto: U.R.A.M Regis College, 2000): "Notice Plantinga's strategy here: it turns out that any atheological objector has the greater burden of proof. All Plantinga needs to do is provide a plausible model of warrant, if Christianity is true. To show that his model of warrant (or any model of warrant) for belief in God is mistaken, however, the objector must prove that Christianity is false."

64 Plantinga, *Warranted Christian Belief*, 498.

Christian Belief to presenting and contesting the main arguments that underlie the various *de jure* objections to Christian belief (which in a generic way he calls the Freud-and-Marx complaint: the *F&M complaint*). In the last two parts, he applies his theory of warrant to human knowledge of God and to the central affirmations of Christian faith, aiming to show that the Christian faith indeed has warrant.

Warranted Christian Belief is an important work from the perspective of this present research. Even if it doesn't deal directly with theology as an academic discipline, its scope is related to questions belonging to the field of this inquiry. A careful study of chosen aspects of this work will help in developing the model in the last chapter of this book. Yet, it is important to note that Plantinga, remarkably perhaps, does not elaborate an *argument* or *case* in favor a of realist conception of the Christian faith and (by extension) Christian theology. Presumably this is for the same reason that prevented him from arguing directly for the *truth* of Christian belief. Conceiving of Christian faith and theology in a realist way seems so self-evident and unavoidable to him, that it is hard to defend by means of independent arguments. Instead, he can only (a) explain his realist stance as best as he can, and (b) rebut any objections that are brought forward against it. And that is exactly what Plantinga does. Leaving aside his rebuttals of counter-arguments, in what follows I concentrate on his more constructive work, which takes the form of a couple of "models."[65] In this section, I first study the application of Plantinga's theory of knowledge to theistic beliefs in general, namely the *A/C model* (3.1). I then present the second extension of his system, which deals with specifically Christian beliefs, that is the *Extended A/C model* (3.2).

3.1 The A/C Model *as an Extension of the Theory of Warrant*
I start by showing how the first model developed in *Warranted Christian Belief*, the *Aquinas/Calvin (A/C) model*, can be interpreted as an extension of Plantinga's general theory of warrant. First, I formulate two general preliminary remarks. Second, I present Plantinga's *A/C model* and show how it fits perfectly the criteria of warrant as presented in *Warrant and Proper Function*.

In the subsection devoted to *Where the Conflict Really Lies* (2.3), I presented Plantinga's realist conception of science based on the theory of warrant. *Warranted Christian Belief* starts with a similar realistic

---

65 It is for this reason that my proposal in Chapter 4 will also take the form of a model or account.

description of human knowledge, only this time specifically focused on knowing God:

> Christian belief involves not only that there is such a being [as God] but also that we are able to address him in prayer, *refer* to him, *think* and *talk* about him, and predicate properties of him. We have some kind of cognitive access to and grasp of him. [...]
> Furthermore, it must be possible, if I can think about God and predicate properties of him, not only that there be such a being but also that *my concepts apply to it*.[66]

From the very first page of the book, the reader is presented with a strong affirmation of a metaphysical, epistemological and semantic realist understanding of human knowledge of God.[67] One can thus observe deep realist continuity between Plantinga's general theory of knowledge, based on his theory of warrant, his understanding of the natural sciences, and his conception of the knowledge of God in particular.

The second observation to be made before turning to the *A/C model* is that, as in his theory of warrant, Plantinga unambiguously affirms the deep connection between epistemology and metaphysics, and even, in a classical way the precedence of metaphysics (including religious assumptions) over epistemology, when dealing with the question of the knowledge of God:

> What you properly take to be rational, at least in the sense of warranted, depends on what sort of metaphysical and religious stance you adopt. It depends on what kind of beings you think human beings are, what sorts of beliefs you think their noetic faculties will produce when they are functioning properly, and which of their faculties or cognitive mechanisms are aimed at the truth. Your view as to what sort of creature a human being is will determine or at any rate heavily influence your views as to whether theistic belief is warranted or not warranted, rational or irrational for human beings. And so the dispute as to whether theistic belief is rational (warranted) can't be settled just by attending to epistemological

---

66 Plantinga, *Warranted Christian Belief*, 3-4.
67 It is worth noting that in *Warranted Christian Belief* Plantinga struggles explicitly with the two major anti-realist trends described in the first chapter of this book. Thus, the thought of Gordon Kaufman is addressed in the second chapter of his book, and Lindbeck's postliberal theology is opposed at the beginning of the presentation of the concept of "faith" (see page 247).

considerations; it is at bottom not merely an epistemological dispute, but an ontological or theological dispute.[68]

This stance is important from the perspective of this research for two reasons. First, it provides the basic orientation of my interpretation of the work of Plantinga (see the next section of this chapter). Secondly, my Bavinck/Plantinga model will partly rely on such a conjunction of metaphysics, religious belief and epistemology (see the last chapter of this book).

Having presented these two important general observations, I move towards what Plantinga calls the *Aquinas/Calvin (A/C) model* of theistic beliefs having warrant.[69] The basic assumption of this model is that, just as we humans have belief-producing mechanisms such as perception, memory, introspection etc.—mechanisms which, if functioning properly, lead us to accept true beliefs of the relevant kind—we have also been equipped with a cognitive mechanism which, if functioning properly, leads us to accept true beliefs *about God*. This mechanism is traditionally called the *sensus divinitatis*, or "sense of divinity." Here is Plantinga's own description of this mechanism: "This capacity for knowledge of God is part of our original cognitive equipment, part of the fundamental epistemic establishment with which we have been created by God."[70] Why does Plantinga refer to Aquinas and Calvin in this connection? Because he holds that "Thomas Aquinas and John Calvin concur on the claim that there is a kind of natural knowledge of God (and anything on which Calvin and Aquinas are in accord is something to which we had better pay careful attention)."[71]

As indicated, a key-concept of the *A/C model* is the *sensus divinitatis*. Plantinga mentions this concept in *Warrant and Proper Function*, but he does not develop it in that context. As stated above, he instead works there with the idea of the *imago Dei* as he describes human beings as able

---

68 Plantinga, *Warranted Christian Belief*, 190.
69 Plantinga's use of the concept of *model* is very close to the method employed in *Warrant and Proper Function*. It indeed shows the same probabilistic coloration: "To give a model of a proposition or state of affairs S is to show how it could be that S is true or actual. The model itself will be another proposition (or state of affairs), one such that it is clear (1) that it is possible and (2) that if it is true, then so is the target proposition. From these two, of course, it follows that the target proposition is possible" (Plantinga, *Warranted Christian Belief*, 168).
70 Plantinga, *Warranted Christian Belief*, 180.
71 Plantinga, *Warranted Christian Belief*, 170.

to know something about the world.⁷² In *Warranted Christian Belief*, Plantinga affirms that the *sensus divinitatis* is a part of the wider *imago Dei*,⁷³ and that this specific part is particularly devoted to the production of some knowledge of God: "There is a kind of faculty or cognitive mechanism, which Calvin calls a *sensus divinitatis* or sense of divinity, which in a wide variety of circumstances produces in us beliefs about God."⁷⁴ One can observe a conceptual evolution from the use of the *imago Dei* concept in *Warrant and Proper Function* to that of the *sensus divinitatis* in *Warranted Christian Belief*. This move from one theological anthropological concept to another does not represent a break in Plantinga's thought, but is the expression of a will to use a narrower theological concept to deal with the specific question of the knowledge of God (and not only with the wider metaphysical explanation that humans are knowing beings).

My hypothesis that the *A/C model* is best interpreted as an extension of the theory of warrant is made obvious by Plantinga's use of warrant terminology when dealing with the *sensus divinitatis* as a belief-producing faculty. The following quotation strikingly applies the definition of warrant proposed in *Warrant and Proper Function* to the *sensus divinitatis*:

---

72 On page 48 of *Warrant and Proper Function*, there is nevertheless a passage in which Plantinga mentions the *sensus divinitatis* as a part of his project: "Our project for the next six chapters or so is a whirlwind tour of some of the main modules of our epistemic establishment: self-knowledge, memory, perception, knowledge of other persons, testimony, a priori knowledge, induction, and probability. I make no claim to completeness; indeed, I claim incompleteness, and that in two different directions. First, I shall stick to modules about whose existence there is fairly wide agreement. As I see it, however, there are other main modules, modules whose existence is a matter of controversy: there is our way of knowing moral truths, for example, as well as our means of perceiving beauty; and there is the *sensus divinitatis* of which John Calvin speaks, as well as what some theologians refer to as the Internal Testimony of the Holy Spirit."

73 See *Warranted Christian Belief*, 204. Plantinga introduces the abovementioned distinction between the broad and the narrow image of God, and includes the *sensus divinitatis* in the narrow image.

74 Plantinga, *Warranted Christian Belief*, 172. Plantinga's use of the *sensus divinitatis* has generated much secondary literature. See among others: Paul Helm, "Natural Theology and the *Sensus Divinitatis*," in *John Calvin's Ideas* (Oxford: Oxford University Press, 2004), 209-245; Georg Plasger, "Does Calvin Teach a Sensus Divinitatis? Reflections on Alvin Plantinga's Interpretation of Calvin," in *Plantinga's "Warranted Christian Belief,"* ed. Dieter Schönecker (Berlin and Boston: Walter de Gruyter, 2015), 169-189; Aleksandar S. Santrac, *A Comparison of John Calvin and Alvin Plantinga's Concept of* Sensus Divinitatis. *Phenomenology of the Sense of Divinity* (Lewiston: The Edwin Mellen Press, 2011).

The *sensus divinitatis* is a belief-producing faculty (or power, or mechanism) that under the right conditions produces belief that isn't evidentially based on other beliefs. On this model, our cognitive faculties have been designed and created by God; the design plan, therefore, is a design plan in the literal and paradigmatic sense. It is a blueprint or plan for our ways of functioning, and it has been developed and instituted by a conscious, intelligent agent. The purpose of the *sensus divinitatis* is to enable us to have true beliefs about God; when it functions properly, it ordinarily does produce true beliefs about God.[75]

Placing the question of human knowledge of God within the context of the theory of warrant leads to valuable observations. First, it confirms the idea that the *sensus divinitatis* as a belief-producing faculty, can be interpreted as an extension of the general theory of warrant. In Plantinga's mind, there is no opposition between knowledge of the world and knowledge of God. Second, it proposes a precise way of extending the general realist conception of knowledge that underlies the theory of warrant to the specific question of our knowledge of God. This transition is noteworthy, since one can adhere to the one without adopting the latter. Finally, it allows us to activate the *adequatio* epistemological theme mentioned in *Where the Conflict Really Lies* and apply it in an analogical way to human knowledge of God.

3.2 The Extended A/C Model

The *A/C model* may seem convincing and one may adhere to the idea that the *sensus divinitatis* can, in a natural and common way, generate accurate theistic beliefs. It is nevertheless obvious that theistic beliefs are far from being shared by everyone. The questions are therefore: if the *A/C model* is true, how does Plantinga explain that not all people develop theistic beliefs? Shouldn't the results of this model be more obviously universal? Plantinga doesn't miss the point and in order to address these questions,

---

75 Plantinga, *Warranted Christian Belief*, 179. It is interesting to notice that Plantinga refers to two lexical fields when defining the *sensus divinitatis*. The first is that of warrant, which is of direct interest in this chapter; the second is that of properly basic beliefs, which contributed to making Plantinga famous after the publication of his groundbreaking article "Reason and Belief in God" in 1983. This article is published in: Alvin Plantinga and Nicholas Wolterstorff (eds.), *Faith and Rationality. Reason and Belief in God* (Notre Dame: Notre Dame University Press, 1983), 16-93. From page 175 of *Warranted Christian Belief*, Plantinga explains why the *sensus divinitatis* produces beliefs that are not based on other beliefs, which corresponds to the shortest definition of what basic beliefs are.

develops a further model, calling this second extension of his theory of warrant the *Extended A/C model*. The aim of this subsection is to present this model and show how it can be understood as an extension of the previously-studied facets of Plantinga's theory of warrant.

First of all, here we are entering the thoroughly theistic supernaturalist part of Plantinga's work:

> The extended model will bear some of the earmarks of Reformed theology, but similar models can be constructed for other theological traditions. This model, incidentally, will essentially involve such theological notions as *faith* and the work of the Holy Spirit. Some may find it scandalous that theological ideas should be taken seriously in a book on philosophy; I find it no more scandalous than the ingression into philosophy of scientific ideas from (for example) quantum mechanics, cosmology, and evolutionary biology.[76]

We find ourselves here in the specific methodological context of the contemporary American analytic philosophy of religion described at the end of the first chapter of this book. Proponents of this approach do not hesitate to bring together philosophical and theological concepts in order to develop an overall argument. Plantinga's reference in these lines to Reformed theology is also interesting in the context of my proposal, since it is an explicit recognition of his Dutch neo-Calvinist (and therefore at least in part Bavinckian) spiritual heritage.

The *Extended A/C model* is built on a theological structure that plays an important role in modern Dutch neo-Calvinism, namely the so-called Creation-Fall-Redemption motif.[77] This motif proposes a three-stage description of reality as created by God, affected by sin, and finally restored by the work of Christ and the Holy Spirit. While the *A/C model* affirms that God has created the *sensus divinitatis*, the *Extended A/C*

---

76 Plantinga, *Warranted Christian Belief*, 200.
77 Herman Dooyeweerd was a great twentieth century promoter of this theological structure. It is interesting to notice that Plantinga knows the work of the Dutch philosopher and refers to it in laudatory terms: "Dooyeweerd's work was comprehensive, insightful, profound, courageous, and quite properly influential." (Plantinga, "Christian Philosophy at the End of the 20th Century," 30). This approach is still influential in North American Reformed circles influenced by Dutch Reformed thinking. See among others: Gordon J. Spykman, *Reformational Theology. A New Paradigm for Doing Dogmatics* (Grand Rapids: Eerdmans Publishing, 1992); Albert M. Wolters, *Creation Regained. Biblical Basics for a Reformational Worldview* (Grand Rapids and Cambridge: Eerdmans Publishing, 2005).

model develops how this *sensus* has been damaged by sin and can be restored by faith. In the following paragraphs, I explore Plantinga's presentation of the noetic effects of sin, and how he understands faith as a renewal and an extension of the original *sensus divinitatis*.

Plantinga refers to the theological concept of sin and its noetic effects in order to explain why not everybody believes in God, in spite of the *sensus divinitatis* implanted in every human being. He does not develop this question in a straightforward theological way, however. Interestingly, from the perspective of this interpretation of Plantinga's work, he once more uses the terminology of his warrant theory to describe the problem:

> Due to one cause or another, [a] faculty itself may be diseased and thus partly or wholly disabled. There is such a thing as cognitive disease; there is blindness, deafness, inability to tell right from wrong, insanity; and there are analogues of these conditions with respect to the operation of the *sensus divinitatis*.[78]

The concept of disability (or dysfunction) introduced in *Warrant and Proper Function* is applied here to the *sensus divinitatis*. Plantinga then goes on and presents what he considers the theological explanation of this epistemic dysfunction. He introduces the highly loaded theological concept of *original sin* and describes how this sin has disturbed the cognitive structure of human beings. Plantinga states:

> Original sin involves both intellect and will; it is both cognitive and affective. On the one hand, it carries with it a sort of blindness, a sort of imperceptiveness, dullness, stupidity. This is a cognitive limitation that first of all prevents its victim from proper knowledge of God and his beauty, glory, and love; it also prevents him from seeing what is worth loving and what worth hating, what should be sought and what eschewed. It therefore compromises both knowledge of fact and knowledge of value.[79]

According to Plantinga, both the will and the intellect are damaged by original sin. Given the aims of this present research, I am mainly interested in the effect of sin on human knowledge, which is called in a technical way the *noetic effect(s) of sin*.[80]

---

78 Plantinga, *Warranted Christian Belief*, 184.
79 Plantinga, *Warranted Christian Belief*, 207.
80 On the issue of the noetic effects of sin, see among others: Paul Helm, "John Calvin,

Plantinga suggests that sin has noetic effects on both the *imago Dei* and the *sensus divinitatis*. These realities are damaged in such a way that human beings lose the possibility of knowing God in a straightforward and unproblematic way. Plantinga even argues that we have to do here with "[t]he most serious noetic effects of sin" (214). Without sin and its consequences, we would know God in a spontaneous and obvious way, just like we know that other minds and physical objects exist. But cognitive faculties can get out of order, and that is what has happened with our *sensus divinitatis* as a result of sin.[81] According to Plantinga, this is why many people don't develop theistic beliefs. This answer nevertheless immediately raises new questions: if it is correct, how can we explain that a good number of people *do* develop theistic beliefs? Shouldn't knowledge of God be lost in all human beings? The following paragraphs present Plantinga's answer to these sorts of questions.

In accordance with the creation-fall-redemption motif, Plantinga claims that the cognitive damage generated by sin is not the last word of the story. Thus, after exploring the damage to the *sensus divinitatis* from original sin, and drawing on another locus of classical Christian theology (pneumatology), Plantinga describes its restoration by the supernatural operation of the Holy Spirit:

> Regeneration heals the ravages of sin—embryonically in this life, and with even greater fullness in the next. Just what are the cognitive benefits of regeneration? First, there is the repair of the *sensus divinitatis*, so that once again we can see God and be put in mind of him in the sorts of situations in which that belief-producing process is designed to work. The work of the Holy Spirit goes further. It gives us a much clearer view of the beauty, splendor, loveliness, attractiveness, glory of God. It enables us to see something of the spectacular depth of love revealed in the incarnation and atonement.[82]

In these lines, Plantinga mentions the two aspects of the Holy Spirit's work of restoration: the repair of the *sensus divinitatis* and the possibility of recognizing God's love as revealed in the incarnation and atonement.

---

the Sensus Divinitatis, and the Noetic Effect of Sin," *Journal for Philosophy of Religion* 43 (1998), 87-107; Stephen K. Moroney, *The Noetic Effects of Sin. A Historical and Contemporary Exploration of How Sin Affects our Thinking* (Lanham: Lexington Books, 2000); Rik Peels, "Sin and Human Cognition of God," *Scottish Journal of Theology* 64 (2011), 390-409.

81 Plantinga, *Warranted Christian Belief*, 214.
82 Plantinga, *Warranted Christian Belief*, 280-281.

The first aspect is a restoration of a damaged natural cognitive faculty; the second is a cognitive extension—faith—which allows human beings to grasp specifically Christian truths. While the first aspect can be understood in continuity with what has been studied in this chapter, the second introduces a new epistemological extension that deserves special attention.

The *sensus divinitatis* plays a crucial role in the *A/C model* and its description of natural human knowledge of God; *faith* plays such a role in the *Extended A/C model* and its description of supernatural knowledge of God. As faith is a much-debated theological topic, Plantinga clarifies the way he understands this concept. Unsurprisingly, he adopts the warrant terminology in stressing the cognitive dimension of faith:

> Faith is a belief-producing process or activity, like perception or memory. It is a cognitive device, a means by which belief, and belief on a certain specific set of topics, is regularly produced in regular ways. In this it resembles memory, perception, reason, sympathy, induction, and other more standard belief-producing processes. It differs from them in that it also involves the direct action of the Holy Spirit, so that the immediate cause of belief is not to be found just in her natural epistemic equipment. There is the special and supernatural activity of the Holy Spirit.[83]

Plantinga does not only describe faith as a "cognitive device"; he also adopts a semantic realist stance by insisting that faith has an inescapably propositional dimension:

> What one believes are propositions. To have faith, therefore, is (at least) to believe some propositions. [...] The propositional object of faith is the whole magnificent scheme of salvation God has arranged. To have faith is to know that and how God has made it possible for us human beings to

---

83 Plantinga, *Warranted Christian Belief*, 256. On page 257, he continues: "When these beliefs [Christian theistic beliefs] are accepted by faith and result from the internal instigation of the Holy Spirit, they are produced by cognitive processes working properly; they are not produced by way of some cognitive malfunction. Faith, the whole process that produces them, is specifically designed by God himself to produce this very effect—just as vision, say, is designed by God himself to produce a certain kind of perceptual beliefs." It is noteworthy that here again, as for the *sensus divinitatis*, Plantinga refers to the lexical field of basic beliefs by holding that the deliverances of faith are analogous to those of perception or memory. From page 258 of *Warranted Christian Belief*, he explains why he thinks that Christian beliefs can be understood as properly basic.

escape the ravages of sin and be restored to a right relationship with him; it is therefore a knowledge of the main lines of the Christian gospel.[84]

Faith as a supernatural extension of natural cognitive faculties allows human beings to formulate and accept propositional truths about God and his work of redemption.[85] Even if Plantinga does not call theology a science, I will show in the fourth chapter of this book that it is possible to refer to such a conception of faith and apply it to theology understood as a science.

In conclusion to this presentation of Plantinga's trilogy of warrant, I briefly stress its overall coherency, which is best interpreted from the perspective of what has been said of Bavinck's organic or synthetic method. Plantinga does not oppose common sense knowledge to scientific knowledge; he does not oppose either our knowledge of ourselves or of external reality to our knowledge of God. One can also underline the thoroughly realistic conception of knowledge contained in these works on warrant. Plantinga's realism is altogether metaphysical, epistemological and semantic. And it applies not only to the material world (scientific knowledge), but also to what can be said about God (the theological realm). The convergence between Plantinga's work, Bavinck's argument, and my proposal is thus progressively taking shape.

---

84 Plantinga, *Warranted Christian Belief*, 248. On page 244, Plantinga insists: "Faith [...] involves an explicitly cognitive element; it is, says Calvin, *knowledge*—knowledge of the availability of redemption and salvation through the person and work of Jesus Christ—and it is revealed to our minds. To have faith, therefore, is to know and hence *believe* something or other."

85 It is noteworthy that the *Extended A/C model* relies on two other theological concepts: "revelation" and the "internal testimony of the Holy Spirit" (see pages 242-243 of *Warranted Christian Belief*). I nevertheless do not develop these concepts in this chapter for two reasons. First, I have stressed the facets of Plantinga's argument that are necessary to the development of my proposal by presenting his understanding of faith. Second, Plantinga's understanding of the "faith and revelation tandem" is extremely close to Bavinck's reflection on the principles of theology described in the second chapter of this book. Several scholars have offered good global syntheses of Plantinga's *Extended A/C model*. See chapter 5 of Kevin Diller, *Theology's Epistemological Dilemma. How Karl Barth and Alvin Plantinga Provide a Unified Response* (Downers Grove: InterVarsity Press, 2014); or chapter 6 of Beilby, *Epistemology as Theology*; or chapter 2 of Cornelis van Kralingen, "A Study of Theological Responses to Alvin Plantinga's Aquinas/Calvin Model of Warranted Christian Belief" (PhD diss., Vrije Universiteit Amsterdam, 2018).

4. Critical Issues Related to Plantinga's *Extended A/C Model*

The last section of this chapter is devoted to the discussion of two critical issues related to Plantinga's trilogy of warrant. Almost every facet of the work of the American philosopher has generated academic debates and Plantinga studies are now very lively. In the following pages, I concentrate on two issues directly related to the scope of my research and that challenge the interpretation of Plantinga proposed in this chapter. By discussing these issues, I aim to defend a thoroughly realist Plantinga based on a unified reading of the trilogy of warrant. Therefore, I first deal with debates raised by Plantinga's conditional method and its relation to *truth* (4.1). Second, I discuss Kevin Diller's recent Barthian interpretation of Plantinga's work (4.2), since it raises fundamental questions in relation to the *Bavinck/Plantinga model for a realist conception of theology*, questions that I develop in the last chapter of this book.

4.1 Plantinga's "Unresolved Conditional" Method

A first important point of discussion flows from Plantinga's use of what K. Scott Oliphint calls an "unresolved conditional" method.[86] In the two previous sections of this chapter, I referred to Plantinga's use of a probabilistic or conditional argument, both in *Warrant and Proper Function* and in *Warranted Christian Belief*. In this context, the last lines of *Warranted Christian Belief* have perplexed many readers and raised many questions:

> But *is* [Christian belief] true? This is the really important question. And here we pass beyond the competence of philosophy, whose main competence, in this area, is to clear away certain objections, impedances, and obstacles to Christian belief. Speaking for myself and of course not in the name of philosophy, I can say only that it does, indeed, seem to me to be true, and to be the maximally important truth.[87]

Having developed a wide argument that repudiates the *de jure* objections to Christian faith and having shown that, if true, faith is warranted, Plantinga seems to leave open the crucial philosophical question of the *de facto* objections, which are those questions that challenge the truth of Christian belief. This debate is of first importance from the perspective of

---

86 I borrow the "unresolved conditional" formula from K. Scott Oliphint's article: "Review Essay. Epistemology and Christian Belief," *Westminster Theological Journal* 63 (2001), 151-182 (160).
87 Plantinga, *Warranted Christian Belief*, 499.

this present project, since I have affirmed that Plantinga defends a realist conception of knowledge that is altogether metaphysical, epistemological and semantic. If Plantinga leaves open the question of the effective truth of Christian faith, one can read him as a postmodern coherentist rather than a classical realist thinker, and the argument developed in this chapter threatens to fall down. I hold that Plantinga is not indifferent to the question of the truth of Christian faith and will justify this affirmation in this subsection. First, I present the argument of two Christian thinkers who have criticized Plantinga for leaving the question of the truth of Christian faith open.[88] Then I show how these critiques can be refuted in a convincing way.

I start with the critique of well-known British philosopher, Richard Swinburne. In his review of *Warranted Christian Belief*, he states:

> There is [...] a monumental issue which Plantinga does not discuss, and which a lot of people will consider needs discussing. This is whether Christian beliefs do have warrant (in Plantinga's sense). He has shown that they do, if they are true; so we might hope for discussion of whether they are true.[89]

Swinburne devotes the following pages of his review to clarifying his position. It rapidly appears that he is an internalist epistemologist.[90] He doubts that Plantinga's work on warrant and the *de jure* objection is significant and would prefer seeing him work on deciding whether Christian faith is "probably true, given our evidence."[91] From this

---

88 In relation to the general scope of this book, I only discuss here the affirmations of Christian thinkers. One should nevertheless be aware that agnostic or atheist readers of Plantinga are also concerned by the open end to *Warranted Christian Belief*. See for instance Evan Fales, "Alvin Plantinga, *Warranted Christian Belief*," *Noûs* 2 (2003), 353-370.
89 Swinburne, "Plantinga on Warrant," *Religious Studies* 37 (2001), 206.
90 "Despite what Plantinga seems to say, there is a clear and all-important question about whether a belief is rational (or justified) which has nothing to do with whether it is justified by the believer's own lights or with whether it is produced by 'properly functioning' processes. In a strong internalist sense, a belief of a person S is rational if it is rendered (evidentially) probable by S's evidence." Swinburne, "Plantinga on Warrant," 207.
91 Swinburne, "Plantinga on Warrant," 207. This evidentialist approach characterizes Swinburne's own work. See for instance a work that is indirectly related to the scope of this present research: Richard Swinburne, *Revelation. From Metaphor to Analogy* (Oxford: Oxford University Press, 2007).

perspective, the most important objections to Christian faith are the *de facto* objections and Swinburne laments that Plantinga ends his book as he does. This disagreement highlights the difference between Swinburne and Plantinga's understanding of the work of the Christian philosopher: the evidentialist approach that characterizes the work of the former is indeed radically opposed to the conditional method of the latter.

The second critique is formulated by the American Reformed theologian Scott Oliphint, already mentioned at the end of the previous chapter. In an article in which he claims that most of the modern discussions on faith and its relationship to reason are dominated by the thought of Kant, he interprets the last paragraph of *Warranted Christian Belief* as an illustration of his overall thesis. Just before quoting this paragraph, he suggests that Plantinga's limitation to the *de jure* question is a sign of his Kantian approach, which allows him to avoid the issue of truth.[92] Having cited Plantinga, Oliphint presents his radical interpretation of his Reformed colleague's work in a way that is worth quoting extensively:

> In keeping with Kant's emphasis, the truth question is a question that is "beyond the competence of philosophy." Elsewhere Plantinga says he "resists the temptation to make an excursion from the firm dry ground of epistemology into the misty miasmic morasses of metaphysics." So, Plantinga strikes the Kantian pose and argues for a rational theistic, even a rational Christian-theistic, belief, that itself does not address the question of truth, or the question of the nature of ultimate reality. It is rational, not because it squares with reality, but because we have other beliefs like it in our epistemological box, and so, if we add one more, no harm done. There is a decided aversion, if not a complete ignoring, of things metaphysical. Kant would only cheer such conclusions.[93]

According to Oliphint, the open end of *Warranted Christian Belief* unambiguously shows that Plantinga is ultimately a more-or-less disguised post-Kantian coherentist philosopher. This affirmation may surprise the

---

92 K. Scott Oliphint, "Using Reason by Faith," *Westminster Theological Journal* 73 (2011), 100. Kant famously argued that we cannot know the truth about noumenal reality.

93 Scott Oliphint, "Using Reason by Faith," 100. Oliphint's relation to the work of Plantinga is notably unstable. In 1995, he published a harsh critique of *Warrant and Proper Function* ("Plantinga on Warrant," *Westminster Theological Journal* 57 [1995], 415-435), while the abovementioned 2001 book review of *Warranted Christian Belief* is quite appreciative. Finally, this 2011 article is again very critical. For a synthesis of Oliphint's hesitations, see Van Kralingen, *A Study of Theological Responses to Alvin Plantinga's Aquinas/Calvin Model of Warranted Christian Belief*, 72.

reader of Plantinga, who openly refers, among others, to the works of Thomas Aquinas, John Calvin and Thomas Reid in the elaboration of his thought system.[94] It nevertheless presents the advantage of raising radical interpretative questions that must be addressed.

In *Epistemology as Theology*, James Beilby mentions that Plantinga's "construal of the task of religious epistemology has led him to focus nearly exclusively on negative apologetics and minimalist arguments."[95] He proposes a biographical explanation for this situation. Plantinga has admitted that when he worked at Wayne State University at the beginning of his career, he "was never able to get beyond a sort of defensive posture."[96] According to Beilby, Plantinga's entire philosophical work is marked by those years and that is the reason why "he does not address the reasons to think the Christian worldview is not only permitted but true, persuasive, compelling."[97] In the following paragraphs, I propose a more philosophical interpretation of his choices.

Plantinga himself has given an answer to Swinburne's critique along two main argumentative lines. First, he contests the affirmation that he is uninterested in the question of the truth of Christian faith (the *de facto* objections):

> It isn't at all that on my view believer and unbeliever (and fence sitter) cannot fruitfully discuss and dispute the question whether Christian belief is true and has warrant (but can only issue affirmations and counter-affirmations).

---

[94] Dieter Schönecker rightly states, "It should be noted that Plantinga himself always points out that there are predecessors such as Thomas Reid, Herman Bavinck and, of course, Calvin (and even Aquinas) who already developed some of the principal ideas involved in what has become Reformed Epistemology." See "The Deliverances of Warranted Christian Belief," in *Plantinga's "Warranted Christian Belief." Critical Essays with a Reply by Alvin Plantinga*, ed. Dieter Schonëcker (Berlin and Boston: De Gruyter Gmbh, 2015), 10. From the same perspective, Keith A. Mascord affirms: "Plantinga's position on the epistemology of faith is significantly similar to that of Thomas Aquinas." Keith A. Mascord, *Alvin Plantinga and Christian Apologetics* (Eugene: Wipf and Stock Publishers, 2006), 192. Plantinga himself states in *Warrant: The Current Debate*: "This account of warrant is in some ways similar to that of Thomas Reid; at any rate it is in the spirit of Reid's work (as perhaps also in the spirit of Aquinas and Aristotle)," (viii).

[95] James Beilby, *Epistemology as Theology. An Evaluation of Alvin Plantinga's Religious Epistemology*, 139-140.

[96] Alvin Plantinga, "A Christian Life Partly Lived," in *Philosophers who Believe. The Spiritual Journeys of 11 Leading Thinkers*, ed. Kelly James Clark (Downers Grove: InterVarsity Press, 1993), 65.

[97] Beilby, *Epistemology as Theology*, 141-142.

> In *WCB* [*Warranted Christian Belief*], [...] I devote some six chapters to just that project—the project of refuting arguments (both *de facto* and *de iure*) against Christian belief. To my mind this undertaking is of major importance (and one to which I've devoted much of my career).[98]

This quotation should be taken seriously, since it orientates the interpretation of Plantinga's entire philosophical work. From the perspective of this present research, it is a confirmation that he is, or at least seeks to be, a realist in the metaphysical, epistemological and semantic sense proposed. His use of the conditional method, or the distinction he makes between the *de facto* and the *de jure* objections should not be interpreted as a refined postmodern coherentist anti-realist stance. It is instead a methodological choice that can perfectly fit a wider, deeply realistic philosophical project. Plantinga is indeed able to adhere to a Christian theistic metaphysical intellectual frame while working simultaneously on the knowledge of conditionals, as he calls his exploration of various alternative thought systems: Plantinga's beliefs should not necessarily be confused with his philosophical method. I would add that this distinction is precisely what makes possible the practice of what he has described as the third and fourth tasks of the Christian philosopher (*Christian cultural criticism* and *positive Christian philosophy*).[99]

---

98 Alvin Plantinga, "Rationality and Public Evidence: A Reply to Richard Swinburne," *Religious Studies* 37 (2001), 217. There is an obvious confirmation of this claim in *Warranted Christian Belief*: "So the *de jure* question we have finally found is not, after all, really independent of the *de facto* question; to answer the former we must answer the latter. This is important: what it shows is that a successful atheological objection will have to be to the *truth* of theism, not to its rationality, justification, intellectual respectability, rational justification, or whatever. [...] This fact by itself invalidates an enormous amount of recent and contemporary atheology; for much of that atheology is devoted to *de jure* complaints that are allegedly independent of the *de facto* question" (191). This is the reason why Plantinga devotes all of Part IV of *Warranted Christian Belief* (about 150 pages) to defeating the main defeaters of Christian beliefs.

99 Still writing from a biographical perspective, Beilby stresses the importance of the publication of *God and Other Minds* and *The Nature of Necessity* at the beginning of Plantinga's career. These are two metaphysical books which explore the nature of possibility, necessity, and other modal distinctions. Beilby states on page 10 of *Epistemology of Theology*: "While *The Nature of Necessity* constitutes the most in-depth analysis of the metaphysics of modality in print and is arguably one of the most important works on metaphysics written in the last fifty years, for Plantinga it was a tool." I agree with this statement and hold that Plantinga's ability to work with conditionals as he does probably originates in these two books.

Plantinga's second line of argument consists in a clarification of a fundamental conviction:

> On my view, Christians can quite properly offer any arguments for the truth of Christian belief they think are appropriate. I doubt that these arguments are sufficient to warrant the firmness of belief involved in faith (as traditionally understood) but it doesn't follow that they have no use at all. On the contrary; they can be extremely useful, and in at least four different ways. They can confirm and support belief reached in other ways; they may move fence-sitters closer to Christian belief; they can function as defeater-defeaters; and they can reveal interesting and important connections. My claim here is only that such arguments are not *necessary* for justified, rational and warranted Christian belief.[100]

By answering Swinburne's critique as he does, Plantinga reaffirms his adherence not to postmodern antirealism, as one might think, but to the Augustinian *fides quaerens intellectum* philosophical tradition.[101] By leaving the truth question open at the end of *Warranted Christian Belief*, Plantinga does not display indifference or sloth. He simply recognizes the limitations of philosophy, as many theologians and philosophers before him (including Calvin and Bavinck) have done.[102] The bottom line of this approach is as follows: arguments and evidences for the truth of the Christian faith can play an ancillary role, but from an epistemological point of view they are not decisive.[103]

---

100 Plantinga, "Rationality and Public Evidence: a Reply to Richard Swinburne," 217.
101 IPaul Helm offers a good presentation of this philosophical tradition which includes a chapter on Plantinga (Chapter 8): *Faith and Understanding* (Grand Rapids: Eerdmans Publishing, 1997). This takes us back to Plantinga's programmatic article mentioned in the introduction of this chapter: "Augustinian Christian Philosophy."
102 Plantinga has become increasingly interested in natural theology arguments, yet he continues to adopt the same position as at the end of *Warranted Christian Belief*: "Theistic arguments are not needed for justification, or rationality, or, if true, warrant. But then what are these arguments good for? At least four things. First, they can move someone closer to theism—by showing, for example, that theism is a legitimate intellectual option. Second, they reveal interesting and important connections between various elements of a theist's set of beliefs. [...] Third, the arguments can strengthen and confirm theistic belief. [...] Finally, and connected with the last, these arguments can increase the warrant of theistic belief." *Alvin Plantinga*, "Preface [2006] to Two Dozen (or so) Theistic Arguments," in *Alvin Plantinga*, edited by Deane-Peter Baker (Cambridge: Cambridge University Press, 2007), 209.
103 In addition to Plantinga's direct answer to Swinburne, one might usefully refer to his already mentioned article "Reason and Belief in God," where he states that since belief in God is *properly basic*, the believer is "entirely rational, entirely within his

In conclusion, Plantinga is not indifferent to metaphysical or truth questions. His responses show that he indeed cares for an intimate relation between metaphysics and epistemology, and the importance he gives to the question of truth leads us to understand his work in a thoroughly realistic way. Using his work to propose a model for a realist conception of theology is thus legitimate and, as I aim to show in the last chapter, fruitful.

4.2 A Barthian Reading of Plantinga?
A recently published book deserves a special place in this discussion of critical issues. Kevin Dillers' *Theology's Epistemological Dilemma. How Karl Barth and Alvin Plantinga Provide a Unified Response* is of great interest in the context of this research.[104] He is working in the same field of research, and our methods of inquiry are similar. His book exemplifies the sort of fruitful work that can be done in the context of contemporary American analytic philosophy of religion. But even if I appreciate the clarity and the precision of Diller's argument, I contest his overall interpretative frame. If Diller's construal of Plantinga's *Warranted Christian Belief* is correct, it is impossible to interpret this work as a robust defense of classical realism in theology. I therefore devote the last subsection of this chapter to presenting and discussing it. I first briefly present Diller's interpretation of Plantinga's work, and then address the main debated issues. I end by showing why this difference in interpretation matters from the perspective of this present research.[105]

In the introduction to his book, Diller presents what he interprets as theology's epistemological dilemma. On the one hand, Christian theologians are required to adopt a high view of theological knowledge, since the Christian faith comprises strong belief claims that usually come with a high degree of epistemic confidence. On the other, they have to maintain a low view of all human knowledge claims, since the noetic part

---

epistemic rights, in *starting with* belief in God, in accepting it as basic, and in taking it as premise for argument to other conclusions" (72). It is noteworthy to stress here (and also from the perspective of the next subsection of this chapter), that already in 1983 Plantinga affirms that "one who holds this view need not to suppose that natural theology is of no use" (73).

104 Kevin Diller, *Theology's Epistemological Dilemma. How Karl Barth and Alvin Plantinga Provide a Unified Response* (Downers Grove: InterVarsity Press, 2014).

105 For two good general presentations of the content of Diller's book, see Rik Peels, "Kevin Diller. *Theology's Epistemological Dilemma: How Karl Barth and Alvin Plantinga Provide a Unified Response,*" *Journal of Analytic Theology* 4 (2016), 421-427; and Van Kralingen, *A Study of Theological Responses to Alvin Plantinga's Aquinas/Calvin Model of Warranted Christian Belief*, 73-90.

of our life (as well as all others) is deeply affected by sin.¹⁰⁶ Diller proposes a convergent reading of the works of Karl Barth and Alvin Plantinga in order to overcome this epistemological dilemma: "I contend that the mutually informed Barth/Plantinga theological epistemology provides a cogent, sustainable and philosophically nuanced solution to the core epistemological issues" that beset Christian theology.¹⁰⁷ Even if this thesis may surprise the reader versed in Barthian and/or Plantinga studies, since Barth is well-known for his total rejection of natural theology, whereas Plantinga (as we have seen) makes use of it, Diller's careful work is interesting and of heuristic value.

Diller's thesis relies on a radical interpretative choice that orientates *Theology's Epistemological Dilemma* in its entirety:

> [Plantinga] provides not just *a* model, but two models. The first is intended to show how generally theistic belief might have warrant. This model is extended into a second model, giving an account of how explicitly Christian belief could have warrant.¹⁰⁸

From Diller's perspective, the first model is Plantinga's *A/C model* with its *sensus divinitatis*, and the second model is the *Extended A/C model* with its supernatural concepts, such as faith, revelation, the internal testimony of the Holy Spirit, etc. On the following page, Diller unveils his radical methodological choice: "I will only be referring to Plantinga's argument with respect to his extended model for how specifically Christian belief may have warrant."¹⁰⁹ This choice is based on the following conviction:

> The A/C model is not a premise in an argument for theistic belief. And since, due to sin, the A/C model is dependent on and largely replaced by the extended A/C model, it is in fact the case that defending any role for the *sensus divinitatis* is unnecessary to Plantinga's wider argument. If Plantinga is right, there cannot be a warranted theistic belief that is not the work of the Spirit's giving birth to faith in Jesus Christ.¹¹⁰

This decision to interpret the *A/C model* as "largely replaced" by the *Extended A/C model* is important, since it isolates the *Extended A/C model* from the rest of the trilogy of warrant. Thus, *Warrant and Proper*

---

106 Diller, *Theology's Epistemological Dilemma*, 17.
107 Diller, *Theology's Epistemological Dilemma*, 22.
108 Diller, *Theology's Epistemological Dilemma*, 129.
109 Diller, *Theology's Epistemological Dilemma*, 130.
110 Diller, *Theology's Epistemological Dilemma*, 148.

Function and the *A/C model* are of little interest in the resolution of theology's great dilemma, and all the attention is to be focused on the theologically-loaded *Extended A/C model*. As a consequence of this fundamental methodological choice, Diller's work in bringing together the works of Barth and Plantinga is rewarding and makes possible the writing of numerous interesting theological pages on concepts such as faith, revelation, the work of the Holy Spirit, etc.

It is noteworthy that Diller does not avoid dealing with questions that may challenge his attempt to propose a unified reading of Barth and Plantinga. He devotes two entire chapters to the questions of the *sensus divinitatis* and the role played by natural theology in Plantinga's work. His decision to interpret the *A/C model* (which includes the *sensus divinitatis* and the arguments in favor of natural theology) as having been largely replaced by the *Extended A/C model* leads him to the conclusion that there is no serious opposition between Barth and Plantinga, even on these potentially tricky issues. Thus, after devoting his seventh chapter to the question of natural theology, Diller confidently concludes:

> If we understand the arguments of natural theology to function as catalysts to or extensions of the deliverances of faith, there is nothing independently natural about them. My proposal is not only that this gives us a way to understand Plantinga's notion of the positive role of natural theology in a way that does not conflict with Barth's theology of revelation or epistemological *sola gratia*. It also provides the best way to understand Plantinga's direct comments on the matter and their coherence with his wider corpus.[111]

According to Diller, there is thus no contradiction between Barth and Plantinga on the role of natural theology, and the *Extended A/C model*, isolated from the rest of the trilogy of warrant, meets the Barthian standards of "epistemological *sola gratia*."[112]

Diller then devotes Chapter 8 of his book to the notion of the *sensus divinitatis* and the nature of human knowledge of God. His conclusion is that there is concord between Barth and Plantinga on this question also:

> In my view, there is no glaring incompatibility here [i.e. regarding the *sensus divinitatis*] for Barth and Plantinga. Insofar as the *sensus divinitatis*

---

111 Diller, *Theology's Epistemological Dilemma*, 216.
112 I dealt with the important question of the interpretation of the five *solas* of the Reformation in subsection 2.2 of chapter 2.

operates independently of the personal, historical, transformative, reconciling action of God, it delivers only at best an affirmation of some true proposition *about* God. [...] The propositional knowledge delivered by a properly functioning *sensus divinitatis* is narrow and fails to disclose to us *who* God is.[113]

Diller's downplayed *sensus divinitatis*, which belongs, he believes, to the replaced *A/C model*, is sufficiently theologically meaningless to meet Barthian standards on the question of the human natural knowledge of God.

My evaluation of Diller's interpretation of the work of Plantinga is that it is flawed by a sort of argumentative circle and also by a historical misunderstanding.[114] I start my critique with what I understand as an argumentative circle. Having started his reading of Plantinga with a Barthian premise (the decision not to read the trilogy of warrant as a coherent whole, but from the perspective of the replacement of the *A/C model* by the *Extended A/C model*), Diller concludes his argument with the presentation of a Barthian Plantinga. If one follows the typology proposed in the first chapter of this book, Diller's Barth and Plantinga are both *radical theological realists* who agree that natural theology and the *sensus divinitatis* are quite meaningless from a theological point of view. I believe that this argumentative circle is the origin of the problem underlined by Rik Peels:

> It is hard to deny that Barth seems to suggest that natural theology ought to be abandoned altogether. This is a significantly stronger claim than Plantinga's assertion that natural theology isn't necessary to be rational, epistemically justified, or warranted in believing that God exists. Plantinga has become increasingly positive about the value of arguments for God's existence. In fact, his paper "Two Dozen (or so) Theistic Arguments," is one of the most cited papers on this point. This is something Diller fails to acknowledge or even misunderstands.[115]

---

113 Diller, *Theology's Epistemological Dilemma*, 259-260.
114 It is not without apprehension that I criticize Diller's thesis, since he has the *imprimatur* of Plantinga himself, who wrote a very short but appreciative "Foreword" to his book (11). I nevertheless believe that my conclusions are strong and that they are sufficiently important to be shared with the reader.
115 Rik Peels, "Kevin Diller. *Theology's Epistemological Dilemma: How Karl Barth and Alvin Plantinga Provide a Unified Response*," *Journal of Analytic Theology* 4 (2016): 425. On the value of the *sensus divinitatis*, Plantinga doesn't seem as pessimistic as

If one doesn't start from Barthian premises, one is in a better position to understand way the role played by natural theology and the *sensus divinitatis* in Plantinga's thought.

As Diller affirms, Plantinga indeed mentions two models in *Warranted Christian Belief*. Yet contrary to Diller's hermeneutical key, he doesn't oppose them or replace one with the other. Plantinga unambiguously affirms that his "extended model [...] will *complete and deepen* the previous account [the A/C model] of our knowledge of God."[116] This affirmation should not surprise, since the entire preceding presentation of Plantinga's trilogy of warrant has shown that it is constructed in a coherent and progressive way. Every new concept—and even the supernatural notions of the *Extended A/C model*—is presented against the background of the previously-defined elements of the wider theory. Plantinga's philosophical method has little to do with the oppositions on which Barth's dialectical thought is founded. As stated above, Plantinga instead consistently adopts a sort of Bavinck-style synthetic or organic method which seeks to tie together the different facets of his overall argument.

In addition to this philosophical critique, one might notice that Diller's thesis is also problematic from a historical point of view. He devotes interesting pages to the 1930s Barth-Brunner debate on natural theology and describes the two positions in a clear way.[117] I nevertheless hold that the situation is somehow ironical, since Diller does not seem to realize

---

Diller: "So according to Calvin, there is a natural knowledge of God. In a wide variety of circumstances—upon beholding the starry heavens above, when in danger, upon seeing that we have done something deeply wrong—we human beings find ourselves aware of God's presence, realizing that we owe him obedience and allegiance. We praise him for his glory, or ask for his help, or see him as disapproving. This is not a knowledge of God that depends upon regeneration or faith; it is a knowledge we have by virtue of our created nature. Of course it has been spoiled, suppressed, damaged by sin. We don't know God the way we would if there were no sin; if it weren't for sin, Calvin thinks, we would all believe in God with the same spontaneous and simple trust with which we believe in other human persons, our own existence, the past, and so on. *Still, we do have this natural knowledge.*" Plantinga, "The Twin Pillars of Christian Scholarship," 154 (italics mine).

116 Plantinga, *Warranted Christian Belief*, 242 (italics mine).
117 Diller interestingly states: "The uniqueness of God creates a problem for any revelation that moves from creation to Creator. In fact, the uniqueness of God is problematic for revelation in general. This problem is often discussed as a problem of theological reference or the problem of the inadequacy of human language and concepts for the knowledge of God. For Brunner, the solution seems to be found in the *imago Dei* as the point of contact for human beings." Diller, *Theology's Epistemological Dilemma*, 188.

that if one were to choose, one would rather relate Plantinga's work to that of Brunner than that of Barth. As Georg Plasger writes in conclusion to his article, "like Plantinga, Brunner also sees a continuity in humanity by virtue of our being created in God's image."[118] Diller's thesis is original, but I believe it lacks historical evidence.

I conclude this discussion by raising the core question that underlies this subsection: why does Diller's Barthian interpretation of Plantinga matter from the perspective of this present research? Diller rightly states that "Plantinga takes a fundamentally realist stance, affirming that there is a truth to be known about the world and about God."[119] I fully agree with this affirmation. I nevertheless hold that an important question flows from it: what *sort of* realist is Plantinga, or what sort of argument in favor of a realist conception of theology can be built upon his thought? This question matters from the perspective of my research, since it is important to know precisely upon which sort of realism I should build my own defense of a realist conception of theology.

If one were to read Diller's pages devoted to Plantinga's realism at face value, it would be necessary to affirm that "like Barth, Plantinga's view is properly understood as a kind of critical realism."[120] Diller obviously follows Bruce McCormack's interpretation of Barth here, which he then applies to Plantinga in a straightforward way. According to McCormack, Barth is a *critical realist* (in its *post-Kantian* meaning—see the typology in the first chapter of this book), since the Swiss theologian regularly insists on the *indirect* character of human knowledge of God. Without discussing McCormack's interpretation of Barth, even a rapid survey of Plantinga's work shows that it is impossible to interpret the trilogy of warrant from this perspective. I believe that the post-Kantian critical realist Plantinga is a mere chimera.

I would rather interpret Diller's Plantinga as a *radical theological realist*. By artificially isolating the *Extended A/C model* from the rest of the trilogy of warrant, Diller proposes a Plantinga who only works with strictly theological concepts while dealing with the question of human knowledge of God. This observation is confirmed by the following affirmation:

---

118 Plasger, "Does Calvin Teach a Sensus Divinitatis? Reflections on Alvin Plantinga's Interpretation of Calvin," 188.
119 Diller, *Theology's Epistemological Dilemma*, 110.
120 Diller, *Theology's Epistemological Dilemma*, 109.

> From the perspective of Christian theology these two models [the *A/C model* and the *Extended A/C model*] represent the classical though potentially distorting division between general and special revelation—the Book of Nature and the Book of Scripture.[121]

Diller's decision to concentrate on the *Extended A/C model* thus implies a will to focus on *special revelation* and the *Book of Scripture* and to abandon *general revelation* and the *Book of Nature* while doing theology. As noted previously in this book, these are unambiguous marks of radical theological realism.

I am contesting this interpretation, since I hold that Diller's approach is not necessary, even "from the perspective of Christian theology," and that it weakens Plantinga's overall argument by downplaying its coherency and its originality. The *Extended A/C model* is strong precisely when read against the background of the whole trilogy of warrant. An isolated *Extended A/C model* fits the post-Barthian theological standards, but weakens what makes *Warranted Christian Belief* an internationally recognized original work in philosophy of religion.

Finally, I believe that my reading of Plantinga's work makes clear that it is not only more relevant to relate Plantinga to Bavinck, but that the result of such an intellectual operation is also more valuable in light of the research question. It indeed leads to a consistent classical Christian argument in favor of a realist conception of theology. The last chapter of this book is devoted precisely to the positive exposition of this proposal.

---

121 Diller, *Theology's Epistemological Dilemma*, 129. By mentioning a "potentially distorting division," Diller indirectly refers to the Barthian critique of Article 2 of *The Belgic Confession of Faith*, which affirms that God can be known by two means, the creation and the biblical Scriptures. For a short presentation of this issue, see the section 5.3 of the second chapter of this book.

Chapter 4

A Realist Conception of Theology for the Contemporary Western Context

1. Introduction

Having introduced the context, the scope and the relevance of this research in the first chapter, before examining relevant facets of Bavinck and Plantinga's work in the second and third chapters, I am now in a position to propose a detailed answer to the main research question:

> In what ways might the conjunction of Bavinck's prolegomena to dogmatic theology and Plantinga's theory of warrant (with its theistic extensions) strengthen the contemporary case in favor of a realist conception of theology?

In this last chapter, I answer this question in a way that leads to a strong synthesized classical realist conception of theology for the context of contemporary Western philosophical and theological thought. More precisely, I show how the contributions of both Bavinck and Plantinga not only have many points of convergence, but also have some weaknesses that can be remedied by their synthesis. Thus, the *lacunae* that are visible in Bavinck's theory can be filled in by Plantinga's account, and vice versa.

This chapter is organized in three concentric circles. In the first main section, I bring together the content of the second and third chapters of this book, present the contours of a combined *Bavinck/Plantinga model for a realist conception of theology*, and show that there is an added value in bringing them together (2). I then show how this combined proposal interacts with existing contemporary defenses of a realist conception of theology. By going beyond the works of these two thinkers, the aim is to formulate cogent propositions that can enrich the current discussion (3). Thirdly, I adopt a more hermeneutical approach and question the wider meaning and issues raised by my proposal in the context of contemporary Western thought. Among other things, I extend the Bavinck/Plantinga synthesis and extrapolate from it by sketching the contours of a viable realist form of theology that is geared to our contemporary Western context, and that addresses the vexed question of the status of theology (4). Having done this, I briefly conclude by pointing to some further research avenues elicited by the results of the project (5).

2. The *Bavinck/Plantinga Model for a Realist Conception of Theology*

The aim of this section is to reap what has been sown in the two previous chapters by drawing the contours of a *Bavinck/Plantinga model for a realist conception of theology*. From the first chapter of this book, I have affirmed that there is an important compatibility between Bavinck's *Reformed Dogmatic 1: Prolegomena*[1] and Plantinga's works on warrant and on the science-religion relationship. In the second and third chapters, I sketched here and there some points of convergence between these works, but without developing them. The time has come to flesh out the argument by showing how these two works effectively work together towards the construction of a unified account.

In the first subsection, I present in a systematic way the main points of convergence between the works of Bavinck and Plantinga and show how my proposal relies on these points (2.1). Secondly, I show how bringing together these two works simultaneously improves both and leads to a strong overall presentation of a realist conception of theology (2.2).

2.1 Points of Convergence

My thesis is that bringing together the works of Bavinck and Plantinga in relation to realism issues is not only possible, but also desirable. The aim of this subsection is to give weight to this argument by stressing in a systematic way five important points of convergence that tie these two works together. In so doing, I will draw some important specific contours of my proposal, since these points are far from being commonplaces or mere coincidences in the Western contemporary context.[2] The first point of convergence lies in Bavinck and Plantinga's shared interdisciplinary approach of philosophy and theology. The next three points can be understood in the light of what has been written on Bavinck's organization of the three principles of theological knowledge (the *principium essendi,*

---

1 Herman Bavinck, *Reformed Dogmatics 1: Prolegomena* (Grand Rapids: Baker Academic, 2003).
2 To avoid the redundancy of quoting numerous passages of Bavinck and Plantinga already cited in the second and third chapters of this book, I quote Bavinck and Plantinga as little as possible in this subsection. I also decline to present an explicit justification for all my affirmations, for doing so would generate many repetitions and increase the length of this chapter in an undesirable way.

the two *principiae cognoscendi*, and how they are articulated together): the overall precedence of metaphysics over epistemology, the importance of the metaphysics of creation, and the common organic or analogical approach to knowledge. Finally, the fifth point of convergence is a common definition of faith.

The first point of convergence is Bavinck and Plantinga's common interdisciplinary approach of philosophy and theology. While Bavinck is a theologian interested in philosophy, Plantinga is a philosopher who deals with numerous theological concepts. This situation has generated incomprehension on both sides, but James Beilby's following statement on Plantinga's work can also be applied in a reverse way to that of Bavinck:

> Most of the misunderstandings of Plantinga's project arise because of the uniquely interdisciplinary nature of his work. Often philosophers fail to fully appreciate the theological context of Plantinga's assumptions and theologians/religious scholars fail to understand the philosophical content of his arguments.[3]

At the end of the first chapter of this book, I indicated a choice not to oppose what Wolterstorff has called "philosophical theology" and "theological theology." This methodological decision allows me to avoid the misunderstandings mentioned by Beilby and instead to stress the deeply interdisciplinary character of Bavinck and Plantinga's works. This approach makes possible the outlining of an important convergence between these two thinkers on this methodological question and legitimates the idea of having them interact.

The aim is therefore to present a realist conception of theology which is altogether based on both philosophy and theology. This approach has characterized Christian thought over the centuries and makes possible a mutual enrichment that is much needed today.

---

3 Beilby, *Epistemology as Theology*, viii. As an illustration of this quotation applied to Bavinck, we have Henk van den Belt's perplexed statement: "Bavinck fits his general epistemology into his theological framework via the concept of the divine *Logos*. It seems as if he approaches philosophy from a theological perspective, but his prolegomena are so influenced by his philosophical epistemology, that in reality he approaches theology from a philosophical perspective." Henk van den Belt, *The Authority of Scripture in Reformed Theology. Truth and Trust* (Leiden and Boston: Brill, 2008), 266.

The second point of convergence is that both Bavinck and Plantinga affirm the precedence of metaphysics over epistemology. In the post-Kantian and post-Wittgensteinian traditions, metaphysics is somehow despised and the focus is on specifically epistemological questions. By contrast, Bavinck clearly states that the two epistemological principles of theological knowledge (*principium cognoscendi internum* and *externum*) flow directly from the most fundamental metaphysical principle (*principium essendi*, which is God as the essential foundation of theology). On his side, Plantinga repeatedly states in his trilogy of warrant that there is an intimate connection between epistemology and metaphysics, and that major epistemological stances directly depend upon "what sort of creatures you think human beings are."[4] In *Where the Conflict Really Lies* Plantinga unashamedly presents the metaphysical foundations of scientific knowledge, since he believes that the concept of science first of all raises metaphysical rather than epistemological questions.[5]

This second point of convergence is important from the perspective of this research, since I propose a realist understanding of theology which is altogether metaphysical, epistemological and semantic. I contest the commonplace assertion of much Continental philosophy and theology that classical metaphysics is a vain or even harmful discipline. On the contrary, I believe that metaphysical thought is fundamental and unavoidable, and that it is better to face it in a conscious way.

The third point of convergence is that Bavinck and Plantinga work from the perspective of a theistic metaphysics, since they understand the world and human beings as created by God. This stance specifies the more general second point of convergence and provides for a *principium essendi* that orientates their entire work. At the end of his argument in favor of realist conception of theology, Bavinck proposes a theology of the divine Logos that functions as the keystone of his whole case. Human knowledge in general and theological knowledge in particular is made possible by the fact that all of reality is created by the divine Logos. This is the ultimate reason why human beings can know something about external reality and about God. Plantinga also refers to the world as created by God, both in his trilogy of warrant and in *Where the Conflict Really Lies*. After defining the concept of warrant, he affirms that the best metaphysical

---

4 Alvin Plantinga, *Warrant and Proper Function* (Oxford: Oxford University Press, 1993), 183.
5 Alvin Plantinga, *Where the Conflict Really Lies. Science, Religion and Naturalism* (New York: Oxford University Press, 2011). See chapter 3 of this book for more details.

explanation is that the world was created by God.⁶ He also affirms that the reason why there is a correspondence between our scientific theories and the world is because God created both human beings and the world.⁷ Even if Plantinga doesn't refer to the theology of divine Logos, the convergence of his work with that of Bavinck is obvious in these theistic metaphysical affirmations.⁸

This third point of convergence is important from the perspective of this research, since it substantiates the theistic metaphysical dimension of my defense of a realist conception of theology. The possibility and the effectiveness of human knowledge of the world and of God are first of all based on the reality of a world and human beings created by God. Apart from such a theistic metaphysical basis, defending a realist conception of theology is arguably a fragile and unstable intellectual enterprise.

Fourthly, Bavinck's organic method and Plantinga's multileveled (or analogical) analysis of human knowledge display important similarities. From the perspective of Bavinck's three principles of knowledge, the point of convergence relates to the two epistemological principles, the *principium cognoscendi internum* and *externum*. Bavinck is very much opposed to any epistemological method that works with oppositions in a dualistic way. On the contrary, he proposes an organic or synthetic method that is sensible of the unity and interconnected character of human knowledge. His definition of theology as a science is based on the rejection of modern dualistic (or dialectical) epistemological standards and can be understood from the perspective of an analogical approach of science. Plantinga's work on warrant is also marked by an utterly non-dualistic conception of knowledge. As studied above, he regularly insists on the multi-leveled character of knowledge and invites the reader to "pause for a moment to marvel at the enormously articulate, subtle, and complex nature of our cognitive faculties,"⁹ which allows us to know the external environment, thoughts of others, of ourselves, mathematics and logic, beauty, right and wrong, God, etc.

The importance of this fourth epistemological point of convergence for this present proposal lies in the methodological rejection of both univocal and dualist conceptions of knowledge. Such perspectives lead to

---

6 See *Warrant and Proper Function*, 197-198, 214-215.
7 See *Where the Conflict Really Lies*, 269.
8 I had the privilege of meeting Alvin Plantinga twice in 2013. It was interesting to find him agreeing when I mentioned the hypothesis that Bavinck's use of the theology of the divine Logos could fit and enhance the metaphysical foundation of his work.
9 Plantinga, *Warrant and Proper Function*, 42.

insurmountable difficulties when dealing with issues related to a realist conception of theology. By contrast, the rigorous flexibility offered by these two thinkers makes possible the formulation of a proposal that is both subtle and strong.

Finally, the fifth point of convergence directly flows from the fourth and concerns the definition of *faith* in Bavinck and Plantinga's works. Bavinck and Plantinga both hold that faith is not opposed to reason since it belongs to the rational part of the human soul. It is a cognitive faculty that gives access to propositional truths. In an anti-dualistic way, they both affirm that faith is altogether a natural and supernatural faculty; it is grounded in the subtle analogical human cognitive structure, even if it ultimately has its origin in the operation of the Holy Spirit.

This point of convergence is meaningful from the perspective of this work since it helps in characterizing theology in its various dimensions in a precise way. This question is closely related to that of realism in theology, especially in its semantic dimension. The affirmation that theology is in a position to formulate truth-content propositions is indeed partly based on such a conception of faith.

In conclusion to this subsection, these significant points of convergence between the works of Bavinck and Plantinga on issues related to the formulation of a realist conception of theology strengthen in an important way my own case. By presenting these points, I have shown how they improve the realist stance in its metaphysical, epistemological and semantic dimensions.

2.2 The Benefit of the Bavinck/Plantinga Model
Having outlined the points of convergence between the works of Bavinck and Plantinga on which my synthetic model relies, this subsection demonstrates how bringing these two works together extends and improves them both, and leads to the elaboration of a realist conception of theology. By doing this, I will start to formulate a thoughtful answer to the main research question. Furthermore, as indicated, this proposal contributes to Bavinck and Plantinga studies, since it overcomes some blind spots that may weaken their works when taken in isolation.

To employ a spatial metaphor, the points of convergence noted in the previous subsection lie at the center of this proposal. They are indeed the core affirmations upon which it relies. The improvements proposed in this subsection apply to the two extremities of the argument. By "extremities" I mean, on the one hand, the most basic general theory of human knowledge on which the specific question of the knowledge of God is based; and on the other, questions related to theology considered as a science. In short, Bavinck shows how sensible and intellectual knowledge functions, before transiting too rapidly to the theistic foundation which makes this knowledge possible. At the other extreme, Plantinga deals with faith and knowledge of God, but not explicitly with theology as an academic discipline. The aim of this subsection is to display how both gaps can be filled in light of the work of the other.

2.2.1 How Plantinga Improves Bavinck's General Theory of Knowledge

Two weaknesses in Bavinck's argument can be strengthened by bringing his line of reasoning together with Plantinga's work, and this improvement will enrich the wider case in favor of a realist conception of theology. The first weakness is the hasty character of Bavinck's general defense of a realist conception of knowledge. The second is the somewhat dated character of his argument.

The first weakness in Bavinck's argument is probably due to its location in a prolegomena volume of a dogmatic theology. An inherent difficulty with this sort of book is finding the right balance. If one writes too much, and in a technical way, the reader might be discouraged and move too quickly to the core sections of the dogmatic work. If one writes too little, it becomes easy to find weaknesses in the presentation of the subject, since the matter is quite complex. Paradoxically, both criticisms can be made about Bavinck's *Prolegomena*. On the one hand, theologians not versed in philosophical issues might say it is too long and too technical; on the other, thinkers interested in philosophical theology may criticize Bavinck's rapid epistemological justification of his theological realism. My aim now is to address the second critique.

My thesis is that Bavinck's synthetic Aristotelian presentation of the nature of sensible and intellectual knowledge can be improved by adding the content of Plantinga's *Warrant and Proper Function*.[10] If one applies Plantinga's four criteria definition of warrant and the numerous chapters devoted to the precise description of how human beings concretely know something about themselves and the world to Bavinck's canvas, one

---

10 This is not just to say that Plantinga has a better account of knowledge than Bavinck, for that implies that both accounts are in fundamental agreement. Plantinga's epistemology is just much more elaborate, refined and shored up against all sorts of objections. This is to some extent a difference in detail and precision that can be expected between a theologian and a philosopher, given the philosophical nature of the theme.

immediately understands how sensible and intellectual knowledge effectively function. Plantinga's presentation of the good design plan, oriented towards the production of true beliefs about external reality, reinforces Bavinck's crucial affirmation that by forging concepts we don't distance ourselves from the world, but work on knowing it better. Plantinga's work provides a detailed model that helps in bridging the idealist gap between external reality and human knowledge in a decisive way. When one reads Bavinck and Plantinga together on this question, it is no longer easy to argue that human beings have no access, or have only a schematic indirect access, to external reality.

A second weakness resulting from the hasty character of Bavinck's presentation lies in the transition from an Aristotelian (or, in this case, Thomistic) general epistemology to its explicitly theistic foundation (the theology of the divine Logos and its ramifications), which may not convince an antirealist thinker. Plantinga's work on warrant, which starts with observations based on a naturalist epistemology, and, after a careful step-by-step argument, ends with a theistic metaphysical model, fits Bavinck's argument perfectly and fleshes out this transition. I have shown in the third chapter of this book that Plantinga's overall argument is careful, progressive, and coherent. These qualities can be applied to Bavinck's one page transition in order to transform it into a thoughtful intellectual movement. The task of the anti-realist thinker is again complicated by this proposal. Even if an atheist thinker is not convinced by the theistic foundation of (the possibility of) knowledge, Plantinga's argument cannot be rejected without careful study.

A second major critique that can be formulated against a contemporary use of Bavinck's work is that it is dated. Bavinck worked in the late nineteenth and early twentieth century Continental intellectual world, which was deeply influenced by post-Kantian thought. In that context the main philosophical challenge for a realist thinker was to bridge, in one way or another, the idealist gap between external reality and its representation in the human mind as defined by Kant a century before. Bavinck was very much aware of this difficulty and he answered it by integrating much of the main realist philosophy of his time, i.e., neo-Thomism. When one studies nineteenth century theology, one realizes that neo-Thomist theologians, who were encouraged by Pope Leo XIII's encyclical *Aeterni Patris*, developed the strongest defenses of a realist conception of theology. It is therefore no great surprise to see Bavinck referring to it. Given this present research is a contemporary systematic work, this second critique needs to be addressed.

I hold that my proposal opens reading avenues into the work of Bavinck that have a modest resemblance to what happened to the work of Thomas Reid in the late twentieth century analytic philosophy context. Thomas Reid was an almost-forgotten eighteenth-century philosopher when analytic philosophers rediscovered him in the context of the internalism vs. externalism epistemological debate.[11] They found in his work a strong case in favor of externalism and started to study this in order to give philosophical and historical weight to their own case.[12] I believe that the recent English translation of Bavinck's work makes a similar intellectual movement possible.

The way Bavinck deals with the question of sensible and intellectual knowledge is shaped by the nineteenth-century context and may be perceived as slightly fusty. But when one starts to read his work, and especially his use of the theology of the divine Logos, in light of Plantinga's theory of warrant, one realizes that it is still vivid. As noted in chapter 3, Plantinga's definition of warrant indeed shifts the internalist epistemological issues from the knowing subject to the wider structure and environment of human cognition. This shift can be applied successfully to Bavinck's century-old defense of realism. When read in light of the four criteria of Plantinga's definition of warrant, Bavinck's work is emancipated from its neo-Thomistic terminology and brought in line with contemporary debates. Relating Bavinck's use of the theology of the divine Logos to Plantinga's concepts of proper function or design plan, and understanding Bavinck's affirmations on human sensible and intellectual knowledge in this light, allows him to enter contemporary analytic philosophy debates. It also shifts the generally blocked contours of the traditional Continental philosophical realism debate and hence renews the debate.

2.2.2 How Bavinck Improves Plantinga's Theological Thought
If my proposal improves Bavinck's work by merging it with Plantinga's, the converse is also observable for two main reasons. First, and most importantly, my proposal makes it possible to move from Plantinga's reflections on faith to the elaboration of a realist understanding of

---

11 Nicholas Wolterstorff's *Thomas Reid and the Story of Epistemology* (Cambridge: Cambridge University Press, 2001) is a perfect illustration of this movement. In the Preface, Wolterstorff claims that his book "is an *interpretation* of Reid's epistemology" (xi), and not a full treatment or an exegetical study.

12 This interpretation has been challenged by René van Woudenberg, "Thomas Reid between Externalism and Internalism," *Journal of the History of Philosophy* 51 (2013), 75-92, who observes that Reid also clearly had internalist leanings.

theology as an academic discipline. Secondly, it strengthens Plantinga's use of theological concepts and therefore improves his *Extended A/C model*.

The first benefit this proposal makes possible is an extension of Plantinga's system—from faith as proposed in the *Extended A/C model* to theology understood as a science from a realist perspective. A noteworthy aspect of Plantinga's philosophical work is his interest in questions related to Christian faith. He regularly works with theological concepts, but he does not develop an explicit reflection on theology as a scientific or academic discipline. The contrast with his works on the natural sciences is obvious here. On the one hand, he carefully develops the transition from his theory of warrant to a sustained reflection on scientific knowledge; on the other, he is attentive to the cognitive dimension of faith and refers to it in the context of his *Extended A/C model*, but he doesn't go further in the direction of conceiving theology as a science. This is probably due to the fact that Plantinga adheres to an Anglo-Saxon conception of science, which assimilates science in general to the natural sciences in particular. It is nevertheless unsatisfying for philosophers or theologians who would rather propose a definition of science (as *Wissenschaft*, or academic scholarship broadly conceived) that includes their discipline. This situation is even more frustrating since the application of Plantinga's rigorous and original philosophical thought to theology seems promising.

Of course, we might reflect on what Plantinga's view of the nature and tasks of theology would look like, extrapolating perhaps from what is implicit in his writings. Would he join his friend Nicholas Wolterstorff (who did write about the topic) in saying that there is no structural difference between philosophy and theology, or philosophical and theological theology?[13] Would he be willing to label his own work on warranted Christian belief an exercise in theology as well as in philosophy? Or would he, perhaps, ascribe a different methodology to theology, allowing for the fact that, apart from philosophical considerations, theologians have to take biblical studies and the history of doctrine into account, something that might make their task much more complex? Or does Plantinga not see any use for theology at all? The simple answer is: we just do not know, and it makes little sense to speculate.

What we do know is that Plantinga proposes a coherent and progressive intellectual movement that starts with a general theory of knowledge (the theory of warrant) and ends with its application to natural sciences. The

---

13 See Chapter 1, section 4.2.

result of this overall argument is a book—*Where the Conflict Really Lies*—which enriches the contemporary science and religion debates in a remarkable way. Plantinga could have applied a similar argument to theology, but he stops at the penultimate stage, that of faith. He has therefore never written a book in which he argues that the conflict is not between, for instance, theology as an academic discipline and rationality, but between classical theology and the contemporary anti-realist trends which transform theology into derived forms of anthropology, psychology or sociology.

My proposal lays the foundation for such an imaginary book. According to Bavinck, the specific task of the theologian is to organize the cognitive content of faith in a trustworthy, coherent and cogent way ("to think God's thoughts after him and to trace their unity"). In order to achieve this goal, the theologian should take into account the three principles of theological science (in short: God-revelation-faith, see chapter 2) and adopt an organic method. As displayed in the previous subsection of this chapter, not only is there a convergence between Bavinck's principles of theology and the *Extended A/C model* as developed in *Warranted Christian Belief*,[14] but also between Bavinck's organic method and Plantinga's multi-leveled conception of knowledge. Bavinck's reflections on the principles and method of theology can be plugged into *Plantinga's Extended A/C model* to generate what could be called the *Expanded extended A/C model*. This model adopts the content of the *Extended A/C model* and extends it from faith to theology. As noted above, Plantinga often deals with theological concepts, but he never develops meta-reflections on theology as he does with the natural sciences. This proposal fills that gap.

This so-called *Expanded extended A/C model* strengthens a realist conception of theology by importing the philosophical rigor of Plantinga's theory of warrant into the epistemology of theological studies. Whether one defines (dogmatic) theology as the study of God and all things in relation to God, or, like Bavinck, as an attempt to think God's thoughts after him and to trace their unity, Plantinga's work provides a robust and wide-ranging epistemological foundation for a realist understanding of this discipline, on which Bavinck's prolegomena to theology can flourish. Thus, my model proposes a comprehensive argument for a realist understanding of theology that goes from most basic observations of how human beings know something about themselves, external reality, and

---

14 Alvin Plantinga, *Warranted Christian Belief* (New York: Oxford University Press, 2000).

God to complex meta-reflections on theology. Nowadays, one typically reads that realism is a *naïve* position and that well-informed people know that anti-realism is far more accurate. My proposal invites Plantinga into this debate and holds that this "intrusion" moves the intellectual frontlines. The realist theologian who puts forward Bavinck's three principles of theological science enriched by Plantinga's work of warrant proposes a complete argument which cannot be easily refuted.

The second benefit of reading Plantinga in light of Bavinck lies in the potential improvement of the former's use of theological concepts, and therefore of his overall theory of warrant as developed in his trilogy. As noted in the previous chapter of this book, Plantinga often refers to theological concepts while developing his philosophical work. He employs concepts such as the *imago Dei*, the *sensus divinitatis*, the noetic effect of sin, faith, the internal testimony of the Holy Spirit, God's revelation in the Bible, etc. From the point of view of a contemporary systematic or historical theologian, his use of theological concepts may be perceived as insufficiently informed. Plantinga indeed does not interact with contemporary theological scholarship (except in chapter 12 of *Warranted Christian Belief*, which is devoted to biblical scholarship), and the way he refers to these concepts is very straightforward.

However, Plantinga is not destabilized by such a critique. For instance, his use of Calvin's *sensus divinitatis* has raised many scholarly discussions, notably its faithfulness to Calvin. His answer to this sort of critique is bold: his aim is not to do historical or systematic theology, but to develop his own philosophical work. In this context, he allows himself some freedom in the way he employs these concepts. Responding to Georg Plasger, who has criticized his use of the *sensus divinitatis*, Plantinga writes:

> Calvin wasn't an epistemologist. In the effort to develop an adequate epistemology of Christian and/or theistic belief, therefore, one can't simply present Calvin's view as such an epistemology. My aim was to develop such an epistemology, and Calvin played into this effort as a source of some general ideas—ideas that I proposed to develop in my own way, whatever Calvin had in mind. As I said somewhere, it's my model, not Calvin's.[15]

---

15 Alvin Plantinga, "Replies to my Commentators: Ad Plasger," in *Plantinga's "Warranted Christian Belief": Critical Essays with a Reply by Alvin Plantinga* (Berlin and Boston: Walter de Gruyter, 2015), 255.

Plantinga's answer is satisfying from the perspective of his work, since he has no pretensions about improving contemporary historical or systematic theological scholarship. It may nevertheless leave theologians who work in these areas hungry for more.

My proposal makes possible the improvement of the historical and systematic cogency of Plantinga's use of theological concepts. Reading Plantinga from a Bavinck-informed perspective indeed helps to improve our understanding of his use of theological concepts. Plantinga's intellectual background is that of Calvin College's Dutch neo-Calvinism, a background which has been unambiguously influenced by the thought of Bavinck. Even a rapid glance at Plantinga's work shows that his use of the above-mentioned theological concepts is in accordance with this background. A reference to this theological tradition may thus enrich the understanding of Plantinga's use of theological concepts.

Even if some of its aspects are dated, Bavinck's *Reformed Dogmatics* is still acknowledged as a theological work of historical, biblical and systematic rigor. Even his detractors generally recognize that Bavinck develops his thought and refers to theological concepts with great precision and care. It is noteworthy that all the theological concepts employed by Plantinga (as mentioned above) are developed in the four volumes of Bavinck's *Reformed Dogmatics*. We could thus plug Bavinck's careful theological work into Plantinga's argument and considerably improve its theological cogency. It would be anachronistic to suggest that the reference to Bavinck solves the entire problem raised by Plantinga's use of theological concepts. Nor can one affirm that reading Plantinga in light of Bavinck would place the American philosopher at the center of contemporary systematic theology debates. Nevertheless, bringing together these two works increases Plantinga's legitimacy as a valuable discussion partner on the theological issues related to the scope of this present research.

In conclusion to this section, I can propose a first provisional answer to my research question. My synthesized model strengthens the case in favor of a realist conception of theology for the following two reasons. First, it is comprehensive: it starts with a strong theory of knowledge based on Bavinck's presentation of sensible and intellectual knowledge improved by Plantinga's theory of warrant, and ends with Bavinck's thoughtful definition of theology plugged into Plantinga's *Extended A/C model* (which is itself rooted in his whole theory of knowledge). Secondly, the argument is consistent: it gives weight to a realist conception of theology that is altogether metaphysical, epistemological and semantic by explaining why these three dimensions matter and by proposing a step-by-step justification of this position. It does so in an original way: by synthesizing the works of Bavinck and Plantinga it combines theology and philosophy, Continental and analytic methods, and proposes insights that unblock some classical frontlines of the *realism in theology* debate.

3. The *Bavinck/Plantinga Model* in the Contemporary Realism Debate

Having outlined in the previous subsection the main facets of the *Bavinck/Plantinga Model for a realist conception of theology*, I now embed this model in the current debate on realism in theology, so as to elucidate the difference it makes in the contemporary scene. More precisely, the aim of this section is to display how the model can be understood as a positive contribution to an up-to-date account of a realist conception of theology. I do so by having the Bavinck/Plantinga model interact critically with the contemporary defenses of a realist conception of theology

In the following pages, I thus relate the proposal to the various forms of realism described in the first chapter of this book; first to the diverse forms of contemporary *critical realism* (3.1), and then to the different forms of *theological realism* (3.2). Finally, I propose a synthesis that stresses some specific contributions of this proposal in the contemporary context (3.3). This will lead to a second provisional answer to the research question.

3.1 The Bavinck/Plantinga Model *and* Critical Realism
In the first chapter of this book, I described *critical realism* in theology and presented two different tendencies within this movement: methodological (or scientific) critical realism and post-Kantian critical realism. This subsection explains why my proposal is on the one hand favorable to critical realism understood in its methodological sense, contributing to its improvement by proposing a model that is methodologically comprehensive and well-informed; and why, on the other hand, it is opposed to critical realism understood in its post-Kantian form, since I interpret this stance as an elegant disguised form of anti-realism that generates confusion.

I start by describing why my proposal fits perfectly the methodological critical realist ambition to propose a theory of knowledge that interacts with contemporary scientific issues. Critical realists, understood as methodological or scientific realists, are not interested in a defense of a realist conception of theology developed separately from the rest of human fields of knowledge, and neither am I. Both Bavinck and Plantinga share this worry, and the present proposal can be understood from this perspective.

As shown in the third chapter of this book, Plantinga is very much interested in questions related to science. He has been on the front line of the American science and religion debates, and this has led him to develop a sustained reflection on science, its foundation, scope and method. Even if Plantinga has not been directly interested in discussing the epistemological standards of theology as a science, if one were to merge his work with that of Bavinck, one might obtain an *Expanded extended A/C model* that develops a scientific conception of theology. This observation brings Plantinga close to critical realist thinkers such as Barbour, Polkinghorne, Torrance, McGrath or van den Brink—works marked by the will to make the natural sciences and theology interact on an epistemological level.

Furthermore, Plantinga's work on warrant meets the critical realists' scientific methodological standards. It is indeed obvious that *Warrant and Proper Function* and *Warranted Christian Belief* are written with a constant epistemological awareness that is far from *naïve* (in the sense of the despised *naïve realism*). Plantinga constantly seeks to be as precise as possible in the formulation of his observations; he builds his global argument step-by-step in an extremely careful way. These qualities have established Plantinga's philosophical reputation even among his opponents.

Bavinck's work also displays an important scientific awareness, as shown in the second chapter of this book. In writing *Reformed Dogmatics 1: Prolegomena*, in which he defines theology as a science with great precision and works on locating it within the field of other forms of human knowledge, he displays a methodological and reflexive awareness above the average. Even if Bavinck works with a definition of science that is wider than that usually employed by critical realist theologians, the questions raised by their work (especially concerning the relation between theology and other sciences, and the articulation of the activity of the knowing subject vis-à-vis the objectivity of external reality) as well as their methodological insights are highly compatible. Finally, if one employs the work of Plantinga to strengthen the epistemological foundation of that of Bavinck, one obtains a highly reflexive epistemological model that can be interpreted as a critical realist contribution to the contemporary debates.

The second reason why this present proposal can be understood from the perspective of critical realism is that, like scientific critical realists, it seeks the right balance between the knowing subject and the known object in the act of knowledge. Critical realists are working on developing an understanding of human knowledge that avoids both naïve objectivist realism and subjectivist instrumentalism. When applied to theology, methodological critical realism insists on the partial and provisional character of human knowledge of God, even if it is real. This modest but confident attitude is close to that displayed by Bavinck in his *Reformed Dogmatics* and is opposed to both the univocal overconfidence of naïve realism and the skepticism of anti-realism. From this perspective, as well as that of Bavinck, the reference to *models* or *metaphors* to describe human knowledge does not need to be assimilated to the post-Kantian mental screens, but rather to the Pauline affirmation that we see God "in a mirror dimly."

The present proposal not only pursues the same goal, but also enriches the overall argument. Bavinck's description of how human beings know something about the world stresses altogether the fact that there is an external reality which is not structured by the activity of the knowing subject, and that the knowing subject nevertheless plays an active role by forging concepts and theories. This is made possible by Bavinck's use of an organic method. Plantinga's definition of warrant goes in the same direction, since it takes into account the structure of external reality and the cognitive faculties of the knowing subject. As shown in the previous section, these two descriptions of how human beings acquire knowledge are highly compatible and lead to a proposal that strengthens the critical realist ambition.

My proposal also provides for a metaphysical model that gives weight to the critical realist project. Plantinga's understanding of human beings as created in the image of God, the structure of external reality and the correspondence between the two provides for an understanding of reality that makes the critical realist project cogent.[16] Bavinck's theology of the

---

16 It is worth comparing Plantinga's metaphysical proposal with that of John Polkinghorne. The convergence is striking: "There is the remarkable and fortunate fact that we are people of such an intellectual kind, living in a universe of such rationally transparent kind, that we are enabled to understand a great deal of the pattern and process of the world that we inhabit. Theologically, this is to be understood as due to the universe's being a creation and ourselves as creatures made in the image of the Creator. The possibility of science is then the consequence of the deposit of the imago dei within humanity. The critical realism which I have been seeking to defend is thus found in one of those circularities which we have discovered to be inherent in the human search for knowledge, to be undergirded by a theological belief in the faithfulness of God, who has not created a world whose appearances will mislead the honest enquirer. The unity of knowledge is underwritten by the unity of the one true

divine Logos goes even further and synthesizes in a striking way all metaphysical affirmations that make possible a methodologically informed understanding of human knowledge. It stresses that external reality and God are intelligible (at least to a certain extent), and that the active cognitive faculties of the human being are fitted to seize this intelligibility. In this connection, this *Bavinck/Plantinga model* and methodological critical realism share a similar "abductive method," which is neither purely inductive nor deductive, but is based on an "inference to the best explanation." In critical realism, models are not deduced in a straightforward way from reality, but are used because of their capacity to explain different phenomena in a coherent way. The reference to the divine Logos, even if it introduces an explicitly theistic concept into the argument, can be seen as a model that provides for an enlightening metaphysical background to critical realism.

Having explained how the present proposal strengthens the argument of a critical realist understanding of theology, as far as it is understood in its methodological (or scientific) sense, I now show why it is opposed to the work of thinkers who claim to be critical realists in the post-Kantian sense of the label. First, the concept of critical realism, when understood from this perspective, is a sort of philosophical oxymoron. In modern philosophy, the adjective *critical* is closely related to the work of Immanuel Kant, which is, at least on the epistemological and semantic levels, antirealist. In France of the 1930s, two important Roman Catholic philosophers, Etienne Gilson and Jacques Maritain, debated the question of critical realism. Gilson, who was deeply opposed to Maritain's critical realist stance, affirmed boldly: "Le problème de trouver un réalisme critique est en soi contradictoire comme la notion de cercle carré."[17] I will develop why I agree with Gilson's polemic statement (if critical realism is understood in a post-Kantian way) in the following paragraphs.

The post-Kantian critical realist theologians often claim to be faithful to the classical Christian teaching on the transcendence of God and its epistemological consequences. Nevertheless, their insistence on the indirect character of human knowledge (which flows, they hold, from the

---

God; the veracity of well-motivated belief is underwritten by the reliability of God." John Polkinghorne, *Belief in God in an Age of Science* (New Haven and London: Yale University Press, 1998), 122.

17 Etienne Gilson, *Le Réalisme Méthodique* (Paris: Pierre Téqui, 1937), 10. See: Etienne Gilson, *Methodical Realism. A Handbook for Beginning Realists* (San Francisco: Ignatius Press, 2011) and Jacques Maritain, *The Degrees of Knowledge* (Notre Dame: University of Notre Dame Press, 1995).

unavoidable use of models, metaphors, cultural frameworks, etc.) has little to do with classical Christianity, and much more with the modern philosophies of representation. I interpret post-Kantian critical realism as a contemporary resurgence of Duns Scotus' *esse repraesentatum* described in the first chapter of this book. (Duns Scotus affirmed that when confronted with external reality, the knowing subject produces a mental image—the *esse repraesentatum*—that becomes the effective object of knowledge instead of reality itself.) Thomas Torrance, introducing this stance in an interesting essay on realism, unveils the break this new epistemology represents in the history of Christian thought:

> In Western medieval thought an Aristotelian epistemology, governed by the principle that there is nothing in the mind but what was first in the senses and grafted on to an Augustinian basis with its disjunction between the sensible and the intelligible, the temporal and the eternal, resulted, for the most part, in ways of thinking through the medium of images and ideas that intervened between the mind and reality, the so-called *objecta mentis*, which rendered the relation between the mind and reality or between sign and thing signified *oblique*. This bit so deeply even into would-be realist epistemology that a master idea such as *adaequatio intellectus ad rei* became quite ambiguous, for it could be interpreted either as the conformity of the mind to its object or the conformity of the object to the mind.[18]

I understand contemporary post-Kantian critical realism as a resurgence of what Torrance describes in this paragraph: would-be realist epistemologies that renounce in a subtle way the *adaequatio intellectus ad rei* master idea, by considering it as conforming the object to the mind rather than the other way around.

Against this philosophical ambiguity, the present model suppresses the above-mentioned confusing third element in the act of knowledge (the mental screen) on which the post-Kantian critical realist model is based. While this model insists on the *indirect* character of knowledge, in the end it leaves us with no knowledge of the external world at all. There is no necessity, however, to fabricate such an ambiguous philosophical tool in order to find the point of contact between the intelligibility of the external reality and the active role played by the knowing subject in the

---

18 Thomas F. Torrance, "Theological Realism," in *The Philosophical Frontiers of Christian Theology* (Cambridge: Cambridge University Press, 1982), 174.

act of knowledge. Plantinga's work on warrant is a striking illustration of this affirmation. My proposal is hospitable to reflections on the activity of the knowing subject in the act of knowledge that are so appreciated by post-Kantian critical realists. It nevertheless makes possible the understanding of this activity, not as a screen or a lens between the human mind and external reality, but as the proper way for the human mind to acquire knowledge of the world and of God.

In conclusion and in opposition to post-Kantian critical realism, I adhere to the more restrictive view of realism Torrance proposes in opposition to the above-described philosophical evolution:

> We shall use the expression "realist" to describe the orientation in thought that obtains in science, philosophy or theology on the basis of a non-dualist or unitary relation between the empirical and theoretical ingredients in the structure of the real world and in our knowledge of it. It may be noted at this point that it was a realist orientation of this kind which Greek patristic theology, especially from the third to the sixth century, struggled so hard to acquire and which it built into the foundations of classical theology.[19]

In light of this, it is obvious that the classical realist conception of theology has little to do with post-Kantian critical realism and its ancestors.

3.2 The Bavinck/Plantinga Model and Theological Realism
In the first chapter of this book, I presented the contemporary theological realist defenses of theology as a reaction against the hegemony of modern philosophical or scientific epistemological standards, and an affirmation of the need for theology to claim its right to work with its own specific criteria. In this subsection, I show that my proposal is, on the one hand, favorable to classical theological realism and contributes to its improvement by proposing a coherent and cogent approach to theology. On the other hand, my proposal is opposed to radical theological realism, since this stance goes too far in its longing for methodological independence and leads to the isolation of theology from the rest of the sciences.

If one compares the presentation of classical theological realism in subsection 3.4 of the first chapter of this book and Bavinck's careful work of definition of theology by its object, principles and method in chapter 2,

---

19 Torrance, "Theological Realism," 173.

one immediately observes three striking points of convergence. First, the theological realist insistence on the primacy of God as the ultimate foundation of theology, and the correlated insistence on revelation and faith (which are, as studied in chapters 2 and 3, in accordance with human faculties) as the most basic epistemological principles of theology, finds powerful support in Bavinck's *Reformed Dogmatics*. His reflection on the three principles of theology (God as the *principium essendi*, the revelation as the *principium cognoscendi externum*, and faith as the *principium cognoscendi internum*) represents a precise and structured case in favor of the core affirmations of classical theological realism. Secondly, classical theological realism's ambition to access an effective and direct knowledge of God (as opposed to the indirect knowledge of the post-Kantian critical realists—if it is knowledge at all) is also corroborated by Bavinck's development on realism. I even hold that his reflection on archetypal and ectypal theologies improves the general classical theological realism case by reworking in a thoughtful way the classical tension between God's knowability and incomprehensibility. Thirdly, just as classical theological realists generally affirm the importance of human reasoning and of metaphysical thought while doing theology, so does Bavinck. The latter's definition of theology as the "interpretation of the *gratia Dei* in the arena of science" perfectly fits the classical theological realist claim of a specifically theological approach to theology that is not hostile to commonly shared rational approaches to external reality. *Gratia non tollit naturam, sed perficit.*

Plantinga's intellectual world is quite foreign to the questions raised by these theological realist subjects of interest. Nevertheless, his *A/C model* and his *Extended A/C model* can be interpreted—*via* the work of Bavinck—as compatible with classical theological realism. As shown above, he indeed bases this part of his theory on theological concepts in a way that is highly compatible with Bavinck's approach. The role played by concepts such as revelation, faith, and the internal testimony of the Holy Spirit indeed perfectly fits the intellectual frame of classical theological realism. As stated above, integrating Plantinga's work with theological studies, by merging it with Bavinck's *Prolegomena*, represents a potentially valuable improved elaboration of classical theological realism. Theological realists are sometimes suspected of being more or less irrational fideists by scholars of other disciplines. In this context, the support of Plantinga's careful work on the epistemology of Christian belief should not be ignored, even if it has not been produced in an intellectual context familiar to classical theological realists.

Having shown how this proposal strengthens the argument of a classical theological realist understanding of theology, I now demonstrate how it is opposed to radical theological realism. My thesis is that by reversing the traditional order of creation and redemption, by opposing theology to philosophy and its intellectual tools, by attempting to develop an ontology based on Christology rather than on creation, radical theological realism isolates theology from the rest of sciences in a way that leads it, whether consciously or not, to abandon realism in favor of a subtle form of *cultural-linguistic* anti-realism.

We can develop this idea by making a detour and referring briefly to Hans Frei's "types" of theology.[20] Frei's fourth type draws the contours of theological systems that tend to make theology interact with external reality in order to show that Christian faith is the best (or at least a good) explanatory system. This type of theology is animated by a realist ethos and seeks a real and deep interaction of theology with the most recent discoveries in the human and natural sciences. Frei's fifth type represents trends that tend to push forward the inner logic of Christian faith, without searching interactions with other fields of knowledge. These systems rely on the idea that Christian faith and other thought systems are incommensurable, and that Christian theology is mainly an attempt to depict what Christians believe. Their overall ethos is that of post-Wittgensteinian anti-realism.

Classical theological realism belongs to Frei's fourth type of theology, since its insistence on grounding theology in theological principles doesn't prevent it from having a reality-depicting ambition. It is also animated by the desire to interact with other fields of knowledge. It aims to formulate true propositions about God that are not limited to the scope of self-depicting Christian belief. By contrast, *radical* theological realism cannot be placed in the fourth type of theology but should paradoxically be moved into the fifth. The intellectual tools used by these theologians are so radically theological (and so they proudly claim) that they are barely intelligible to scholars who are not working in a Christian perspective. Then, the main scope tends to be Christian self-description rather than the formulation of true propositions about God.

This motion from the fourth to the fifth type of theology is problematic, since it leads Christian theology to an intellectual isolationism which is damaging both to the church and to the world. As for post-Kantian critical realism, I believe that radical theological realism is ultimately a

---

20 See chapter 4 of Hans W. Frei, *Types of Christian Theology* (New Haven and London: Yale University Press, 1992).

disguised form of anti-realism. It is proposed by thinkers who probably try to overcome a strong intellectual discomfort generated by an attraction for fashionable forms of anti-realism, and a will not to bridge what is perceived as a theological Rubicon for anyone who works from a more-or-less conservative perspective—the explicit adoption of theological anti-realism.[21] By contrast, the present proposal displays how it is possible to be a consistent classical theological realist, without having to look ambiguously in the direction of post-Wittgensteinian forms of antirealism. I therefore agree with the following affirmation from John Bolt and hold that my proposal gives weight to such a way of understanding the scope of theology:

> It is the theologian's responsibility to present the full knowledge of God and his revelation as *reality, as a truth claim, as an argument for the truth about God and his world*. In other words, Christian theology is not only—and certainly not in the first place—a summary of what Christians *believe*, but an attempt to state what is really true about God and the world.[22]

3.3 Concluding Observations

Having worked on placing my proposal in the context of the contemporary realist trends in theology, I now formulate some wider concluding thoughts. I have observed that my proposal is congruent with both methodological critical realism and classical theological realism. This observation is far from insignificant, since it leads one to realize that even if these two trends are not identical, they manifest noteworthy points of convergence. One indeed observes in these two trends a deep common will to develop a realist conception of theology that is unambiguously metaphysical, epistemological and semantic. One can also notice a shared recognition of the need for theology to develop its own methodological tools in a lucid and reflexive way.

---

21 I acknowledge that there is a grey zone between Frei's fourth and fifth types of theologies and hold that this has its origin in the work of Lindbeck (see chapter 1, section 3.3). The latter has indeed always been ambiguous when dealing with the question of the objective external reference of theology. This maintained ambiguity has exercised a deep influence on the *narrative theology* movement and later on radical theological realists. For instance, Andrew Moore's *narrative realism* is quite ambiguous and could probably be located in both the fourth and fifth types. See Andrew Moore, *Realism and Christian Faith. God, Grammar, and Meaning* (Cambridge: Cambridge University Press), 2003.

22 John Bolt, "Sola Scriptura as an Evangelical Theological Method?" in *Reforming or Conforming? Post-Conservative Evangelicals and the Emerging Church*, ed. Gary L.W. Johnson and Ronald N. Gleason (Wheaton: Crossway Books, 2008), 82.

This observation explains why it is now not so easy to label the works of contemporary classical Christian realist thinkers such as Thomas Torrance[23] or Alister McGrath.[24] The attention they give to the twentieth century developments of scientific epistemology, coupled with an affirmation of the need to ground theology in theological principles, indeed leads one to wonder whether they are critical or theological realists. Working on locating the present proposal helps one realize that in such cases, this question of label is not so important, since the points of convergence between methodological critical realism and classical theological realism are much more important than the differences (which, in short, mainly lie in the way one interprets the specificity of theology within the arena of the sciences). I therefore plead for the abandonment of useless label discussions and for the opening of common research avenues in the context of contemporary *realism in theology* studies.

My proposal provides a good illustration of this convergence between methodological critical realism and classical theological realism, since it merges important themes of these two trends. It is a model that starts with Plantinga's basic observations on human knowledge and ends with Bavinck's ultimate foundation on the divine Logos in a way that meets the standards of methodological critical realism. It displays a will to develop a realism driven by an important methodological worry, and by the will to make theology interact with the rest of the human sciences. The overall scope and coherency of my proposal is indeed far from being naïve in the sense of being unaware of the issues raised by the studied question. But my proposal also displays a sensitivity to crucial theological concepts that meet the exigencies of classical theological realism. As shown in the second and third chapters of this book, the works of both Bavinck and Plantinga rely deeply on explicitly theological concepts.

---

23 The work of Torrance on this question is vast. For instance, in *Theological Science* (Oxford: Oxford University Press, 1969), he shares the worries of methodological critical realists. But while he deals with patristic theology, he seems to be closer to classical theological realists. See among others "Theological Realism," in *The Philosophical Frontiers of Christian Theology. Essays Presented to D.M. MacKinnon*, ed. Brian Hebblethwaite and Stewart Sutherland (Cambridge: Cambridge University Press, 1982), 169-196.

24 Alister E. McGrath, *A Scientific Theology: Reality. Vol. 2* (London and New York: T&T Clark, 2006). In this book, McGrath develops a vast argument in favor of a critical realist conception of theology (see especially chapter 10 titled "Critical Realism: Engaging with a Stratified Reality"). Nevertheless, at the end of the book, he develops typically theological realist themes (see especially pages 297ff, in which he develops a Christocentric understanding of scientific theology).

A second observation that flows from the two previous subsections is that post-Kantian critical realism and radical theological realism are working in opposing directions, even if they both lead to cryptic forms of anti-realism. On the one hand, the opposition to the objectivist standards of positivism has led post-Kantian critical realists to adopt the contrary unbalanced stance, that of a barely hidden post-Kantian philosophy of representation. On the other hand, resistance to the contemporary hegemony of secular intellectual disciplines (natural or social sciences, philosophy, etc.) has led radical theological realists to oppose the practice of theology to other forms of human knowledge, which leads this discipline into intellectual isolation. It has also contributed to blurring the lines between classical theological realism and post-Wittgensteinian forms of anti-realism. By contrast, my proposal also rejects modern positivist objectivism as an unbalanced critical realist answer. It rejects any form of secular intellectual hegemony on theology as well as the retreat into a conception of theology mainly understood as Christian self-description.

In conclusion to this section, it is possible to formulate a second provisional answer to the research question. Having shown that my proposal provides a realist conception of theology that is altogether comprehensive and consistent, I am now in a position to state why it is also *cogent* in the contemporary Western context: it has the capacity to interact with the major contemporary realist trends in a fruitful way. My proposal is sympathetic to *methodological critical realism* and *classical theological realism*, and opposed to both *post-Kantian critical realism* and *radical theological realism*. The sympathies as well as the oppositions are instructive, since they suggest that the intellectual frontlines may not be exactly where we think they are at first sight. This proposal has indeed shown that the contemporary frontlines ultimately don't oppose critical realism and theological realism but divide these two forms of realism from the inside. The next section will deepen this observation and progressively lead to the final conclusion of this book.

4. The Wider Scope of the *Bavinck/Plantinga Model*

Having described the Bavinck/Plantinga model for a realist conception of theology in conjunction with the contemporary realism in theology debates, this last section offers a more hermeneutical approach and questions the wider scope of the proposal in the context of modernity and postmodernity. Defending a realist conception of theology is not simply a technical theological or philosophical enterprise. On the contrary, it questions in a radical way the impact of the Western cultural movements labeled modernity and postmodernity on the understanding of the nature and meaning of theology.

In the first subsection, I depart from the technical aspects of the works of Bavinck and Plantinga and study how these thinkers interpret what happened to the epistemology of theology in the modern (and, for Plantinga, postmodern) age. First, this will lead to an interpretation of their work—and therefore of this proposal also—as works of theological and philosophical *retrieval* (4.1). I then oppose this retrieval approach to that which underlies both post-Kantian critical realism and radical theological realism (4.2). Finally, I show how my proposal helps present theology as a meaningful truth-seeking discipline in the context of the church, the academy, and society, and why it matters (4.3).

4.1 The Bavinck/Plantinga Model *as a Work of Retrieval*

In a synthetic article written in the "Prospects" section of a handbook of systematic theology, John Webster describes what he calls *theologies of retrieval*.[25] This label has been used to group diverse and heterogeneous trends in contemporary theology which "tend to agree that mainstream theological response to seventeenth and eighteenth-century critiques of the Christian religion and Christian religious reflection needlessly distanced theology both from its given object and from the legacies of its past."[26] The concept of retrieval displays the will to "resist this view of the situation of theology by proposing different genealogies of modernity and by treating pre-modern Christian theology as resource rather than problem."[27] Webster then traces the contours of various theologies of retrieval (Jüngel, de Lubac, Milbank, Buckley, Dupré, T. F. Torrance, Frei, Farley) and ends by stressing the potential weaknesses of these kinds of approaches. He affirms that a "temptation for theologians of retrieval is to subscribe to a myth of the fall of theology from Christian genuineness at some point in its past (fourteenth-century nominalism, the sixteenth-century Reformation, seventeenth-century Cartesianism, or wherever 'modernity' is considered to have first presented itself)."[28] He ends by stating that theologies of retrieval "can fail to grasp that the problem is not *modern* theology but simply *theology*. All talk of God is hazardous.

---

25 John Webster, "Theologies of Retrieval," in *The Oxford Handbook of Systematic Theology*, ed. John Webster, Kathryn Tanner and Ian Torrance (Oxford: Oxford University Press, 2007), 583-599.
26 Webster, "Theologies of Retrieval," 584.
27 Webster, "Theologies of Retrieval," 585.
28 Webster, "Theologies of Retrieval," 596.

Modern constraints bring particular challenges which can be partially defeated by attending to a broader and wiser history, but there is no pure Christian past whose retrieval can ensure theological fidelity."[29]

Webster's synthesis of retrieval theologies is enlightening, even if the last quotation is questionable (and will be questioned in the next subsection). In the following paragraphs, I display how my proposal can be interpreted from such a perspective, by adhering to Kevin Vanhoozer's definition of retrieval and aiming to follow this track:

> We ought not to confuse retrieval with either retrenchment or repristination: retrieval is not a simple return to the past (it can't be done). [...] No, the main purpose of retrieval is the revitalization of biblical interpretation, theology, and the church today. *To retrieve is to look back creatively in order to move forward faithfully.*[30]

A noteworthy facet of Bavinck and Plantinga's thought I haven't stressed yet is their view of the history of Christian theology and of the impact of modernity and postmodernity on this discipline, particularly in relation to the topic of this present research. Their views are convergent, and, when brought together, consist in a good piece of retrieval work. First, I describe Bavinck's understanding of tradition and modernity, and then pay attention to the view of the history of Christian theology conveyed by Plantinga's *A/C model*.

In a dense programmatic text, the "Foreword" to the first edition of his *Reformed Dogmatics,* Bavinck formulates his view on the intellectual climate of his time. On the one hand, his assessment is rather pessimistic: "At the present time, dogmatic theology does not get much respect; our age is not amenable to Christian dogma. For good reason, then, many of us feel isolated and forsaken."[31] The impact of modernity on theology is perceived as negative, mainly because of anti-realist trends which void theology from its content. But on the other hand, Bavinck is not without hope. If the theologian may feel isolated among his contemporaries, this isolation disappears when he looks at the tradition of the church:

---

29 Webster, "Theologies of Retrieval," 596-597.
30 Kevin J. Vanhoozer, *Biblical Authority after Babel. Retrieving the* Solas *in the Spirit of Mere Protestant Christianity* (Grand Rapids: Brazos Press, 2016), 24.
31 Herman Bavinck, "Foreword to the First Edition (Volume 1) of the *Gereformeerde Dogmatiek*," *Calvin Theological Journal* 45 (2010): 9.

However, this is all the more reason to be grateful that we can underscore our communion and fellowship with generations past. That is why more attention is paid in this work to Patristic and Scholastic theology than is often the case in a Protestant dogmatics. Irenaeus, Augustine, and Thomas do not belong exclusively to Rome; they are Fathers and Doctors to whom the whole Christian church has obligations.[32]

The retrieval of the tradition of the Christian church will help the theologian to do his work despite the difficult modern context. This observation places Bavinck within Webster's definition of theologies of retrieval.

Reading the work of Bavinck as a theology of retrieval makes possible the formulation of some interesting observations. First, while exposing the principles of theology, Bavinck repeats that along with the Holy Scripture and the Christian conscience, there is a third basic principle: the church's confession.[33] Thus, "the dogmatician will be most fully equipped to carry out this task if he lives in communion of faith with the church of Christ."[34] This is why he often calls his theological method the synthetic-genetic method.[35] It is a genetic method, since it constantly attempts to work from the perspective of the history of the church.

Secondly, Bavinck's reference to the theology of the divine Logos is a vivid illustration of his will to work from the perspective of the tradition of the Christian church. As stated in the second chapter of this book, this theological locus has played an immense role in patristic theology and Bavinck's work of retrieval is far from naïve. Against the pervasive influence of the anti-realist understandings of theology of his time, which make the classical dogmatic theologian feel isolated, he seeks inspiration in the tradition of the church and develops his case by reworking central beliefs of the ancient church.

Thirdly, this approach clarifies why Bavinck is not afraid to redefine the theological fronts in a way that may surprise his reader at first sight.[36]

---

32 Bavinck, "Foreword to the First Edition (Volume 1) of the *Gereformeerde Dogmatiek*," 9.
33 Bavinck, *Reformed Dogmatics 1: Prolegomena*, 61.
34 Bavinck, *Reformed Dogmatics 1: Prolegomena*, 93.
35 Bavinck, *Reformed Dogmatics 1: Prolegomena*, 93.
36 This surprise is expressed in George Puchinger's comment on Bavinck's *Reformed Dogmatics*: "History has its ironies but it cannot be denied: the most ecumenical protestant dogmatic theology in fact appeared in Kampen, the place where theology was practiced in the most isolationist manner." Quoted by James Eglinton, *Trinity and Organism. Towards a New Reading of Herman Bavinck's Organic Motif* (London and New York: T&T Clark, 2012), 93.

It indeed appears from his work that on questions related to this present research, the opposition is not between Protestants and Roman Catholics anymore, but between modern anti-realists and classical realists. Bavinck states:

> In general, Protestants know far too little about what we have in common with Rome and what divides us. Thanks to the revival of Roman Catholic theology under the auspices of Thomas, it is now doubly incumbent on Protestants to provide a conscious and clear account of their relationship to Rome.[37]

This affirmation takes concrete shape in the parts of Bavinck's *Reformed Dogmatics* studied in the second chapter of this book. As stated above, his general epistemology is obviously marked by the influence of Thomas Aquinas and of the nineteenth century neo-Thomistic movement.[38] Bavinck perceived this movement not as a danger for his *Reformed Dogmatics* project, but as an ally against the anti-realist trends of his time that led many to dismiss dogmatic theology as a truth-seeking discipline.[39]

Plantinga's work on the *A/C model* and the *Extended A/C model* can also be interpreted as a work of retrieval in the sense defined by Webster, even if he has not always worked from this perspective. At the beginning of his career, in 1983, Plantinga published an article titled "Reason and Belief in

---

37 Bavinck, "Foreword to the First Edition (Volume 1) of the *Gereformeerde Dogmatiek*," 9. Bavinck develops a similar idea in another article: "The Catholicity of Christianity and the Church," in *Calvin Theological Journal* 27 (1992): 220-251.

38 Bavinck probably has in mind the publication of Leo XIII's encyclical *Aeterni Patris*, in which this pope pleads in favor of Thomas Aquinas's realism against the modern trends which threaten the classical understanding of theology. In the first volume of the *Reformed Dogmatics*, Bavinck also quotes several times Matteo Liberatore's neo-Thomistic epistemological sum: *Traité de la connaissance intellectuelle* (Paris: Berche et Tralin, 1885) (I haven't found the English version). From a historical theology point of view, it could be valuable to study in more detail the relation between Bavinck and neo-Thomistic thought (exemplified for instance by the work of the French theologian Réginald Garrigou-Lagrange).

39 From this perspective, Karl Barth's immense polemic against natural theology can only be perceived as deeply misguided. He uses modern philosophical tools (a dualistic opposition between general and special revelation) to fight against classical Christian positions in the name of Reformed faith. Yet, since modernity, Bavinck would say, the main epistemological conflicts have moved: they don't chiefly oppose Protestants to Catholics, but classical Christian faith to modern Christian faith.

God."[40] This text has been progressively interpreted as the manifesto of the intellectual movement founded by Plantinga and his friend Wolterstorff, the "Reformed epistemology" movement. In this article, Plantinga clearly opposes Calvin to Thomas Aquinas on epistemological questions, criticizing Aquinas as a foundationalist thinker who paved the way to modern epistemological errors, and praising Calvin for his non-foundationalist religious epistemology. This manifesto-article gave birth to international and inter-denominational debates. Nevertheless, since being hired by the Catholic University of Notre Dame, he has progressively abandoned the inter-denominational epistemological polemics generated by the Reformed epistemology movement and has started to work from another perspective.[41]

Warranted Christian Belief and its *A/C model* and *Extended A/C model* are an obvious result of this change in perspective. This entire work is indeed underlain by an important redefinition of the epistemological frontlines. On the one side there are thinkers like Locke, Kant, and what Plantinga calls the *Freud-and-Marx Complaint* opposed to the possibility of religious belief or knowledge. On the other side, there is the above studied *A/C model*, which is a combination of the epistemologies of Calvin and Thomas Aquinas.[42] In 2000, the opposition on theological

---

40 Alvin Plantinga, "Reason and Belief in God," in Alvin Plantinga and Nicholas Wolterstorff (eds.), *Faith and Rationality. Reason and Belief in God* (Notre Dame: University of Notre Dame Press, 1983), 1-93.

41 In 1998, Plantinga indeed states in an autobiographical text: "I am inclined to regret the choice of the name [that of *Reformed Epistemology*]: some have apparently thought the idea was to cast a gauntlet at the feet of Roman Catholic philosophers. Nothing could be further from the truth. As a matter of fact I think Calvin and Thomas Aquinas are very close on matters epistemological, in particular on matters concerning the epistemology of Christian belief." Alvin Plantinga, "Afterword," in *The Analytic Theist. An Alvin Plantinga Reader*, edited by James F. Sennett (Grand Rapids: Eerdmans Publishing, 1998), 354. Plantinga's work has generated interesting reactions among analytical Thomists. See among others: Linda Zagzebski (ed.), *Rational Faith: Catholic Responses to Reformed Epistemology* (Notre Dame: University of Notre Dame Press, 1993) and, more specifically, John Greco, "Catholics vs. Calvinists on Religious Knowledge," *American Catholic Philosophical Quarterly* 1 (1997): 13-34.

42 Cf. chapter 3 of this book, and the above quoted page 170 of *Warranted Christian Belief* (Oxford: Oxford University Press, 2000): "Thomas Aquinas and John Calvin concur on the claim that there is a kind of natural knowledge of God (and anything on which Calvin and Aquinas are in accord is something to which we had better pay careful attention). Here I want to propose a model based on Calvin's version of the suggestion [...] because he presents an interesting development of the particular thought in question. And here, as in several other areas, we can usefully see Calvin's

epistemology questions is thus no longer between Roman Catholics and Reformed Protestants, but between classical (or pre-modern) Christian thinkers and agnostic modern thinkers.

Manfred Svensson and David VanDrunen have stressed in the introduction to a recent book interestingly titled *Aquinas among the Protestants*, that Plantinga is nowadays not isolated in his decision to have Aquinas and Calvin work together:

> Beside ecumenism in the strict sense, we find something which is not wholly unrelated and yet distinct: the fact that Protestants and Roman Catholics face many similar intellectual challenges, and that at least some of these challenges can be faced together while relying on their common tradition. [...] The possibility of such collaboration rests on the fact that a robust Christian philosophical community now exists across the Christian traditions. The well-known renewal of "Christian philosophy" since the latter part of the twentieth century has in fact been a source for a more than historical interest in the thought of Aquinas.[43]

---

suggestion as a kind of meditation on and development of a theme suggested by Aquinas."

43 Manfred Svensson and David VanDrunen, "Introduction: The Reception, Critique, and Use of Aquinas in Protestant Thought," in *Aquinas Among the Protestants*, ed. Manfred Svensson and David VanDrunen (Oxford: Wiley Blackwell, 2018), 8. See also Michael Allen and Scott R. Swain, *Reformed Catholicity. The Promise of Retrieval for Theology and Biblical Interpretation* (Grand Rapids: Baker Academics, 2015). An older significant book on this question, prefaced by the well-known Notre Dame Roman Catholic philosopher Ralph McInerny is: Arvin Vos, *Aquinas, Calvin, and Contemporary Protestant Thought. A Critique of Protestant Views on the Thought of Thomas Aquinas* (Grand Rapids: Eerdmans Publishing Company, 1985). And also prefaced by Ralph McInerny: Norman L. Geisler, *Thomas Aquinas. An Evangelical Appraisal* (Grand Rapids: Baker Book House, 1991). In an article quoted at the end of the second chapter of this book ("*Sola Scriptura* as an Evangelical Theological Method?"), John Bolt works from the same perspective. The Yale theologian William Placher has also worked from this perspective in a book indirectly related to the scope of my research: "This book selects from all the issues Christians faced at the beginning of the modern era one set of interrelated questions: How did theologians and philosophers think about God? How did they define their language about God? What was God's relation to the created world and human moral efforts? I will argue that seventeenth-century thinkers grew more confident about human capacities [...] and narrowed their understanding of what counted as reasonable articulation of an argument for faith. That combination of a kind of confidence in human abilities and constricting definitions of acceptable reasoning led theology astray. Broad generalizations about the Christian tradition are dangerous, so I will be contrasting seventeenth-century developments with three particular earlier theologians—Aquinas, Luther, and Calvin. The three of them certainly would not have agreed about

Among the shared "intellectual challenges" mentioned by Svensson and VanDrunen is certainly that of a realist understanding of theology which is altogether metaphysical, epistemological and semantic. The renewal of Christian philosophy and its interest in the thought of Aquinas is an expression of a denial of "the fundamental premise of Enlightenment philosophy of religion [which is the ideal of a rationally grounded religion], shared alike by Locke and those in his tradition, and by Kant and those in his."[44]

As stated in the first chapter, Nicholas Wolterstorff is one of the main proponents of this contemporary movement (with his friend Plantinga). He has written numerous interesting pages in which he proposes an interpretation of the shift which has occurred during these last decades. While describing the evolution of analytic philosophy during the second half of the twentieth century, he states:

> I think it was the demise of the policing function within analytic philosophy that made possible the extraordinary flourishing in recent years of metaphysics, of philosophy of religion, and of philosophical theology—in particular, of philosophical theology that is theistically realist in its orientation. [...] These developments have contributed, in turn, to the resurgence of interest in medieval philosophy. No longer is the metaphysics or theology of the medieval philosophers dismissed on the ground that they were trying to think the unthinkable or say the unsayable.[45]

The present proposal can be understood from the perspective of the mingling of the above-described emergence of theologies of retrieval and this evolution of analytic philosophy of religion. This intellectual convergence, coupled with the loss of influence of a Continental philosophy

---

everything, but they did manifest patterns of theological thinking that often got lost in the seventeenth century." *The Domestication of Transcendence. How Modern Thinking about God Went Wrong* (Louisville: Westminster John Knox Press, 1996), 2-3.

44 Nicholas Wolterstorff, "Analytic Philosophy of Religion: Retrospect and Prospect," in *Inquiring about God. Selected Essays, Volume 1*, ed. Terence Cueno (Cambridge: Cambridge University Press, 2010), 29.

45 Nicholas Wolterstorff, "Postscript: A Life in Philosophy," in *Practices of Belief. Selected Essays, Volume 2*, ed. Terence Cuneo (Cambridge: Cambridge University Press, 2010), 417. In "Analytic Philosophy of Religion: Retrospect and Prospect," he states: "Most analytic philosophers of religion simply take metaphysical realism for granted, including metaphysical realism concerning God. [...] A second baffling and off-putting feature [from a postmodern non-realist perspective] is their epistemological confidence concerning our ability to gain knowledge of God." (*Inquiring about God*, 18.)

of religion stuck in apophaticism or skepticism, is indeed favorable to enterprises such as this one. By working on thinkers who build their argument on Thomism and Calvinism, and, on Bavinck, who refers to the classical theology of the divine Logos, I consciously join these wider contemporary movements and aim to contribute to their development.

4.2 Retrieval versus "Working under the Conditions of (Post-) Modernity"
This proposal is unambiguously opposed to all the various forms of modern or postmodern anti-realism. But more interestingly, I have outlined in the previous subsection that the main realist conceptions of theology are not homogeneous, and that this proposal is compatible with methodological critical realism as well as classical theological realism but opposed to post-Kantian critical realism and radical theological realism. This divide is significant, and working on interpreting it allows for interesting conclusions on the contemporary context. The aim of this subsection is to show that the convergence between this proposal, methodological critical realism, and classical theological realism is due to a common will to be faithful to classical Christian faith; and that, by contrast, the important divergences between post-Kantian critical realism and radical theological realism are an illustration of the Babelian consequences of modernity and postmodernity on theology.

In order to display this contrast, I briefly refer to one of Bruce McCormack's books on Karl Barth, *Orthodox and Modern. Studies in the Theology of Karl Barth*.[46] In this book, McCormack deals with numerous facets of the twentieth-century Swiss theologian and proposes in the introduction an overall interpretation of his work:

> The truth is that Barth has not simply taken over unchanged any doctrinal formulation of the ancient or the Reformation churches. He has reconstructed the whole of "orthodox" teaching from ground up. [...] My own view is this: what Barth was doing, in the end, was seeking to understand what it means to be orthodox *under the conditions of modernity*.[47]

---

46 Bruce McCormack, *Orthodox and Modern. Studies in the Theology of Karl Barth* (Grand Rapids: Baker Academic, 2008).
47 Bruce McCormack, *Orthodox and Modern. Studies in the Theology of Karl Barth*, 16-17. Two interesting chapters of this book are devoted to issues that closely relate to the scope of my research: chapter 5 ("Beyond Nonfoundationalism and Postmodern Readings of Barth: Critically Realistic Dialectical Theology," 109-165) and chapter 6 ("The Limits of the Knowledge of God: Theses on the Theological Epistemology of Karl Barth," 167-180).

I am not interested in discussing the cogency of this affirmation in the context of Barthian studies. I nevertheless hold that it characterizes in a lapidary way the spirit of many contemporary theological works, and especially both post-Kantian critical realism and radical theological realism. The proper name "Barth" can be replaced by these two realist trends and the question is then: "what does it mean to be realist *under the condition of (post)modernity*?"

By contrast, the present proposal, along with methodological critical realism and classical theological realism, takes the (post)modern context into account, but refuses to work *under the conditions* of this cultural phenomenon. It is possible to work *in the context of* modernity or postmodernity without being *under their conditions*. The theologies of retrieval can be interpreted, as Vanhoozer states, as an illustration of this affirmation. We must therefore ask how we might retrieve the Christian tradition and develop it in a fruitful way in the contemporary philosophical and theological context.[48]

One can work from the perspective of classical Christianity and apply it to contemporary discussions, the strategy being to contest the logic of marginalization of classical realist conceptions of theology. The "tabula rasa" ethos of modernity, which leads modern thinkers to distrust anything that comes from previous centuries, may deafen us to any serious reference to the past. Working from a perspective of retrieval is automatically interpreted as a vain attempt to reach a lost golden-age. I nevertheless hold that such an approach contributes to the revalorization of classical Christian affirmations and unifies works from various centuries and intellectual contexts. Even if defending a metaphysical, epistemological and semantic realist conception of theology may nowadays be perceived as an uncommon attempt, it is a meaningful and common enterprise from the perspective of the lively and age-old Christian tradition of thought.

By contrast, even if they all claim to be realists, it is difficult for post-Kantian critical realists and radical theological realists to find a common ground of discussion. By adopting modern core intellectual stances—the Kantian philosophy of representation or the rejection of thought-categories that come from classical philosophy, such as a metaphysics of

---

48 I thus disagree with Sutanto's statement: "With the organic motif in place, […] it is no longer necessary to choose between an orthodox or modern Bavinck." Nathaniel Gray Sutanto, *God and Knowledge. Herman Bavinck's Theological Epistemology* (London and New York: T&T Clark, 2020), 10. By contrast, I consider it necessary to choose, and the way Bavinck refers to the organic motif shows that he undoubtedly belongs to the family of classical theologians (in the sense defined in Chapter 1).

substance —these trends are themselves a manifestation of the Babelian intellectual character of the contemporary Western context.

In conclusion to this subsection, it is worth remembering Webster's affirmation that the problem is not mainly *modern* theology, but *theology* itself. This statement can be interpreted from the perspective of the classical tension described in the first chapter between the knowability and the incomprehensibility of God. In this case, theology is indeed an always problematic discipline. But if one understands Webster's statement as a minimization of the impact of modernity (and postmodernity) on theology, it should be contested. These cultural trends have indeed made the practice of theology *much* more problematic than it was, and therefore have to be challenged. Our proposal is best interpreted from the former perspective and represents a positive contribution to this project.

4.3 Theology as a Meaningful Truth-Seeking Discipline
A positive sequel of this proposal is that it helps us view theology as a meaningful truth-seeking discipline in the contemporary context. It is indeed obvious that theology, as a discipline aimed at studying God and the world as related to God, is nowadays a broadly contested discipline. This situation is concerning and hence it is important to work on defending the legitimacy of theology. It is often acknowledged that from a professional angle, theology has three main audiences: the Christian churches, academia, and society.[49] Even if the professional theologian chooses to address one or another audience more specifically—since it may be difficult to satisfy simultaneously the varied exigencies of these three audiences—it is worth keeping in mind this triple responsibility. Nowadays, the practice of theology is not well secured in any of these three audiences. In the Christian churches the emphasis is often placed on religious experience, personal development, community life or social work rather than on theological issues. In many Western universities, the academic status of theology is contested and challenged by the comparative approach of secular religious studies. In society, the demands are for theoretical tools that promote interreligious dialogue and fight religious fundamentalism, rather than for the formulation of Christian theological propositions. The aim of this subsection is to study how and to what extent, standing on the shoulders of both Bavinck and Plantinga, we can contribute to strengthening the status of theology in the contemporary Western context.

---

49 Cornelis van der Kooi and Gijsbert van den Brink, *Christian Dogmatics. An Introduction* (Grand Rapids: Eerdmans Publishing Company, 2017), 5-6.

As already said, an important consequence of a synthesized model of a realist conception of theology is that it leads to an understanding of theology as a meaningful truth-seeking discipline. By employing the concept of "truth-seeking," I aim to put forward two equally important affirmations that both flow from this proposal. First, contrary to the contemporary anti-realist phenomenological or pragmatic approaches of theology, I have developed a comprehensive and consistent argument that justifies the idea that theology has an inescapably cognitive and propositional dimension, and that it may formulate *true* or *false* claims about God, the world and human beings. Secondly, theology is a humble discipline, which never comprehends or controls its object of study. The form of realism proposed—by fleshing out fundamental insights of classical theology on God's knowability and incomprehensibility in a contemporary context—substantiates this stance. I now briefly apply the understanding of theology which flows from this proposal to the three above-mentioned audiences.

An immediate consequence of phenomenological or pragmatic antirealist conceptions of theology in the Christian churches is an indifference towards dogmatic theological questions. The antirealist trends lead to a valorization of practical, experiential or community life quests rather than intellectual issues. As a limited but significant illustration of this statement, we can refer to the work of two sociologists of religion, Christian Smith and Melinda Lundquist Denton. They have studied the religious and spiritual lives of American teenagers and have concluded that what they call *Moralistic Therapeutic Deism* "is colonizing many historical religious traditions and, almost without anyone noticing, converting believers in the old faiths to its alternative religious vision."[50] These authors have forged this concept in order to describe a faith based on a non-doctrinal spiritual quest for personal happiness and interpersonal "niceness."[51] An important consequence of this shift is described by these authors as follows:

---

50 Christian Smith and Melinda Lundquist Denton, *Soul Searching. The Religious and Spiritual Lives of American Teenagers* (New York: Oxford University Press, 2005), 171.
51 Here is their presentation of what they consider the creed of this form of religion: "1. God exists who created and orders the world and watches over human life on earth. 2. God wants people to be good, nice, and fair to each other, as taught in the Bible and by most world religions. 3. The central goal of life is to be happy and to feel good about oneself. 4. God does not need to be particularly involved in one's life except when God is needed to resolve a problem. 5. Good people go to heaven when they die." (Smith and Denton, *Soul Searching. The Religious and Spiritual Lives of American Teenagers*, 162-163)

The language, and therefore experience, of Trinity, holiness, sin, grace, justification, sanctification, church, Eucharist, and heaven and hell appear, among most Christian teenagers in the United States at the very least, to be supplanted by the language of happiness, niceness, and an earned heavenly reward.[52]

Smith and Lundquist Denton's 2005 teenagers are now adults and one can observe that *Moralistic Therapeutic Deism* is alive in contemporary Western Christianity, and not only in the United States.

Since Christian religion is altogether ritualistic, moral and intellectual,[53] I interpret the loss of theological interest in the churches as an at least problematic evolution. A cogent model for a realist understanding of theology contributes to the appreciation of theological inquiry within the Christian church. My argument secures the possibility of acquiring some theological knowledge and encourages church ministers and theologians to develop a comprehension of the Christian faith with confidence. If one interprets dogmatic work as something more than forging a symbolic language about an unknowable transcendence, or more than providing for the grammar (or rules) of the language game of a specific religious tradition, it immediately becomes much more meaningful. Seeking the truth is a natural activity of the human mind and characterizes every scientific enterprise. *Real* issues are at stake while one is doing theology, and deserve sustained and careful work as part of a collective truth-seeking discussion.

A particular interest for the church in this proposal is that it works on retrieving the classical realistic heritage of the Christian church against theological anti-realism, which, as noted, is a mainly modern phenomenon. Both Bavinck and Plantinga explicitly plead for a unified interpretation of Calvin and Thomas Aquinas against phenomenological symbolism or pragmatism. As Todd Billings states, such an approach

---

52 Smith and Denton, *Soul Searching. The Religious and Spiritual Lives of American Teenagers*, 171.
53 The historian of the church Robert Louis Wilken sums up this idea nicely: "The Christian religion is inescapably ritualistic (one is received into the church by a solemn washing with water), uncompromisingly moral ('be ye perfect as your Father in heaven is perfect,' said Jesus), and unapologetically intellectual (be ready to give a 'reason for the hope that is in you,' in the words of I Peter). Like all the major religions of the world, Christianity is more than a set of devotional practices and a moral code: it is also a way of thinking about God, about human beings, about the world and history." Robert Louis Wilken, *The Spirit of Early Christian Thought* (New Haven and London: Yale University Press, 2003), xiii.

"opens up a place for ecclesial life and theological reflection that is wide and spacious, yet specified in its worship of the Triune God and rooted in theological conviction."[54]

The second audience of theology as a professional activity is the academy, even if this audience is probably now the most challenged. In numerous Western countries, state universities have been hosting a faculty of theology for many centuries. Nevertheless, since the birth of modern universities in the nineteenth century, the academy has become a somehow problematic audience for theology.[55] One can indeed observe a tension between the secular character of the modern university and the religious character of theology. Some theologians are glad to practice theology within state universities, even if they can consider leaving the academy if the secularist pressure encroaches on their discipline: "Theology can exist and flourish within or without the academy, and has done so in a large number of ways. No institutional locale is wholly adequate; each exposes theology to a set of vices as well as affording opportunities."[56] Other theologians, such as Gijsbert van den Brink, are insisting on maintaining theology faculties within state universities, arguing that "if it is possible to *know* God, as Christians hold, then surely God should not be absent from the contemporary centres of knowledge production *par excellence*—the universities."[57] They are therefore working on clarifying and defending the methodological standards of the

---

54 Todd Billings, "Rediscovering the Catholic-Reformed Tradition for Today: A Biblical, Christ-Centered Vision for Church Renewal," in *Reformed Catholicity. The Promise of Retrieval for Theology and Biblical Interpretation*, ed. Michael Allen and Scott R. Swain (Grand Rapids: Baker Academics, 2015), 144.
55 I mentioned this question in the introduction of chapter 2. For an insightful overview of this development, see Thomas A. Howard, *Protestant Theology and the Making of Modern German University* (New York: Oxford University Press, 2006).
56 John Webster, "*Regina Artium*: Theology and the Humanities," in *The Domain of the Word. Scripture and Theological Reason* (London and New York: T&T Clark, 2012), 192. Before this, Webster states on page 171: "As theology acquires some of the properties of an academic discipline, and especially after the growth of the modern research university from the mid-eighteenth century, the question [of the relation between theology and the humanities] shifts to become one about the relation of theology as one discipline to the humanities as another cluster of disciplines. This more recent way of asking the question, forms of which remain the conventional approach in the modern university, has rarely proved fruitful; the very terms in which the question is asked defeat in advance any theologically satisfactory answer."
57 Gijsbert van den Brink, "The Future of Theology at Public Universities," *In die Skriflig* 54, no. 2 (2020): 2 (https://doi.org/10.4102/ids.v54i2.2583). This article provides interesting reflections on this question and an up-to-date bibliography.

discipline from an academic perspective.[58] In this context, Van den Brink insists that "theology is directed at giving a scientifically responsible account of faith, which does not, of course, transform faith itself into a scientific theory."[59] One notices here an explicit desire to find a right balance between the critical-scholarly exigencies of the academy and the specific character of the discipline.[60]

In the first chapter, I affirmed that the adoption of a phenomenological or a pragmatic antirealist conception of theology leads this discipline to its dissolution into other human sciences, such as philosophy, psychology, sociology, anthropology or literary criticism. I thus hold that adopting an antirealist theological discourse that waters down the metaphysical claims of theology in order to safeguard a position within contemporary academies is a losing strategy. By contrast, a realist approach (which includes metaphysical claims) is an essential part of a meaningful practice of theology within the academy, even if it may disturb defenders of academic secularism. Viewing theology as a truth-seeking discipline stimulates the activity of the intellect and leads to a view of theological research as something serious.

Even if this proposal may not convince a defender of a strongly secularist university, it meets the standards of academic scholarship and therefore may contribute to strengthening theology within contemporary state universities. Some aspects of the present research may play this role. First, the study of Bavinck's careful defense of a realist conception of theology is valuable, since he faced similar academic issues and proposed an informed, subtle, well-balanced answer. Second, the integration of the work of Plantinga represents a philosophical strengthening of the proposal. His recognized epistemological work plays an important role in the consolidation of Bavinck's proposal without leading to an abandonment of the specific nature of theology. Third, the model provides a complete intellectual framework that encourages cogent and fruitful academic theological work. In short, it represents an application of theology as "a scientifically responsible account of faith."

---

58 As shown in chapter 1, this is a difference between the theological realists and the critical realists.
59 Gijsbert van den Brink, *Philosophy of Science for Theologians. An Introduction* (Frankfurt am Main: Peter Lang, 2009), 155. See pages 149-159 titled "The relevance of theology as an academic discipline."
60 Whether this balance is acceptable in the contemporary Western context is of course ultimately an academic policy question and depends on the mandate given to the university by society.

The third audience of theology as a professional activity is society. And as for the first two audiences, the position of theology in society today is not an easy one. Contemporary Western societies indeed manifest important concerns towards religions. A first concern is related to the multicultural and religiously pluralistic character of our societies. What role should religion play in society? How should society organize the cohabitation of its numerous religious communities? A second concern lies in the fear of religious fundamentalism and fanaticism. The distinction between adhering with conviction to a religion and being a fanatic is not always clear in the minds of our contemporaries. In this context, the development of a public theological discourse may be perceived as somehow worrying, or even dangerous for the stability of a society.

In this context and as mentioned in Chapter 1, theological realism is sometimes perceived as a potential source of fundamentalism and intolerance.[61] On the contrary, the comparative and anti-realist character of religious studies is seen as a useful antidote to religious fanaticism, which makes it possible to study religious phenomena in a way that encourages interreligious dialogue and weakens any form of radicalism.[62] One can thus reasonably ask whether developing a cogent model for a realist conception of theology is a fruitful way of strengthening theology's position in society, or whether one shouldn't instead develop anti-realist arguments in order to calm contemporary anxieties. I think that advocating a realist conception of theology doesn't necessarily lead to intolerance or fanaticism and that it may, on the contrary, help theologians reach their third audience.

It is historically established that there was a correlation in seventeenth-century Europe between the emergence of theological skepticism (or relativism, or anti-realism) and that of religious tolerance.[63] We

---

61 This thesis is developed by Harriet A. Harris in *Fundamentalism and Evangelicals* (Oxford: Oxford University Press, 1998), for instance. According to this scholar, adhesion to a sort of Reidian common-sense realism is an important component of what she calls the "fundamentalist mentality" (see chapter 3 of her book).

62 For an illustration of this affirmation see the following article of John Hick, a well-known defender of post-Kantian anti-realism in theology: John Hick, "Religious Pluralism," in *The Routledge Companion of Philosophy of Religion*, ed. Chad Meister and Paul Copan (London and New York: Routledge, 2013), 240-249.

63 See Susan E. Schreiner's interesting study: *Are You Alone Wise? The Search for Certainty in the Early Modern Era* (New York: Oxford University Press, 2011). Without entering this immense historiographical debate, I think that the emergence of religious skepticism and anti-realist conceptions of theology between the sixteenth and the eighteenth centuries is a result of the confessional wars that occurred in Europe. These wars deeply changed the perception of religion (seen as a phenomenon which

nevertheless live in a very different historical situation. Nowadays, indifference towards Christian theology is no longer a support for religious tolerance but can be considered fertile soil for unhealthy religious tensions. It is indeed possible to formulate the following hypothesis: religious fundamentalism in Western countries today is not first of all a consequence of theological realism (even if that may have been the case in Western history), but is a religious or identity reaction against the relativism and theological indifference generated by the contemporary anti-realist trends. In psychological terms, these phenomena can be interpreted as a sort of overreaction against trends that are perceived as destabilizing the faith of people not versed in the study of theology, and as leading to theological illiteracy.[64]

From this perspective, I hold that the theological realism I propose is not an obstacle to religious peace and intelligence in our pluralist and multicultural societies, but that it may improve the comprehensibility of theological discourse (even if it will not lead, of course, to a general agreement). Religious multicultural dialogue based on a phenomenological or pragmatic antirealism often leads to cozy declarations based on indifference towards disturbing truth-questions. Grounding the interreligious dialogue on a realist conception of theology undoubtedly makes it more difficult, but also more fruitful. More difficult, since the question of theological truth is not avoided and the disagreements are clearly identified. But also more fruitful, since both the explicit agreements and disagreements are the result of a demanding process that helps with understanding other religious stances in a better way, and that leads to a socially viable solution where protagonists "agree to disagree" on well-defined questions. Even if this solution is not perfect, it avoids a superficial consensus that may hide deep tensions, notably religious ones, within society. Finally, when this work of dogmatic clarification is done in a realistic way, the place is left to the politicians, who have the task of deciding what sort of society they want to promote on a religious level.

This proposal, with its insistence on the classical distinction between the incomprehensibility and the knowability of God clarifies both the possibilities and the limits of Christian theology. It therefore allows the professional theologian to develop a discourse that is altogether confident

---

generates fanaticism, hatred and extreme violence), and led people to distance themselves from realist conceptions of theology.
64 Even if the context has changed, it is possible to interpret the nineteenth century emergence of fundamentalism as a similar reaction against the claims of modern science. This is a central thesis of Harriet A. Harris's *Fundamentalism and Evangelicals*.

and modest. Theological issues are perceived as serious, since theology is a truth-seeking discipline and ideas do matter. But at the same time, the theologian remains in a humble position, since the object of his study is incomprehensible. This balance helps to overcome the contemporary unsound dialectic that opposes religious indifferentism to fanaticism and makes possible mature public discussions on religious issues.

5. Conclusion: Avenues for Further Research

The aim of this book has been to show in what way bringing together parts of the works of Bavinck and Plantinga strengthens the contemporary case for a realist conception of theology. It was found that synthesizing both streams of thought leads to a model for theological realism that is both comprehensive and consistent, that interacts in an enlightening way with other contemporary realist trends, and that provides an intellectual framework which encourages the practice of theology as a truth-seeking discipline.

Achieving this goal, however, involved many limitations as well as the avoidance of raising or developing too many questions at the same time. I thus devote the brief last subsection of this book to delineating some possible further research avenues. I am indeed aware that even if this work contributes to a contemporary realist conception of theology, it leaves numerous interesting questions open.

The first and most immediate research avenue would be further development of the *Bavinck/Plantinga model* for a realist conception of theology. For instance, it would be interesting to develop in detail the content of subsection 2.2 of this chapter. I hold that the model has been described with enough precision to be convincing, but that its accuracy could be further tested and demonstrated with more material evidence.

A second research avenue lies in the retrieval of the patristic Logos theology and its application to this proposal. As presented in chapter 2, this theological locus plays an important role in Bavinck's system, even if he doesn't develop it in a very precise way. A more careful study of this theological theme could strengthen the present proposal on both systematic and historical levels. On the systematic level, the richness of the locus, the way it brings philosophy and theology together, and the polysemy of the patristic use of the concept of Logos could probably improve the integration of the metaphysical, epistemological and semantic dimensions of the proposal.[65] On the historical level, the

---

65 One would nevertheless have to deal carefully with the Neo-Platonist participation metaphysics that has sometimes accompanied the theology of the divine Logos, and that potentially threatens the Christian doctrine of the transcendence of God.

strengthening of the connection between patristic theology and this proposal could give substance to the theology of retrieval put forward in the previous subsection.

A third fruitful avenue for further research might consist in studying more attentively the work of some important twentieth century theologians who have also dealt with the theology of the divine Logos in order to develop more or less realist conceptions of theology: Erich Przywara[66] and Hans Urs von Balthasar[67] on the Roman Catholic side, and Thomas Torrance[68] and Carl Henry[69] on the Protestant side. Interaction with their work would probably help in refining this model for a realist conception of theology, notably in the way it discusses other existing stances, such as various forms of critical and theological realism. The multiplication of the perspectives on contemporary approaches of the Logos theology could certainly help in clarifying with greater precision the ins and outs of the proposal. Studying the work of these thinkers could also help in testing the validity of the hypothesis of a convergence between Catholics and Protestants on the questions dealt with above.

A fourth avenue might consist in discussing the results of this research in light of the works of Karl Barth[70] and Wolfhart Pannenberg.[71] These two thinkers have exerted an immense influence on contemporary theological thought and have both developed original (and different)

---

66 Erich Przywara, *Analogia Entis. Metaphysics. Original Structure and Universal Rhythm* (Grand Rapids and Cambridge: Eerdmans Publishing, 2014).
67 Hans Urs von Balthasar, *Theo-Logic. Theological Logical Theory: Truth of God*. Vol. II (San Francisco: Ignatius Press, 2004).
68 The works of Torrance on this question are abundant. See among others: *Theological Science* (Oxford: Oxford University Press, 1969); *The Ground and Grammar of Theology* (Charlottesville: University Press of Virginia, 1980); *Reality and Scientific Theology* (Edinburgh: Scottish Academic Press, 1985); *The Christian Frame of Mind. Reason, Order, and Openness in Theology and Natural Science* (Colorado Springs: Helmers and Howard, 1989).
69 Carl F. H. Henry, *God, Revelation and Authority: God who Speaks and Shows. Fifteen Theses*, Part Two. Vol. III (Waco: Word Books Publishers, 1979).
70 Karl Barth, *Church Dogmatics. The Doctrine of God*, Vol. II. 1, trans. T. H. L. Parker, W. B. Johnston, Harold Knight and J. L. M. Haire, ed. G. W. Bromiley and T. F. Torrance. (London and New York: T&T Clark, 1957). Karl Barth, "Fate and Idea in Theology," in *The Way of Theology in Karl Barth. Essays and Comments*, edited by H. Martin Rumscheidt, 25-61 (Eugene: Wipf and Stock Publishers, 1986).
71 Wolfhart Pannenberg, *Systematic Theology*, Vol. 1, trans. Geoffrey W. Bromiley. (Grand Rapids: Eerdmans Publishing Company, 1991). Wolfhart Pannenberg, *Theology and the Philosophy of Science*, trans. Francis McDonagh (Philadelphia: Westminster Press, 1976).

realist conceptions of theology. The study of the convergences and the divergences between this proposal and their work could help with refining and enriching the contemporary elaboration of a realist conception of theology.

A fifth research avenue to be explored with more precision is the way this proposal can be related to the classical Reformed theological locus termed the *noetic effects of sin*.[72] I have referred here and there to this systematic theology issue (as well as the interconnected one of natural theology),[73] but was unable to devote the attention to this question it deserves. It would have taken the discussion too far away from the careful presentation of the *Bavinck/Plantinga Model*. Once the cogency of this proposal is acknowledged, it could be fruitful to interact with this theological theme through a dialogue with the work of moderate post-Barthian theological realists.[74]

As can be seen, the last three research avenues pursue the reflection started in the previous subsection. It is obvious that affirmations of the relation between this proposal and the status of theology in the church, in the academy and in society are not sufficiently developed. Each of these affirmations raises questions that should be dealt with in a careful way, notably by interacting with scholars who are currently working on those issues.

---

72 See for instance: Stephen K. Moroney, *The Noetic Effects of Sin: A Historical and Contemporary Exploration of How Sin Affects Our Thinking* (Lanham: Lexington Books, 2000); Paul Helm, "John Calvin, the *Sensus Divinitatis*, and the Noetic Effects of Sin," in *International Journal for Philosophy of Religion* 43 (1998), 87-107. Rik Peels, "Sin and Human Cognition of God," in *Scottish Journal of Theology* 64 (2011), 390-409.

73 Michael Sudduth, *The Reformed Objection to Natural Theology* (Farnham and Burlington: Ashgate Publishing, 2009).

74 Notably, recently published works of John Webster deal carefully with issues related to this research. See John Webster, *The Domain of the Word. Scripture and Theological Reason* (London and New York: T&T Clark International, 2012); *God Without Measure: Working Papers in Christian Theology. Vol. II. Virtue and Intellect* (London and New York: T&T Clark International, 2016). It could also be interesting to study from this perspective the work of Colin Gunton. See among others: *Revelation and Reason. Prolegomena to Systematic Theology*, ed. P. H. Brazier (London and New York: T&T Clark, 2008).

Bibliography

Allen, Michael and Scott R. Swain. *Reformed Catholicity. The Promise of Retrieval for Theology and Biblical Interpretation*. Grand Rapids: Baker Academic, 2015.

Alston, William P. "Realism and the Christian Faith." *International Journal for the Philosophy of Religion* 3 (1995): 37-55.

Alston, William P. *A Realist Conception of Truth*. Ithaca and London: Cornell University Press, 1996.

Alston, William P. *A Sensible Metaphysical Realism*. Milwaukee: Marquette University Press, 2007.

Alston, William P. *Divine Nature and Human Language. Essays in Philosophical Theology*. Ithaca and London: Cornell University Press, 1989.

Alston, William P., ed. *Realism and Antirealism*. Ithaca and London: Cornell University Press, 2002.

Anscombe, Elizabeth. *Faith in a Hard Ground. Essays on Philosophy and Ethics*. Saint Andrews: Imprint Academic, 2008.

Anscombe, Elizabeth. *From Plato to Wittgenstein*. Saint Andrews: Imprint Academic, 2011.

Aquinas, Thomas. *On the Unity of the Intellect against the Averroists*, translated by Beatrice H. Zedler. Milwaukee: Marquette University Press, 1968.

Aquinas, Thomas. *Summa Theologiae*, translated by T. McDermott. Garden City: Image Books/Doubleday, 1969.

Aristotle. *De Anima*, edited and translated by Robert D. Hicks. New York: Arno Press, 1976.

Aristotle. *Metaphysics*, edited and translated by W. D. Ross. Oxford: Oxford University Press, 1924.

Aristotle. *Posterior Analytics*, edited by Jonathan Barnes. Oxford: Clarendon Press, 1993.

Armstrong, A. H., ed. *The Cambridge History of Later Greek and Early Medieval Philosophy*. Cambridge: Cambridge University Press, 1967.

Asselt, Willem J. van. "The Fundamental Meaning of Theology: Archetypal and Ectypal Theology in Seventeenth-Century Reformed Thought." *Westminster Theological Journal* 64 (2002): 319-335.

Auerbach, Erich. *Mimesis*. Princeton: Princeton University Press, 1968.

Baç, Murat and Renée Elio. "Scheme-Based Alethic Realism: Agency, the Environment, and Truthmaking." *Minds and Machines* 14 (2004): 173-196.

Baker, Deane-Peter, ed. *Alvin Plantinga*. Cambridge: Cambridge University Press, 2007.

Baker, Deane-Peter. *Tayloring Reformed Epistemology. Charles Taylor, Alvin Plantinga and the de jure Challenge to Christian Belief*. London: SCM Press, 2007.

Balserak, Jon. *Divinity Compromised. A Study of Divine Accommodation in the Thought of John Calvin*. Dordrecht: Springer, 2006.

Balthasar, Hans Urs. *Theo-Logic. Theological Logical Theory: Truth of God*, translated by Andrian J. Walker. Vol. 2. San Francisco: Ignatius Press, 2004.

Barbour, Ian G. *Issues in Science and Religion*. Englewood Cliffs: Prentice-Hall Inc., 1966.

Barbour, Ian G. *Myths, Models, and Paradigms. A Comparative Study in Science & Religion*. New York: Harper and Row Publishers, 1976.

Barth, Karl. "Fate and Idea in Theology." In *The Way of Theology in Karl Barth. Essays and Comments*, edited by H. Martin Rumscheidt, 25-61. Eugene: Wipf and Stock Publishers, 1986.

Barth, Karl. *Church Dogmatics. The Doctrine of God*, translated by T. H. L. Parker, W. B. Johnston, Harold Knight and J. L. M. Haire, edited by G. W. Bromiley and T. F. Torrance. Vol. II. 1. London and New York: T&T Clark, 1957.

Barth, Karl. *The Knowledge of God and the Service of God According to the Teaching of the Reformation*, translated by J. L. M. Haire and Ian Henderson. London: Hodder and Stoughton Publishers, 1938.

Bauckham, Richard. "Eschatology." In *The Oxford Handbook of Systematic Theology*, edited by John Webster, Kathryn Tanner and Iain Torrance, 306-322. Oxford: Oxford University Press, 2007.

Bavinck, Herman. "Calvin and Common Grace." In *Calvin and Reformation. Four Studies*, edited by William Park Armstrong, 99-130. Eugene: Wipf and Stock, 2004.

Bavinck, Herman. "Common Grace." *Calvin Theological Journal* 24 (1989): 35-65.

Bavinck, Herman. "Foreword to the First Edition (Volume 1) of the *Gereformeerde Dogmatiek*." *Calvin Theological Journal* 45 (2010): 9-10.

Bavinck, Herman. "The Catholicity of Christianity and the Church." *Calvin Theological Journal* 27 (1992): 220-251.

Bavinck, Herman. "Theology and Religious Studies in Nineteenth-Century Netherlands." In *Essays on Religion, Science, and Society*, edited by John Bolt. Translated by Harry Boonstra and Gerrit Sheeres, 281-288. Grand Rapids: Baker Academic, 2008.

Bavinck, Herman. "Theology and Religious Studies." In *Essays on Religion, Science, and Society*, edited by John Bolt. Translated by Harry Boonstra and Gerrit Sheeres, 49-60. Grand Rapids: Baker Academic, 2008.

Bavinck, Herman. *Christian Worldview*, translated and edited by Nathaniel Gray Suranto, James Eglinton and Cory C. Brock. Wheaton: Crossway, 2019.

Bavinck, Herman. *Gereformeerde Dogmatiek. Eerste Deel*. Kampen: J. H. Kok, 1928.

Bavinck, Herman. *Reformed Dogmatics: God and Creation*. Edited by John Bolt. Translated by John Vriend. Vol. 2. Grand Rapids: Baker Academic, 2004.

Bavinck, Herman. *Reformed Dogmatics: Holy Spirit, Church, and New Creation*. Edited by John Bolt. Translated by John Vriend. Vol. 4. Grand Rapids: Baker Academic, 2008.

Bavinck, Herman. *Reformed Dogmatics: Prolegomena*. Edited by John Bolt. Translated by John Vriend. Vol. 1. Grand Rapids: Baker Academic, 2003.

Bavinck, Herman. *Reformed Dogmatics: Sin and Salvation in Christ*. Edited by John Bolt. Translated by John Vriend. Vol. 3. Grand Rapids: Baker Academic, 2006.

Bavinck, Herman. *The Philosophy of Revelation. A New Annotated Edition, Adapted and Expanded from the 1908 Stone Lectures Presented at Princeton Theological Seminary*. Edited by Cory Brock and Nathaniel Gray Sutanto. Peabody: Hendrickson Publishers, 2018.

Beilby, James. "Plantinga's Model of Warranted Christian Belief." In *Alvin Plantinga*, edited by Deane-Peter Baker, 125-165. Cambridge: Cambridge University Press, 2007.

Beilby, James. *Epistemology as Theology. An Evaluation of Alvin Plantinga's Religious Epistemology*. Burlington: Ashgate, 2005.

Bellah, Robert N. "Christianity and Symbolic Realism." In *Journal for the Scientific Study of Religion* 2 (1970): 89-106.

Belt, Henk van den. *The Authority of Scripture in Reformed Theology. Truth and Trust*. Leiden and Boston: Brill, 2008.

Berkhof Louis. *Systematic Theology*. Edinburgh: The Banner of Truth Trust, 1958.

Berkhof, Hendrikus. *Christian Faith. An Introduction to the Study of Faith*, translated by Sierd Woudstra. Grand Rapids: Eerdmans Publishing Company, 1979.

Berkouwer, Gerrit C. *General Revelation*. Grand Rapids: Eerdmans Publishing Company, 1955.

Berlin, Isaiah. *The Roots of Romanticism*. Princeton: Princeton University Press, 2001.

Billings, J. Todd. "Rediscovering the Catholic-Reformed Tradition of Today: A Biblical, Christ-Centered Vision for Church Renewal." In *Reformed Catholicity. The Promise of Retrieval for Theology and Biblical Interpretation*, edited by Michael Allen and Scott R. Swain, 143-161. Grand Rapids: Baker Academic, 2015.

Boersma Hans. *Heavenly Participation. The Weaving of a Sacramental Tapestry*. Grand Rapids: Eerdmans Publishing Co., 2011.

Boersma, Hans. *Nouvelle Théologie and Sacramental Ontology. A Return to Mystery*. Oxford: Oxford University Press, 2009.

Boghossian, Paul A. *Fear of Knowledge. Against Relativism and Constructivism*. Oxford: Oxford University Press, 2006.

Bolt, John. "Doubting Reformational Anti-Thomism." In *Aquinas Among the Protestants*, edited by Manfred Svensson and David VanDrunen, 129-147. Oxford: Wiley Blackwell, 2018.

Bolt, John. "Grand Rapids Between Kampen and Amsterdam: Herman Bavinck's Reception and Influence in North America." In *Calvin Theological Journal* 38 (2003): 263-280.

Bolt, John. "*Sola Scriptura* as an Evangelical Theological Method?" In *Reforming or Conforming? Post-Conservative Evangelicals and the Emerging Church*, edited by Gary L.W. Johnson and Ronald N. Gleason, 62-92. Wheaton: Crossway Books, 2008.

Bolt, John. "The Bavinck Recipe for Theological Cake." *Calvin Theological Journal* 45 (2010): 11-17.

Bonhoeffer, Dietrich. *Letters and Papers from Prison*, 3rd ed. London: SCM Press, 1967.

Brink, David O. "Moral Realism." In *The Cambridge Dictionary of Philosophy*, edited by Robert Audi, 511-512. Cambridge: Cambridge University Press, 1995.

Brink, Gijsbert van den and Marcel Sarot. "Contemporary Philosophical Theology." In *Understanding the Attributes of God*, edited by Gijsbert van den Brink and Marcel Sarot, 9-32. Frankfurt am Main: Peter Lang, 1999.

Brink, Gijsbert van den. "A Most Elegant Book. The Natural World in Article 2 of the Belgic Confession." *Westminster Theological Journal* 73 (2011): 273-292.

Brink, Gijsbert van den. "On Certainty in Faith and Science: the Bavinck-Warfield Exchange." *The Bavinck Review* 8 (2017): 65-88.

Brink, Gijsbert van den. "The Future of Theology at Public Universities." *In die Skrifkig* 54, no. 2 (2020): 1-9 (https://doi.org/10.4102/ids.v54i2.2583).

Brink, Gijsbert van den. *Philosophy of Science for Theologians. An Introduction*. Frankfurt am Main: Peter Lang, 2009.

Brümmer Vincent. *Speaking of a Personal God. An Essay in Philosophical Theology*. Cambridge: Cambridge University Press, 1992.

Brümmer, Vincent. *Brümmer on Meaning and the Christian Faith. Collected Writings of Vincent Brümmer*. Aldershot and Burlington: Ashgate Publishing, 2006.

Brümmer, Vincent. *The Model of Love. A Study in Philosophical Theology*. Cambridge: Cambridge University Press, 1993.

Brunner, Emil and Karl Barth. *Natural Theology. Comprising "Nature and Grace" by Professor Dr. Emil Brunner and the Reply "No!" by Dr. Karl Barth*, edited by John Baillie and translated by Peter Fraenkel. Eugene: Wipf and Stock Publishers, 2002.

Brunner, Emil. *The Christian Doctrine of God*, translated by Olive Wyon. Vol. 1. Philadelphia: Westminster Press, 1980.

Buckley, Michael J. *At the Origins of Modern Atheism*. New Haven and London: Yale University Press, 1987.

Butchvarov, Panayot. "Conceptualism." In *The Cambridge Dictionary of Philosophy*, edited by Robert Audi, 148. Cambridge: Cambridge University Press, 1995).

Byrne, Peter. *God and Realism*. Aldershot and Burlington: Ashgate Publishing, 2003.

Calvin, John. *Institutes of Christian Religion,* translated by Henry Beveridge. Peabody: Hendrikson, 2007.

Capelle-Dumont, Philippe, Jean Greisch, Richard Kearney, Jean-Luc Marion, Andreas Speer, and David Tracy. *Métaphysique et Christianisme. Vingtième Anniversaire de la Chaire Etienne Gilson*. Paris: Presses Universitaires de France, 2015.

Cathey, Robert Andrew. *God in Postliberal Perspective. Between Realism and Non-Realism*. Farnham and Burlington: Ashgate Publishing, 2009.

Chakravartty, Anian. "Scientific Realism." *Stanford Encyclopedia of Philosophy* (Summer 2017 Edition), edited by Edward N. Zalta. URL = <https://plato.stanford.edu/archives/-sum2017/entries/scientific-realism/>.

Chalmers, Alan F. *What is this Thing Called Science?* 4th ed. Maidenhead: Open University Press, 2013.

Cochrane, Arthur C., ed. *Reformed Confessions of the 16th Century*. Louisville: Westminster John Knox Press, 2003.

Craig, Edward. "Realism and Antirealism." In *Routledge Encyclopedia of Philosophy Online* (2020), doi 10.4324/9780415249126-N049-1.

Crisp, Oliver D. and Michael C. Rea, eds. *Analytic Theology. New Essays in the Philosophy of Theology.* Oxford, Oxford University Press, 2009.

Crisp, Oliver D., ed. *A Reader in Contemporary Philosophical Theology.* London: T&T Clark, 2009.

Crowder, Colin, ed. *God and Reality. Essays on Christian Non-Realism.* London: Mowbray, 1997.

Cueno, Terence and René van Woudenberg, eds. *The Cambridge Companion to Thomas Reid.* Cambridge: Cambridge University Press, 2004.

Cunningham, Conor and Peter M. Candler, eds. *Belief and Metaphysics.* London: SCM Press, 2007.

Cupitt, Don. "Free Christianity." In *God and Reality. Essays on Christian Non-Realism,* edited by Colin Crowder, 14-25. London: Mowbray, 1997.

Cupitt, Don. *Taking Leave of God.* London: SCM Press, 1980.

Cupitt, Don. *The Sea of Faith.* 2nd ed. London: SCM Press, 1994.

Dalferth, Ingolf U. "Karl Barth's Eschatological Realism." In *Karl Barth: Centenary Essays,* edited by S. W. Sykes, 14-45. Cambridge: Cambridge University Press, 1989.

Dalferth, Ingolf U. "Wittgenstein: The Theological Reception." In *Religion and Wittgenstein's Legacy,* edited by D. Z. Phillips and Mario von der Ruhr, 273-302. Aldershot and Burlington: Ashgate Publishing, 2005.

Dalferth, Ingolf U. *Theology and Philosophy.* Eugene: Wipf and Stock Publishers, 2001.

Dawes, Hugh. *Freeing the Faith: A Credible Christianity for Today.* London: SPCK, 1992.

Dennett, Daniel C. and Alvin Plantinga. *Science and Religion. Are They Compatible?* New York and Oxford: Oxford University Press, 2011.

Dillenberger, John. *God Hidden and Revealed. The Interpretation of Luther's Deus Absconditus and its Significance for Religious Thought.* Philadelphia: Muhlenberg Press, 1953.

Diller, Kevin. *Theology's Epistemological Dilemma. How Karl Barth and Alvin Plantinga Provide a Unified Response.* Downers Grove: InterVarsity Press, 2014.

Duby, Steve. "Working with the Grain of Nature: Epistemic Underpinnings for Christian Witness in the Theology of Herman Bavinck." *The Bavinck Review* 3 (2012): 62-74.

Dummett, Michael. *Thought and Reality.* Oxford: Oxford University Press, 2006.

Echeverria, Eduardo J. "The Reformed Objection to Natural Theology: A Catholic Response to Herman Bavinck." *Calvin Theological Journal* 45 (2010): 87-116.

Eglinton, James P. *Response to "Working with the Grain of Nature: Epistemic Underpinnings for Christian Witness in the Theology of Herman Bavinck" by Steve Duby*. Unpublished Document.

Eglinton, James P. *Trinity and Organism. Towards a New Reading of Herman Bavinck's Organic Motif*. London and New York: T&T Clark, 2012.

Eglinton, James. *Bavinck: A Critical Biography*. Grand Rapids: Baker Books, 2020.

Ellis, Fiona. *Concepts and Reality in the History of Philosophy. Tracing a Philosophical Error from Locke to Bradley*. Abingdon: Routledge, 2005.

Ellis, Fiona. *God, Value, and Nature*. Oxford: Oxford University Press, 2014.

Eshleman, Andrew. "Can an Atheist Believe in God?" *Religious Studies* 2 (2005): 183-199.

Eshleman, Andrew. "Religious Fictionalism Defended: Reply to Cordy." *Religious Studies* 1 (2010): 91-96.

Fales, Evan. "Alvin Plantinga, *Warranted Christian Belief*." *Noûs* 2 (2003): 353-370.

Fine, Arthur. "Fictionalism." *Midwest Studies in Philosophy* 18 (1993) : 1–18

Flint, Thomas P. and Michael C. Rea, eds. *Oxford Readings in Philosophical Theology*. 2 Vols. Oxford: Oxford University Press, 2009.

Fodor, James. "Postliberal Theology." In *The Modern Theologians. An Introduction to Christian Theology since 1918*, edited by David F. Ford and Rachael Muers, 229-248. 3rd ed. Malden and Oxford: Blackwell Publishing, 2005.

Ford, David F. and Rachel Muers, eds. *The Modern Theologians. An Introduction to Christian Theology since 1918*. 3rd ed. Malden and Oxford: Blackwell Publishing, 2005.

Ford, David F. *Theology. A Very Short Introduction*. 2nd ed. Oxford: Oxford University Press, 2013.

Fraassen, Bas C. van. *The Scientific Image*. Oxford: Oxford University Press, 1980.

Frame, John M. *The Doctrine of the Knowledge of God*. Phillipsburg: Presbyterian and Reformed, 1987.

Freeman, Anthony. *God in Us: A Case for Christian Humanism*. London: SCM Press Ltd, 1993.

Frei, Hans W. *The Eclipse of Biblical Narrative. A Study in Eighteenth and Nineteenth Century Hermeneutics.* New Haven and London: Yale University Press, 1974.

Frei, Hans W. *Theology and Narrative. Selected Essays*, edited by George Hunsinger and William C. Placher. New York and Oxford: Oxford University Press, 1993.

Frei, Hans W. *Types of Christian Theology.* New Haven and London: Yale University Press, 1992.

Geest, Paul van. *The Incomprehensibility of God. Augustine as a Negative Theologian.* Leuven: Peeters, 2011.

Geisler, Norman L. *Thomas Aquinas. An Evangelical Appraisal.* Grand Rapids: Baker Book House, 1991.

Gettier, Edmund. "Is Justified True Belief Knowledge Belief?" *Analysis* 23 (1963): 121-123.

Gilson, Etienne. *Methodical Realism. A Handbook for Beginning Realists*, translated by Philip Trower. San Francisco: Ingatius Press, 2011.

Gisel, Pierre. *La Théologie.* Paris: Presses Universitaires de France, 2007.

Gootjes, Nicolaas H. *The Belgic Confession. Its History and Sources.* Grand Rapids: Baker Academic, 2007.

Greco, John. "Catholics vs. Calvinists on Religious Knowledge." *American Catholic Philosophical Quarterly* 1 (1997): 13-34.

Gregersen, Niels Henrik and Wentzel van Huysteen, eds. *Rethinking Theology and Science. Six Models for the Current Dialogue.* Grand Rapids: Eerdmans Publishing Company, 1998.

Gunton, Colin. "The Trinity, Natural Theology, and a Theology of Nature." In *The Trinity in a Pluralistic Age. Theological Essays on Culture and Religion*, edited by Kevin J. Vanhoozer, 88-103. Grand Rapids: Eerdmans Publishing Company, 1997.

Gunton, Colin. *Revelation and Reason. Prolegomena to Systematic Theology*, edited by P.H. Brazier. London and New York: T&T Clark, 2008.

Gunton, Colin. *The Barth Lectures*, transcribed and edited by P. H. Brazier. London and New York: T&T Clark, 2007.

Gunton, Colin. *The Christian Faith. An Introduction to Christian Doctrine.* Oxford: Blackwell, 2002.

Harris, Harriet A. *Fundamentalism and Evangelicals.* Oxford: Oxford University Press, 1998.

Hart, David A. *Faith in Doubt: Non-Realism and Christian Belief.* London: Mowbray, 1993.

Hauerwas, Stanley and L. Gregory Jones, eds. *Why Narratives? Readings in Narrative Theology.* Grand Rapids: William B. Eerdmans Publishing Co., 1989.

Helm, Paul. "John Calvin, the *Sensus Divinitatis*, and the Noetic Effects of Sin." *International Journal for Philosophy of Religion* 43 (1998): 87-107.

Helm, Paul. "Nature and Grace." In *Aquinas Among the Protestants*, edited by Manfred Svensson and David VanDrunen, 229-247. Oxford: Wiley Blackwell, 2018.

Helm, Paul. "*Warranted Christian Belief* by Alvin Plantinga." *Mind* 110 (2001): 1110-1115.

Helm, Paul. *Faith and Understanding*. Grand Rapids: William B. Eerdmans Publishing, 1997.

Helm, Paul. *John Calvin's Ideas*. Oxford: Oxford University Press, 2004.

Hendrikse, Klaas. *Croire en un Dieu qui n'existe pas. Manifeste d'un pasteur athée*. Genève: Labor et Fides, 2011.

Henry, Carl F. H. *God, Revelation and Authority: God who Speaks and Shows. Fifteen Theses, Part Two*. Vol. III. Waco: Word Books Publisher, 1979.

Hepburn, Ronald W. "Poetry and Religious Belief." In *Metaphysical Beliefs. Three Essays*, edited by Stephen E. Toulmin, Alasdair C. MacIntyre and Ronald W. Hepburn. London: SPCK, 1957.

Herrmann, Eberhard. *Religion, Reality, and a Good Life. A Philosophical Approach to Religion*. Tübingen: Mohr Siebeck, 2004.

Hick, John. "Religious Pluralism." In *The Routledge Companion to Philosophy of Religion*, edited by Chad Meister and Paul Copan, 240-249. 2nd ed. London and New York: Routledge, 2013.

Hick, John. *An Interpretation of Religion. Human Responses to the Transcendent*. 2nd ed. Basingstoke and New York: Palgrave Macmillan, 2004.

Hodge, Charles. *Systematic Theology*. Vol. 1. Grand Rapids: Eerdmans Publishing Company, 1982.

Hoitenga, Dewey J. Jr. "Christian Theism: Ultimate Reality and Meaning in the Philosophy of Alvin Plantinga." *In American Philosopher's Ideas of Ultimate Reality and Meaning*, edited by Tibor Horvath, 211-237. Toronto: U.R.A.M Regis College, 2000.

Holmes, Stephen R. "The Attributes of God." In *The Oxford Handbook of Systematic Theology*, edited by John Webster, Kathryn Tanner and Iain Torrance, 54-71. Oxford: Oxford University Press, 2007.

Howard, Thomas A. *Protestant Theology and the Making of the Modern German University*. New York: Oxford University Press, 2006.

Hunsinger, George. "Postliberal Theology." In *The Cambridge Companion to Postmodern Theology*, edited by Kevin J. Vanhoozer, 42-57. New York: Cambridge University Press, 2003.

Hunsinger, George. *Disruptive Grace. Studies in the Theology of Karl Barth*. Grand Rapids: Eerdmans Publishing Company, 1999.

Hunsinger, George. *How to Read Karl Barth. The Shape of his Theology.* New York and Oxford: Oxford University Press, 1991.

Huyssteen, Wentzel van. *Alone in the World? Human Uniqueness in Science and Theology.* Göttingen: Vandenhoeck & Ruprecht, 2006.

Huyssteen, Wentzel van. *The Shaping of Rationality. Toward Interdisciplinarity in Theology and Science.* Grand Rapids: Eerdmans Publishing Company, 1999.

Huyssteen, Wentzel van. *Theology and the Justification of Faith. Constructing Theories in Systematic Theology*, translated by H. F. Snijders. Grand Rapids: Eerdmans Publishing Company, 1989.

Insole, Christopher J. "Realism and Anti-realism." In *The Oxford Handbook of the Epistemology of Theology*, edited by William J. Abraham and Frederick D. Aquino, 274-289. Oxford: Oxford University Press, 2017.

Insole, Christopher J. *The Realist Hope. A Critique of Anti-Realist Approaches in Contemporary Philosophical Theology.* Aldershot and Burlington: Ashgate Publishing, 2006.

Inwagen, Peter van. *Metaphysics.* 3rd ed. Boulder: Westview Press, 2009.

Inwood, Michael. *A Hegel Dictionary.* Oxford: Blackwell Publishers, 1992.

Janz, Paul D. *God, the Mind's Desire. Reference, Reason and Christian Thinking.* Cambridge: Cambridge University Press, 2004.

Jenson, Robert W. *Systematic Theology. The Triune God.* Vol 1, Oxford: Oxford University Press, 1999.

Johannesson, Karin. *God Pro Nobis. On Non-Metaphysical Realism and the Philosophy of Religion.* Leuven: Peeters, 2007.

Jüngel, Eberhard. *God as the Mystery of the World. On the Foundation of the Theology of the Crucified One in the Dispute Between Theism and Atheism.* London and New York: Bloomsbury T&T Clark, 2014.

Jüngel, Eberhard. *The Doctrine of the Trinity. God's Being is in Becoming.* Grand Rapids: Eerdmans Publishing Company, 1976.

Kant, Immanuel. *Prolegomena to any Future Metaphysics*, translated by G. Hatfield. Cambridge: Cambridge University Press, 1997.

Kant, Immanuel. *The Critique of Pure Reason*, translated by Norman Kemp-Smith. London: Macmillan, 1933.

Kaufman, Gordon D. "Mystery, God and Constructivism." In *Realism and Religion*, edited by Andrew Moore and Michael Scott, 11-29. Aldershot and Burlington: Ashgate Publishing, 2007.

Kaufman, Gordon D. *Essay on Theological Method.* Montana: Scholars Press, 1975.

Kaufman, Gordon D. *God the Problem.* Cambridge: Harvard University Press, 1972.

Kaufman, Gordon D. *In Face of Mystery. A Constructive Theology.* Cambridge and London: Harvard University Press, 1993.

Kelly, Douglas F. *Systematic Theology. The God who is: the Holy Trinity.* Vol. 1. Fearn: Christian Focus Publications, 2008.

Kerr, Fergus. "The Reception of Wittgenstein's Philosophy by Theologians." In *Religion and Wittgenstein's Legacy,* edited by D. Z. Phillips and Mario von der Ruhr, 253-272. Aldershot and Burlington: Ashgate Publishing, 2005.

Kerr, Fergus. *Theology after Wittgenstein.* Oxford and New York: Basil Blackwell, 1986.

Kerr, Fergus. *Twentieth-Century Catholic Theologians. From Neoscholasticism to Nuptial Mysticism.* Malden and Oxford: Blackwell Publishing, 2007.

Kittel, Gerhard, ed. *Theological Dictionary of the New Testament.* Vol. 4. Grand Rapids: Eerdmans Publishing, 1967.

Klima, Gyula. "The Medieval Problem of Universals." *Stanford Encyclopedia of Philosophy* (Winter 2017 Edition), edited by Edward N. Zalta. URL = <https://plato.stanford.edu/-archives/win2017/entries/universals-medieval/>.

Knowles, Stephen. *Beyond Evangelicalism. The Theological Methodology of Stanley Grenz.* Farnham: Ashgate Publishing, 2010.

Kok, John H. "Woltjer on Classical Antiquity." In *In the Phrygian mode. Neo-Calvinism, Antiquity, and the Lamentations of Reformed Philosophy,* edited by Robert Sweetman, 41-64. Lanham: University Press of America, 2007.

Kooi, Cornelis van der and Gijsbert van den Brink. *Christian Dogmatics. An Introduction,* translated by Reinder Bruinsma with James D. Bratt. Grand Rapids: Eerdmans Publishing Company, 2017.

Kooi, Cornelis van der. "The Appeal to the Inner Testimony of the Spirit, Especially in H. Bavinck." *Journal of Reformed Theology* 2(2008): 103-112.

Kooi, Cornelis van der. *As in a Mirror. John Calvin and Karl Barth on Knowing God.* Leiden and Boston: Brill, 2005.

Kralingen, Cornelis van. "A Study of Theological Responses to Alvin Plantinga's Aquinas/Calvin Model of Warranted Christian Belief." Vrije Universiteit Amsterdam: Unpublished PhD Dissertation, 2018.

Kuhn, Thomas S. *The Structure of Scientific Revolutions.* 2nd ed. Chicago: University of Chicago Press, 1970.

Kuyper, Abraham. *Encyclopedia of Sacred Theology. Its Principles.* New York: Charles Scribner's Sons, 1898.

La Montagne, Paul D. *Barth and Rationality. Critical Realism in Theology.* Eugene: Cascade Books, 2012.

Le Poidevin, Robin. *Arguing for Atheism. An Introduction to the Philosophy of Religion.* London and New York: Routledge, 1996.

Lecerf, Auguste. *Introduction to Reformed Dogmatics*, translated by André Schlemmer. Grand Rapids: Baker Books, 1981.

Liberatore, Matteo. *Traité de la Connaissance Intellectuelle.* Paris: Berche et Tralin, 1885.

Lindbeck, George A. *The Nature of Doctrine*, 25th Anniversary edition. Louisville: Westminster John Knox Press, 2009.

Lipton, Peter. "Science and Religion: The Immersion Solution." In *Realism and Religion*, edited by Andrew Moore and Michael Scott, 31-46. Aldershot and Burlington: Ashgate Publishing, 2007.

Malcolm, Norman. *Wittgenstein. A Religious Point of View? Edited with a Response by Peter Winch.* London and New York: Routledge, 1993.

Mallinson, Jeffrey. *Faith, Reason, and Revelation in Theodore Beza (1519-1605).* Oxford: Oxford University Press, 2003.

Maritain, Jacques. *The Degrees of Knowledge.* Notre Dame: University of Notre Dame Press, 1995.

Markham, Ian S. "Truth in Religion." In *The Routledge Companion to Philosophy of Religion.* 2nd ed., edited by Chad Meister and Paul Copan, 217-227. London and New York: Routledge, 2013.

Mascord, Keith A. *Alvin Plantinga and Christian Apologetics.* Eugene: Wipf and Stock Publishers, 2006.

McCabe, Herbert. *Faith within Reason.* London and New York: Continuum, 2007.

McCabe, Herbert. *On Aquinas.* London and New York: Continuum, 2008.

McCormack, Bruce L. *Karl Barth's Critically Realistic Dialectical Theology. Its Genesis and Development 1909-1936.* Oxford: Oxford University Press, 1995.

McCormack, Bruce L. *Orthodox and Modern. Studies in the Theology of Karl Barth.* Grand Rapids: Baker Academic, 2008.

McFague, Sallie. *Metaphorical Theology. Models of God in Religious Language.* Philadelphia: Fortress Press, 1992.

McFague, Sallie. *Models of God. Theology for an Ecological, Nuclear Age.* London: SCM Press, 1987.

McGrath, Alister E. *A Scientific Theology: Reality.* Vol. 2, London and New York: T&T Clark, 2006.

McGrath, Alister E. *Christian Theology. An Introduction.* 5th ed. Oxford: Wiley-Blackwell, 2011.

McGrath, Alister E. *Luther's Theology of the Cross: Martin Luther's Theological Breakthrough*. Oxford: Blackwell, 1985.

McInerny, Ralph. *Praeambula Fidei. Thomism and the God of the Philosophers*. Washington DC: The Catholic University of America Press, 2006.

Meister, Chad and Paul Copan, eds. *The Routledge Companion to Philosophy of Religion*. 2nd ed. London and New York: Routledge, 2013.

Michon Cyrille and Roger Pouivet, eds. *Philosophie de la Religion. Approches Contemporaines*. Paris: Libraire Philosophique J. Vrin, 2010.

Middleton, Richard. *The Liberating Image. The Imago Dei in Genesis 1*. Grand Rapids: Brazos Press, 2005.

Milbank, John and Catherine Pickstock. *Truth in Aquinas*. London and New York: Routledge, 2001.

Moore, Andrew and Michael Scott, eds. *Realism and Religion. Philosophical and Theological Perspectives*. Aldershot and Burlington: Ashgate Publishing, 2007.

Moore, Andrew. *Realism and Christian Faith. God, Grammar, and Meaning*. Cambridge: Cambridge University Press, 2003.

Moroney, Stephen K. *The Noetic Effects of Sin: A Historical and Contemporary Exploration of How Sin Affects Our Thinking*. Lanham: Lexington Books, 2000.

Mouw, Richard J. "Dutch Calvinist Philosophical Influences in North America." *Calvin Theological Journal* 1 (1989): 93-120.

Muller, Richard A. *Dictionary of Latin and Greek Theological Terms. Drawn Principally from Protestant Scholastic Theology*. Grand Rapids: Baker Books House, 1985.

Muller, Richard A. *Post-Reformation Reformed Dogmatics. Prolegomena to Theology*. Vol. 1, Grand Rapids: Baker Books House, 1987.

Muralt, André de. *L'Enjeu de la Philosophie Médiévale*. Leiden: Brill, 1993.

Naugle, David K. *Worldview. The History of a Concept*. Grand Rapids: Eerdmans Publishing Company, 2002.

Niiniluoto, Ilkka. *Critical Scientific Realism*. Oxford: Oxford University Press, 1999.

Nijhoff, Rob. "The World as Whodunit. Jan Woltjer and his Logo-Centric Philosophy in the Early Years of the VU, Amsterdam." *Calvin Theological Journal* 54 (2019): 353-382.

Oliphint, K. Scott. "Bavinck's Realism, The Logos Principle, and *Sola Scriptura*." *Westminster Theological Journal* 72 (2010): 360-390.

Oliphint, K. Scott. "Epistemology and Christian Belief." *Westminster Theological Journal* 63 (2001): 151-182.

Oliphint, K. Scott. "Plantinga on Warrant." *Westminster Theological Journal* 57 (1995): 415-435.
Oliphint, K. Scott. "Using Reason by Faith." *Westminster Theological Journal* 73 (2011): 97-112.
Oppy, Graham and Nick N. Trakakis, eds. *The History of Western Philosophy of Religion*, 5 Vols. Durham: Acumen Publishing, 2009.
Oppy, Graham and Nick N. Trakakis. "Religious Language Games." In *Realism and Religion*, edited by Andrew Moore and Michael Scott, 103-130. Aldershot and Burlington: Ashgate Publishing, 2007.
Pannenberg, Wolfhart. *Basic Questions in Theology*, translated by George H. Kehm. Vol. 2, London: SCM Press, 1971.
Pannenberg, Wolfhart. *Systematic Theology*, translated by Geoffrey W. Bromiley. Vol.1, Grand Rapids: Eerdmans Publishing Company, 1991.
Pannenberg, Wolfhart. *Theologie und Philosophie. Ihr Verhältnis im Lichte ihrer gemeinsamen Geschichte*. Göttingen: Vandenhoeck & Ruprecht, 1996.
Pannenberg, Wolfhart. *Theology and the Philosophy of Science*, translated by Francis McDonagh. Philadelphia: Westminster Press, 1976.
Patterson, Sue. *Realist Christian Theology in a Postmodern Age*. Cambridge: Cambridge University Press, 1999.
Peacocke, Arthur. *Intimations of Reality. Critical Realism in Science and Religion*. Notre Dame: University of Notre Dame Press, 1984.
Peels, Rik. "Kevin Diller. *Theology's Epistemological Dilemma: How Karl Barth and Alvin Plantinga Provide a Unified Response*." *Journal of Analytic Theology* 4 (2016): 421-427.
Peels, Rik. "Sin and Human Cognition of God." *Scottish Journal of Theology* 64 (2011): 390-409.
Pelikan, Jaroslav. *Christianity and Classical Culture. The Metamorphosis of Natural Theology in the Christian Encounter with Hellenism*. New Haven and London: Yale University Press, 1993.
Pelikan, Jaroslav. *The Christian Tradition. A History of the Development of Doctrine. The Emergence of the Catholic Tradition (100-600)*. Chicago and London: The University of Chicago Press, 1971.
Phillips, D. Z. and Mario von der Ruhr, eds. *Religion and Wittgenstein's Legacy*. Aldershot and Burlington: Ashgate Publishing, 2005.
Phillips, D. Z. *Faith after Foundationalism. Plantinga-Rorty-Lindbeck-Berger – Critiques and Alternatives*. (Boulder and Oxford: Westview Press, 1995).
Phillips, D. Z. *Faith and Philosophical Enquiry*. London: Routledge and Kegan Paul, 1970.
Phillips, D. Z. *Wittgenstein and Religion*. London: Macmillan, 1993.

Phillips, Timothy R. and Dennis L. Okholm, eds. *The Nature of Confession. Evangelicals and Postliberals in Conversation.* Downers Grove: InterVarsity Press, 1996.

Placher, William C. *The Domestication of Transcendence. How Modern Thinking about God Went Wrong.* Louisville: Westminster John Knox Press,1996.

Placher, William C. *Unapologetic Theology. A Christian Voice in a Pluralistic Conversation.* Louisville: Westminster John Knox Press,1989.

Plantinga, Alvin and Michael Tooley. *Knowledge of God.* Oxford: Blackwell Publishing, 2008.

Plantinga, Alvin. "A Christian Life Partly Lived." In *Philosophers who Believe. The Spiritual Journeys of 11 Leading Thinkers*, edited by Kelly James Clark, 45-82. Downers Grove: InterVarsity Press, 1993.

Plantinga, Alvin. "Advice to Christian Philosophers." *Faith and Philosophy* 3 (1984): 253-271.

Plantinga, Alvin. "Afterword." In *The Analytic Theist. An Alvin Plantinga Reader*, edited by James F. Sennett, 353-358. Grand Rapids: Eerdmans Publishing, 1998.

Plantinga, Alvin. "Augustinian Christian Philosophy." *The Monist* 3 (1992): 291-320.

Plantinga, Alvin. "Christian Philosophy at the End of the 20th Century." In *Christian Philosophy at the Close of the 20th Century*, edited by Sander Griffioen and Bert M. Balk, 29-53. Kampen: Uitgeverij Kok, 1995.

Plantinga, Alvin. "Evolution and Design." In *For Faith and Clarity. Philosophical Contributions to Christian Theology*, edited by James K. Beilby, 201-217. Grand Rapids: Baker Academic, 2006.

Plantinga, Alvin. "How to be an Anti-Realist." *Proceedings and Addresses of the American Philosophical Association* 1 (1982): 47-70.

Plantinga, Alvin. "Rationality and Public Evidence: a Reply to Richard Swinburne." *Religious Studies* 37 (2001): 215-222.

Plantinga, Alvin. "Reason and Belief in God." In *Faith and Rationality: Reason and Belief in God*, edited by Alvin Plantinga and Nicholas Wolterstorff, 16-93. Notre Dame: University of Notre Dame, 1983.

Plantinga, Alvin. "Replies to my commentators: Ad Plasger." In *Plantinga's "Warranted Christian Belief". Critical Essays with a Reply by Alvin Plantinga*, edited by Dieter Schönecker, 254-257. Berlin and Boston: Walter de Gruyter, 2015.

Plantinga, Alvin. "The Twin Pillars of Christian Scholarship." In *Seeking Understanding. The Stob Lectures, 1986-1998*, 117-161. Grand Rapids: Eerdmans Publishing Co, 2001.

Plantinga, Alvin. *Knowledge and Christian Belief.* Grand Rapids: Eerdmans Publishing, 2015.

Plantinga, Alvin. *Warrant and Proper Function.* New York: Oxford University Press, 1993.

Plantinga, Alvin. *Warrant: The Current Debate.* New York: Oxford University Press, 1993.

Plantinga, Alvin. *Warranted Christian Belief.* New York: Oxford University Press, 2000.

Plantinga, Alvin. *Where the Conflict Really Lies. Science, Religion and Naturalism.* New York: Oxford University Press, 2011.

Plasger, Georg. "Does Calvin Teach a Sensus Divinitatis? Reflections on Alvin Plantinga's Interpretation of Calvin." In *Plantinga's "Warranted Christian Belief". Critical Essays with a Reply by Alvin Plantinga*, edited by Dieter Schönecker, 169-189. Berlin and Boston: Walter de Gruyter, 2015.

Plato. *The Collected Dialogues of Plato Including the Letters*, edited by Edith Hamilton and Huntington Cairns. Princeton: Princeton University Press, 1961.

Plato. *Theaetetus.* Oxford: Clarendon Press, 1973.

Polkinghorne, John. *Belief in God in an Age of Science.* New Haven and London: Yale University Press, 1998.

Polkinghorne, John. *Scientists as Theologians. A Comparison of the Writings of Ian Barbour, Arthur Peacocke and John Polkinghorne.* London: SPCK, 1996.

Popovitch, Justin. *Philosophie Orthodoxe de la Vérité.* Vol. 1, Lausanne: L'Age d'Homme, 1992.

Pouivet, Roger. "Against Theological Fictionalism." *European Journal for Philosophy of Religion* 2 (2011): 427-437.

Pouivet, Roger. "Descartes et la Question d'un Fondement Théologique de l'Epistémologie." In *Théologie et Sciences. Compréhension du Monde et de l'Homme, Regards Croisés. Hommage à Jacques Fantino*, edited by Fabien Faul, 41-50. Paris: Les Editions du Cerf, 2017.

Pouivet, Roger. "Steps Towards an Epistemology of Revelation." In *The Right to Believe. Perspectives in Religious Epistemology*, edited by Dariusz Lukasiewicz and Roger Pouivet, 47-58. Heusenstamm: Ontos Verlag, 2012.

Pouivet, Roger. *Epistémologie des Croyances Religieuses.* Paris: Les Editions du Cerf, 2013.

Pouivet, Roger. *L'Ethique Intellectuelle, une Epistémologie des Vertus.* Paris: Librairie Philosophique J. Vrin, 2020.

Pouivet, Roger. *Philosophie Contemporaine*. Paris: Presses Universitaires de France, 2008.

Pouivet, Roger. *Qu'est-ce que Croire?* Paris: Librairie Philosophique J. Vrin, 2003.

Przywara, Erich. *Analogia Entis. Metaphysics: Original Structure and Universal Rhythm*, translated by John R. Betz and David Bentley Hart. Grand Rapids and Cambridge: Eerdmans Publishing Co, 2014.

Ragusa, Daniel. "The Trinity at the Center of Thought and Life: Herman Bavinck's Organic Apologetic." *Mid America Journal of Theology* 28 (2017): 149-175

Reid, Thomas. *Inquiry and Essays*, edited by Ronald E. Beanblossom and Keith Lehrer. Indianapolis: Hackett Publishing Co, 1983.

Rumscheidt, H. Martin, ed. *The Way of Theology in Karl Barth. Essays and Comments*. Eugene: Pickwick Publications, 1986.

Santrac, Aleksandar S. *A Comparison of John Calvin and Alvin Plantinga's Concept of* Sensus Divinitatis. *Phenomenology of the Sense of Divinity*. Lewiston: The Edwin Mellen Press, 2011.

Geoff Sayre-McCord. "Moral Realism." *Stanford Encyclopedia of Philosophy* (Winter 2020 Edition), edited by Edward N. Zalta. URL = <https://plato.stanford.edu/archives/win2020/entries/moral-realism/>

Schaff, Philip, ed. *The Creeds of Christendom With a History and Critical Notes. Volume 3: The Evangelical Protestant Creeds with Translations*. Grand Rapids: Baker Book House, 1983.

Schönecker, Dieter. "The Deliverances of *Warranted Christian Belief*." In *Plantinga's "Warranted Christian Belief". Critical Essays with a Reply by Alvin Plantinga*, edited by Dieter Schönecker, 1-40. Berlin and Boston: Walter de Gruyter, 2015.

Schreiner, Susan E. *Are You Alone Wise? The Search for Certainty in the Early Modern Era*. New York: Oxford University Press, 2011.

Shaw, Graham. *God in our Hands*. London: SCM Press, 1987.

Smith, Christian and Melinda Lundquist Denton. *Soul Searching. The Religious and Spiritual Lives of American Teenagers*. New York: Oxford University Press, 2005.

Sosa, Ernest and Jaegwon Kim, Jeremy Fantl, Matthew McGrath, eds. *Epistemology. An Anthology*. Oxford: Blackwell Publishing, 2008.

Sosa, Ernest. "The Raft and the Pyramid." In *Midwest Studies in Philosophy*, Vol. 5, edited by P. French, T. Ueling and H.K. Wettstein, 3-25. Minneapolis: University of Minnesota, 1980.

Soskice, Janet Martin. "Theological Realism." In *The Rationality of Religious Belief. Essays in Honor of Basil Mitchell*, edited by William J. Abraham and Steven W. Holtzer. Oxford: Oxford University Press, 1987.

Soskice, Janet Martin. *Metaphor and Religious Language*. Oxford: Oxford University Press, 1985.

Spykman, Gordon J. *Reformational Theology. A New Paradigm for Doing Theology*. Grand Rapids: Eerdmans Publishing Co., 1992.

Sudduth, Michael. *The Reformed Objection to Natural Theology*. Farnham and Burlington : Ashgate Publishing, 2009.

Sutanto, Nathaniel Gray. *God and Knowledge. Herman Bavinck's Theological Epistemology*. London and New York: T&T Clark, 2020.

Sutanto, Nathaniel Gray. "Two Theological Accounts of Logic: Theistic Conceptual Realism and a Reformed Archetype-Ectype Model." *International Journal for Philosophy of Religion* 79 (2016): 239-260.

Svensson, Manfred and David VanDrunen. "Introduction: The Reception, Critique, and Use of Aquinas in Protestant Thought." In *Aquinas Among the Protestants*, edited by Manfred Svensson and David VanDrunen, 1-23. Oxford: Wiley Blackwell, 2018.

Swain, Scott R. "On Divine Naming." In *Aquinas Among the Protestants*, edited by Manfred Svensson and David VanDrunen, 207-227. Oxford: Wiley Blackwell, 2018.

Swinburne, Richard. "Plantinga on Warrant." *Religious Studies* 37 (2001): 203-214.

Swinburne, Richard. *Revelation. From Metaphor to Analogy*. 2nd ed. Oxford: Oxford University Press, 2007.

Systma, David S. "Herman Bavinck's Thomistic Epistemology: The Argument and Sources of his *Principia* of Science." In *Five Studies in the Thought of Herman Bavinck, a Creator of Modern Dutch Theology*, edited by John Bolt, 1-56. Lewiston: The Edwin Mellen Press, 2011.

Taliaferro, Charles and Chad Meister, eds. *The Cambridge Companion to Christian Philosophical Theology*. Cambridge: Cambridge University Press, 2009.

Taliaferro, Charles, Paul Draper and Philip L. Quinn, eds. *A Companion to Philosophy of Religion*. 2nd ed. Oxford: Wiley-Blackwell, 2010.

Thiemann, Ronald F. *Revelation and Theology. The Gospel as Narrated Promise*. Eugene: Wipf and Stock Publishers, 1985.

Thiselton, Anthony C. *The First Epistle to the Corinthians. A Commentary on the Greek Text*. Grand Rapids: Eerdmans Publishing Company, 2000.

Toren, Benno van den. *Christian Apologetics as Cross-Cultural Dialogue*. London and New York: T&T Clark International, 2011.

Torrance, Thomas F. "Theological Realism." In *The Philosophical Frontiers of Christian Theology. Essays Presented to D.M. MacKinnon*, edited by Brian Hebblethwaite and Stewart Sutherland, 169-196. Cambridge: Cambridge University Press, 1982.

Torrance, Thomas F. *Reality and Scientific Theology*. Edinburgh: Scottish Academic Press, 1985.

Torrance, Thomas F. *The Christian Frame of Mind. Reason, Order, and Openness in Theology and Natural Science*. Colorado Springs: Helmers and Howard, 1989.

Torrance, Thomas F. *The Ground and Grammar of Theology*. Charlottesville: University Press of Virginia, 1980.

Torrance, Thomas F. *Theological Science*. Oxford: Oxford University Press, 1969.

Tracy, David and John B. Cobb Jr. *Talking about God. Doing Theology in the Context of Modern Pluralism*. New York: The Seabury Press, 1983.

Tracy, David. *The Analogical Imagination. Christian Theology and the Culture of Pluralism*. New York: Crossroad Publishing Company, 1987.

Trigg, Roger. "Theological Realism and Antirealism." In *A Companion to Philosophy of religion*, edited by Philip L. Quinn and Charles Taliaferro, 213-221. Malden and Oxford: Blackwell Publishers, 1997.

Trueman, Carl E. "Editorial: Some Advantages of Going Dutch." *Themelios* 3 (2000): 1-4.

Turner, Denys. *The Darkness of God. Negativity in Christian Mysticism*. Cambridge: Cambridge University Press, 1995.

Van Til, Cornelius. "Bavinck the Theologian: A Review Article." *Westminster Theological Journal* 24 (1961): 49-64.

Van Til, Cornelius. *Introduction to Systematic Theology*. Phillipsburg: Presbyterian and Reformed Publishing, 1974.

Vanhoozer, Kevin J. *Biblical Authority after Babel. Retrieving the Solas in the Spirit of Mere Protestant Christianity*. Grand Rapids: BrazosPress, 2016.

Vanhoozer, Kevin J., ed. *The Cambridge Companion to Postmodern Theology*. Cambridge: Cambridge University Press, 2003.

Vos, Arvin. "Knowledge According to Bavinck and Aquinas." *The Bavinck Review* 6 (2015): 9-36.

Vos, Arvin. Aquinas, *Calvin, and Contemporary Protestant Thought. A Critique of Protestant Views on the Thought of Thomas Aquinas*. Grand Rapids: Eerdmans Publishing Company, 1985.

Vos, Geerhardus. "The Range of the Logos-Title in the Prologue of the Fourth Gospel." *Princeton Theological Review* 11 (1913): 365-419, 557-602.

Wainwright, William J., ed. *The Oxford Handbook of Philosophy of Religion*. Oxford: Oxford University Press, 2005.

Walton, Kendall. "Fearing Fictions." *Journal of Philosophy* 65(1978): 5-27.

Walton, Kendall. "How Close are Fictional Worlds to the Real World?" *Journal of Aesthetics and Art Criticism* 37 (1978): 11-23.

Warfield, Benjamin B. "A Review of *De Zekerheid des Geloofs*." In *Selected Shorter Writings of Benjamin B. Warfield-II*, edited by John E. Meeter, 106-123. Nutley: Presbyterian and Reformed Publishing Co, 1973.

Warfield, Benjamin B. *Studies in Tertullian and Augustine*. New York: Oxford University Press, 1930.

Webster, John. "On Theology of the Intellectual Life." In John Webster, *God Without Measure: Working Papers in Christian Theology. Vol. II: Virtue and Intellect*, 141-156. London and New York: T&T Clark International, 2016.

Webster, John. "Theologies of Retrieval." In *The Oxford Handbook of Systematic Theology*, edited by John Webster, Kathryn Tanner and Iain Torrance, 583-599. Oxford: Oxford University Press, 2007.

Webster, John. *Barth*. 2nd ed. London and New York: Continuum, 2004.

Webster, John. *God Without Measure: Working Papers in Christian Theology. Virtue and Intellect*. Vol. II, London and New York: T&T Clark International, 2016.

Webster, John. *The Domain of the Word. Scripture and Theological Reason*. London and New York: T&T Clark International, 2012.

Westphal, Merold. "Theological Anti-Realism." In *Realism and Religion*, edited by Andrew Moore and Michael Scott, 131-146. Aldershot and Burlington: Ashgate Publishing, 2007.

Westphal, Merold. *Overcoming Onto-Theology. Toward a Postmodern Christian Faith*. New York: Fordham University Press, 2001.

White, Roger M. *Talking about God. The Concept of Analogy and the Problem of Religious Language*. Farnham: Ashgate, 2010.

Wittgenstein, Ludwig. *Lectures and Conversations on Aesthetics, Psychology and Religious Belief*, edited by C. Barrett. Oxford: Blackwell, 1966.

Wittgenstein, Ludwig. *On Certainty*. Oxford: Blackwell, 1979.

Wittgenstein, Ludwig. *Philosophical Investigations*. Oxford: Blackwell, 1953.

Wolters, Albert M. "Dutch Neo-Calvinism: Worldview, Philosophy and Rationality." In *Rationality in the Calvinian Tradition*, edited by Hendrick Hart, Johan van der Hoeven and Nicholas Wolterstorff, 113-131. Lanham: University Press of America, 1983.

Wolters, Albert M. *Creation Regained. Biblical Basics for a Reformational Worldview.* Grand Rapids and Cambridge: Eerdmans Publishing Co., 2005.

Wolterstorff, Nicholas. "Herman Bavinck – Proto Reformed Epistemologist." *Calvin Theological Journal* 45 (2010): 133-146.

Wolterstorff, Nicholas. "Living within a Text." In *Faith and Narrative*, edited by Keith E. Yandell, 202-213. Oxford: Oxford University Press, 2001.

Wolterstorff, Nicholas. *Divine Discourse. Philosophical Reflections on the Claim that God Speaks.* Cambridge: Cambridge University Press, 1995.

Wolterstorff, Nicholas. *Inquiring about God. Selected Essays*, edited by Terence Cueno. Vol. 1. Cambridge: Cambridge University Press, 2010.

Wolterstorff, Nicholas. *On Universals. An Essay in Ontology* (Chicago: University of Chicago Press, 1970).

Wolterstorff, Nicholas. *Practices of Belief. Selected Essays*, edited by Terence Cueno. Vol. 2. Cambridge: Cambridge University Press, 2010.

Wolterstorff, Nicholas. *Thomas Reid and the Story of Epistemology.* Cambridge: Cambridge University Press, 2001.

Woudenberg, René van. "Thomas Reid between Externalism and Internalism." *Journal of the History of Philosophy* 51 (2013) : 75-92.

Wrathall, Mark A., ed. *Religion after Metaphysics.* Cambridge: Cambridge University Press, 2003.

Wright, Crispin. *Realism, Meaning and Truth.* 2nd ed. Oxford and Cambridge: Blackwell, 1993.

Wright, Crispin. *Truth and Objectivity.* Cambridge and London: Harvard University Press, 1992.

Wright, N. T. *The New Testament and the People of God.* London: SPCK, 1992.

Yandell, Keith E., ed. *Faith and Narrative.* Oxford: Oxford University Press, 2001.

Zagzebski, Linda. "Plantinga's *Warranted Christian Belief* and the Aquinas/Calvin Model." *Analytic Philosophy* 43 (2002): 117-123.

Index of Names

Alston, William P.: 53
Aquinas, Thomas: 27, 91, 115, 136, 142, 153, 189-193, 198
Aristotle: 77, 87, 106
Balthasar, Hans Urs: 204
Barbour, Ian G.: 44-45, 177
Barth, Karl: 46, 49-50, 108, 156-161, 194, 204
Bavinck, Herman: passim
Beilby, James: 153, 165
Belt, Henk van den: 102-104, 107-109
Berkeley, George: 15
Billings, J. Todd: 198-199
Bolt, John: 91, 112, 114-116, 184
Brink, Gijsbert van den: 9, 177, 199-200
Brunner, Emil: 160-161
Bultmann, Rudolf: 23-24
Calvin, John: 24-25, 111, 142-143, 153, 155, 174, 191-192, 198
Cupitt, Don: 34, 36-37
Descartes, René: 120
Diller, Kevin: 150, 156-162
Eglinton, James P.: 63, 70, 107
Fraassen, Bas C. van: 16
Frei, Hans: 39, 41-42, 183-184, 187
Gilson, Etienne: 179
Gunton, Colin: 12
Hartmann, Eduard von: 93
Hegel, Georg Wilhelm Friedrich: 93
Heidegger, Martin: 22
Henry, Carl F. H.: 204
Herrmann, Eberhard: 13
Insole, Christopher J.: 14, 29-30

John (Evangelist): 86, 113-114
Kant Immanuel: 18-20, 26, 33, 38, 56, 75, 83, 93, 106, 120, 152, 170, 179, 191, 193
Kaufman, Gordon D.: 34-37
Kooi, Cornelis van der: 104
Kuyper, Abraham: 54, 118
Le Poidevin, Robin: 39, 42-43
Lindbeck, George: 32, 37-38
Locke, John: 120, 191, 193
Lundquist Denton, Melinda: 197-198
Luther, Martin: 24
Maritain, Jacques: 179
McCormack, Bruce: 161, 194
McFague, Sallie: 46
McGrath, Alister: 45-46, 177, 185
Milbank, John: 12, 187
Moore, Andrew: 51
Muller, Richard A.: 77
Murdoch, Iris: 16
Ockham, William of: 136
Oliphint, K. Scott: 112, 114-116, 150, 152
Pannenberg, Wolfhart: 204
Peacocke, Arthur: 44
Peels, Rick: 159
Pelikan, Jaroslav: 88-89
Phillips, D.Z.: 39-41
Plantinga, Alvin: passim
Plasger, Georg: 161, 174
Plato: 14, 86, 106, 119-121
Polkinghorne, John: 44, 177
Pouivet, Roger: 9, 52, 120
Przywara, Erich: 204
Rea, Michael C.: 9, 55
Reid, Thomas: 19, 105, 120, 153, 171

Scotus, Duns: 20, 180
Smith, Christian: 197-198
Sutanto, Nathaniel Gray: 66, 89-90
Swinburne, Richard: 151-153, 155
Tertullian: 112-113
Toren, Benno van den: 48
Torrance, Thomas F.: 49-50, 177, 180-181, 185, 187, 204
Trueman, Carl E.: 104-105
VanDrunen, David: 192-193
Vos, Geerhardus: 112-114
Warfield, Benjamin B.: 102, 112-113
Webster, John: 187-190, 196, 199
Wittgenstein, Ludwig: 22, 33, 38-40
Wolterstorff, Nicholas: 53, 56, 58-59, 110, 165, 172, 191, 193
Wright, Crispin: 30-31
Wright, N.T.: 47

Index of Subjects

Accommodatio Dei: 25, 27, 79, 95-99
Adequatio intellectus ad rem: 101, 134-136, 180
Analogy: 27, 94-95
Anti-realism, cultural-Linguistic: 37-43, 58-59, 183-184
Anti-realism, experiential-Expressive: 33-36, 58, 97
Anti-realism: 17-18, 20-21, 29-30, 32-43, 58-59
Aquinas/Calvin (AC) model, expanded extended: 173, 177
Aquinas/Calvin (AC) model, extended: 139, 144-149, 157-162, 172-173, 175, 182, 190-191
Aquinas/Calvin (AC) model: 138-144, 157-159, 182, 188, 190-191
Aristotelian: 23, 50, 65-66, 77-87, 99, 105, 125, 169-170, 180
Augustinian: 23, 155, 180
Barthian, post-Barthian: 48, 71, 150, 156-162, 195, 205
Belgic Confession, art. 2: 90, 110-111
Calvinism, Calvinist: 27, 53-54, 90, 96, 99, 105, 112, 114, 194
Catholicity: 98-99, 188-190, 204
Conditional method: 127, 139-140, 150-156
Constructivism: 18, 20, 133
Dualism: 48, 58, 70-73, 111-112, 166-167, 181
Empiricism: 55, 80-84, 87, 133
Epistemology, naturalistic: 124-128

Epistemology, theological: 66, 82-83
Esse repraesentatum: 20, 48, 180
Faith, and reason: 11, 70-74, 94, 100, 104-105, 109, 111, 152, 155
Faith, as knowledge: 25, 49, 65, 68, 75-77, 79, 100, 103, 145, 148-149, 157-158, 165, 168-169, 172-173, 182, 200
Fictionalism: 16, 42-43
Fundamentalism: 201-202
God, doctrine of: 15, 24-25, 35-37
Grace, common and special: 74-75
Hegelian, post-Hegelian: 34, 36, 107
Holy Spirit, work of the: 80, 145, 147, 157-158, 168, 174 182
Idealism: 15, 18, 81-82, 95
Imago Dei: 129-131, 135, 142-143, 174
Instrumentalism: 17, 42, 44-45, 133
Intellect, active: 87-88
Justification, epistemological debate: 120-121, 171
Kantian, post-Kantian: 18, 20, 24, 26, 31-38, 47-48, 53, 58, 63-69, 75, 81-85, 99-108, 152, 161, 166, 170, 176, 178-183, 186-187, 194-195
Logical positivism, positivist: 20, 22, 31, 44, 49, 62, 69, 83, 85, 105, 186
Logos theology: 86-93, 99-101, 109, 112-116, 166, 170-171, 179, 189, 203-204
Metaphysics, and epistemology: 99, 141-142, 166

Metaphysics, theistic (or supernatural): 126-130, 134, 137, 167
Modernity: 11, 27, 41, 61, 65, 101, 104, 186-188, 194-196
Naturalism: 23, 118, 121, 124-128, 131-132, 137
Neo-Calvinism: 68, 105, 112, 145, 175
Nominalism: 15, 84-85
Non-realism: 29, 39
Organicism, organic: 69-75, 80, 86, 89, 92, 94, 96, 98, 107, 109, 111, 149, 160, 165, 167, 173, 178
Philosophy, Christian: 117-119
Philosophy, of religion (analytical): 55-57, 117, 193
Platonism, Platonist: 14, 23
Post-liberalism: 40-42
Post-modernity: 194-196
Pragmatism: 20, 38-39, 197-198
Rationalism: 26, 80-82, 94, 111
Realism, Christocentric: 50-51
Realism, common sense: 19, 29, 49, 83, 105, 133, 149
Realism, critical realism: 20, 43-48, 101-108, 161, 176-181, 185-195
Realism, epistemological: 19-20, 24-26, 99-101, 193, 195
Realism, in theology: 11-12, 17, 28-31, 52, 43-51
Realism, metaphysical: 18-19, 22-24, 99-101, 193, 195
Realism, moderate: 25, 82-85, 100
Realism, naïve: 19, 27, 44-45, 47, 85, 105, 108, 174, 177-178, 185
Realism, semantic: 21, 26-28, 99-101, 193, 195
Realism, theological realism: 14-15, 18, 22, 43, 48-51, 108-116, 181-186, 194-195
Reformation *solas*: 71-72, 158
Religious studies: 12, 63, 65, 72-75, 196, 201-202
Retrieval, theology of: 187-194
Revelation: 23, 25, 27, 35, 49-50, 56, 58, 62, 67-71, 74-82, 88-93, 94-97, 100-103, 108, 111, 113, 116, 157-158, 162, 173-174, 182-184
Science, nature and scope: 16, 44, 81, 131-134, 172
Sensus divinitatis: 90, 142-148, 157-160, 174
Sin, noetic effect of: 105-106, 146-147, 149, 174, 205
Subjectivism: 102-105
Theology, cataphatic and apophatic: 24-27, 35, 55, 194
Theology, ectypal and archetypal: 25, 27, 79-80, 94-96
Theology, method: 68-72, 109-111
Theology, natural: 71, 110-111, 113, 157-160, 205
Theology, nature and scope: 11-12, 23, 41-42, 64-76, 172-174, 196-203
Theology, object: 67-68
Theology, philosophical: 55-56, 110, 165, 172
Theology, principles: 76-80, 182
Theology, prolegomena: 61, 76-77, 169
Thomism, Thomistic: 23, 73, 80-84, 87, 99-100, 105, 136, 170-171
Tolerance, religious: 201-202

Trinity: 70-71, 80, 89
Truth: 21-22, 89-91, 139-141
Warrant, and design plan: 123-124
Warrant, and proper function: 123-124, 128
Warrant: 121-125, 169-171, 178

Wittgensteinian, post-Wittgensteinian: 38-40, 58, 166, 183-184, 186
World, as creation (or *cosmos*): 97, 99, 115, 134-137, 166-167